诸子百家智慧故事
Wisdom of Ancient Chinese Sages

WISDOM of MENCIUS

孟子
智慧故事

主编　陶黎铭　张　英
中文作者　王小曼
英文作者　王晓伟
英文审订　汪榕培

Editors-in-Chief *Tao Liming　Zhang Ying*
Chinese by *Wang Xiaoman*
English by *Wang Xiaowei*
Revised by *Wang Rongpei*

上海外语教育出版社
SHANGHAI FOREIGN LANGUAGE EDUCATION PRESS

图书在版编目(CIP)数据

孟子智慧故事 / 王小曼著；王晓伟译.
—上海：上海外语教育出版社，2011
(诸子百家智慧故事丛书)
ISBN 978-7-5446-1817-5

I. 孟… II. ①王…②王… III. ①孟轲(前372~前289)—生平事迹—通俗读物—汉、英 IV. B222.5-49

中国版本图书馆CIP数据核字(2010)第065599号

出版发行：**上海外语教育出版社**
　　　　　（上海外国语大学内）　邮编：200083
电　　话：021-65425300（总机）
电子邮箱：bookinfo@sflep.com.cn
网　　址：http://www.sflep.com.cn　http://www.sflep.com
责任编辑：陶　怡

印　　刷：上海申松立信印刷有限责任公司
开　　本：890×1194　1/32　印张 10.625　字数 295 千字
版　　次：2011 年 1 月第 1 版　2011 年 1 月第 1 次印刷
印　　数：3 100 册

书　　号：ISBN 978-7-5446-1817-5 / B・0008
定　　价：39.00 元
　　　　本版图书如有印装质量问题，可向本社调换

前　言

　　2 000多年前的春秋战国时代，是中国各种思想流派百花齐放的时期，涌现了孔子、孟子、老子、庄子、墨子、荀子、孙子、韩非子等思想家、哲学家，他们开创了儒、道、墨、法等各具特色、影响深远的思想派别，后世称为"诸子百家"。"诸子百家智慧故事"是一套介绍先秦诸子经典的汉英对照系列丛书，将先秦诸子的生平事迹、哲学思想、格言警句、哲理寓言以及与他们有关的历史故事串联成启迪智慧的短小故事，既能满足中国读者的普及型阅读需求，又照顾到国外读者的文化特点，让大家在轻松愉快的阅读氛围中走近春秋战国时代"百家争鸣"的先哲们。

　　为了让世界更好地了解中国的经典文化，"诸子百家智慧故事"在编写上突出了以下三个特点：

　　轻松阅读——本系列每本书中文不过七八万字，每个故事就是一个相对独立的阅读单位，仅几百字的内容十分钟就能读完，在当今信息爆炸的快节奏时代，这种文本便于读者随时取出翻阅。

　　经济阅读——中国的文字特别是古文字常常是外国人阅读中国经典的障碍，本丛书采取汉英双语对照，中文是浅显易懂的白话体，配以通顺晓畅的英语译文，读者无须钻研艰深的典籍，就能了解先哲的智慧。

　　趣味阅读——本丛书通过一个个短小生动的故事以及古意盎然的插图，为读者深入浅出地解读诸子经典。

　　先秦诸子经典是中国的宝贵精神财富，至今在中国乃至全世界都有广泛的影响。希望本丛书能够引起广大中外读者对先秦诸子百家的兴趣，并能通过书中的故事体会到博大精深的中国智慧。

编者

2009年9月

Preface

Over two millennia ago, China experienced a boom of ideas and philosophies in the form of "100 Schools of Thought". Confucius, Mencius, Laozi, Zhuangzi, Mozi, Xunzi, Han Feizi, Sun Tzu ... These are the stellar names behind the philosophical schools like Confucianism, Taoism, Mohism, Legalism, etc. in the Spring and Autumn Period and the Warring States Period (from 770 BC to 221 BC). The classics of these ancient sages contain great wisdom and have exerted profound influence on Chinese history and thought. While the classics themselves may seem difficult to understand today, you can find lucid and accessible explanations of the ancient philosophies in the books of *Wisdom of Ancient Chinese Sages*. With the help of a collection of short and interesting stories, you can get to know the lives and thoughts of the ancient sages, the axioms and allegories they employed to illustrate their ideas, and some facts about the historical era they lived in.

With the aim of presenting the ancient Chinese classics to the world audience, *Wisdom of Ancient Chinese Sages* boasts three advantages:

Easiness — Each book in the series is comprised of only a few dozen stories, each of which has no more than 2,000 words and can be glanced through in a 10-minute coffee break. Even in your busy life, you can always snatch some time to enjoy a story of wisdom and gain some spiritual nourishment.

Efficiency — The classics may seem a little obscure today since they are written in the ancient Chinese. In this Chinese-English version of *Wisdom of Ancient Chinese Sages*, however, the classics are rendered in simple, everyday English. Without having to tax your brains, you can readily comprehend the profound wisdom of the ancient sages.

Attractiveness — With all the short but lively stories accompanied by beautiful illustrations, *Wisdom of Ancient Chinese Sages* explains (to you) the ancient philosophical ideas in a friendly and agreeable way.

The ancient philosophical classics in the "100 Schools of Thought" are an important spiritual heritage of China and impose great cultural reverberations beyond the Chinese borders. We hope that the series may let the readers develop an interest in the ancient Chinese sages and their philosophies, and appreciate the quintessential Chinese wisdom that may prove useful in present day.

Editors
September 2009

目录

Contents

孟子生平   13
The Life of Mencius

孟子智慧故事   35
Wisdom of Mencius

1. 何必一定要谈利   37
   Why Should You Mention Profits?   38

2. 与民同乐   41
   Sharing Happiness with the People   42

3. 仁者无敌   44
   A Benevolent Ruler Never Meets His Match   45

4. 望之不似人君   47
   Not the Proper Manners of a King   48

5. 见牛未见羊   50
   Seeing the Ox But Not the Sheep   51

6. 不为与不能   53
   Lack of Willingness vs. Lack of Capacity   54

7. 独乐乐不如众乐乐   57
   Enjoying the Music with the People Is Better than Enjoying It by Himself   58

8. 大勇与小勇   60
   Valor vs. Brute Courage   61

9. 胡服骑射   64
   Wearing the Tartar Attires and Training the Cavalries   65

10. 流连忘返   67
   Reluctant to Leave in Indulgence of Pleasures   68
11. 鳏寡孤独   70
   The Widowers, Widows, Orphans and Childless   71
12. 如何识才   74
   How to Spot the Talents   75
13. 何谓一夫   77
   What Is an Autocrat   78
14. 孟子婉拒齐王   80
   Mencius Politely Rejecting the Requests of King Xuan   81
15. 齐人伐燕   83
   The Incursion of the State of Yan by the Qi Army   85
16. 终生奉母教   88
   Following His Mother's Guidance All His Life   89
17. 邹鲁内讧   91
   The Conflict between the States of Zou and Lu   92
18. 从者如归市   94
   Following Someone As Crowds Hastening to the Market   95
19. 臧仓小人   97
   Zang Cang the Vile Man   99
20. 事半功倍   101
   Doubling the Achievements with Half the Efforts   102
21. 四十不动心   105
   Attaining an Unperturbed Mind at Forty   106
22. 何谓圣人   108
   What Is a Sage?   109
23. 心悦诚服   111
   Heartfelt Admiration and Sincere Conviction   112
24. 未雨绸缪   113
   Saving for the Rainy Day   114

25.	天吏无敌	115
	A Heaven-Sent Minister Has No Rivals	116
26.	恻隐之心	117
	The Heart of Sympathy	118
27.	反求诸己	120
	Reflecting and Trying to Find Fault with Oneself	121
28.	孟子装病	123
	Mencius Feigning Illness	125
29.	该要的为何不要	128
	Why Decline What Ought to Be Accepted	129
30.	孔距心知罪	130
	Kong Juxin Realized His Mistake	131
31.	绰绰有余	133
	Act Freely and Without Any Constraints	134
32.	孟子吊丧	136
	A Condolence Visit Paid by Mencius	137
33.	孟子葬母	139
	The Funeral of Mencius' Mother	140
34.	沈同问伐燕	142
	Enquiry of Shen Tong on the Incursion of Yan	143
35.	宣王愧对孟子	145
	King Xuan Is Ashamed Before Mencius	146
36.	孟子辞官	148
	Resignation of Mencius	149
37.	告别齐国之路	151
	Journey Away from Qi	152
38.	此一时彼一时	155
	That Is Then and This Is Now	156
39.	滕文公问丧仪	158
	Duke Wen of Teng Inquiring about Funeral Manners	159

40. 滕文公问政	162
Duke Wen of Teng Inquiring about Political Advices	163
41. 孟子舌战陈相	165
Mencius' Debate with Chen Xiang	167
42. 墨家治丧辩	170
Mencius' Comments upon Mohists' Attitude for Burial Manners	171
43. 枉己者怎能直人	173
How Could Those Who Act Improperly Make Others Behave Properly	174
44. 什么是大丈夫	177
Who Can Be Defined as Great Men	178
45. 父母之命，媒妁之言	180
The Order of Parents and the Word of Matchmakers	181
46. 食志与食功	183
Living on Wishes or Living on Achievements	184
47. 商汤复仇	187
The Revenge of King Tang in the Shang Dynasty	188
48. 难道是我好辩吗？	190
Am I Really Argumentative?	191
49. 陈仲子的廉洁	194
Chen Zhongzi's Honesty and Integrity	195
50. 没有规矩，不能成方圆	197
Nothing Can Be Accomplished Without Norms	198
51. 反躬自问	201
Examine Oneself	202
52. 以道救天下	204
Save the Society with Morality	205
53. 事亲如曾子	207
Treat Parents as Zengzi Did	208

54. 乐正子见孟子 — 210
Yue Zhengzi Visiting Mencius — 211

55. 小惠不足以治国 — 213
Small Favor Not Enough to Govern a State Well — 214

56. 君臣如何相待 — 215
How Should the King and His Officials Treat Each Other? — 216

57. 公行子长子之吊 — 218
The Condolence for Gong Xingzi's Eldest Son — 219

58. 匡章不孝 — 220
Kuang Zhang Was Not Filial — 221

59. 曾子与寇 — 223
Zengzi and the Invaders — 224

60. 终生之忧与一朝之患 — 226
Life-Long Concern and Immediate Worries — 227

61. 大孝终生慕父母 — 229
A Filial Son Adores His Parents for His Whole Life — 230

62. 舜以德报"象"怨 — 232
Shun Returned Xiang's Malice with Grace — 233

63. 民意为天 — 235
The Will of the People Is the Will of Heaven — 236

64. 致君为尧舜 — 239
Assisting the King to Become Saints like Yao and Shun — 240

65. 好事者为之 — 242
Troublemakers Started the Rumor — 243

66. 集大成者 — 245
Epitome of Wisdom and Sanctity — 247

67. 却之不恭 — 249
Not Respectful to Refuse Gifts — 250

68. 君子的人格 — 252
Character of a Man with High Morals — 253

69. 人性与善	255
Human Nature and Benevolence	256
70. 君子与小人	258
The Moral and the Vile	259
71. 礼义与食色	261
Etiquette and Righteousness vs. Food and Beauty	262
72. 人人都可成尧舜	264
Everybody Could Become Sages as Yao and Shun	265
73. 石丘遇宋牼	267
Encountering Song Keng at Shiqiu	269
74. 什么是良臣	271
What Constitutes a Good Official?	272
75. 孟子批评白圭	274
Mencius Criticized Bai Gui	275
76. 乐正子执政	277
Yue Zhengzi to Govern the State	278
77. 生于忧患，死于安乐	280
To Thrive in Calamity and Perish in a Soft Life	281
78. 独善其身	283
Cultivate One's Own Character	284
79. 君子有三乐	286
Three Delights of People with High Morals	287
80. 乡愿之人	289
People Who Try to Please Every Town Folk	290
81. 五十步笑百步	293
Those Who Had Retreated Fifty Paces Laughed at Those Who Had Retreated a Hundred	294
82. 缘木求鱼	296
Climbing the Trees to Catch Fish	297

83. 王顾左右而言他 … 299
    King Looking Aside and Talking about Other Things … 300
84. 拔苗助长 … 301
    Pull Seedlings to Help Them Grow Up … 302
85. 天时地利不如人和 … 303
    People's Support Is More Important than Opportunities Granted by Heaven and Favorable Geographical Positions … 304
86. 一傅众咻 … 306
    One Teaching and Many Disturbing … 307
87. 为何等到明年 … 309
    Why Wait Until Next Year … 310
88. 三年之艾 … 311
    Three-Year-Old Wormwood … 312
89. 逢蒙学射 … 314
    Feng Meng Learnt Archery … 315
90. 齐人骄妻 … 317
    A Man of Qi Boasted in front of His Wife … 318
91. 得其所哉 … 320
    Have Got to the Right Place … 321
92. 牛山之木 … 323
    The Trees on Mount Niu … 324
93. 一暴十寒 … 327
    One Scorch and Ten Colds … 328
94. 鱼与熊掌 … 330
    Fish or Bears' Paws … 331
95. 茅草塞心 … 334
    The Heart Filled Up with Weeds … 335
96. 再作冯妇 … 337
    Do It Again Would Be Acting like Feng Fu … 338

孟子生平
The Life of Mencius

孟子，名轲，字子舆，邹国（今山东邹县）人。关于孟子的生卒年有很多不同的说法。一般认为他生于周烈王四年（公元前372年），死于周赧王二十六年（公元前289年）的说法比较合理。孟子一生活动的年代大约处于战国中期。

孟子是我国古代伟大的思想家、政治家、教育家，年轻时曾师从孔子的孙子子思的门人学习。孔子的学说、思想和人生态度，给孟轲以极大的影响。他悉心钻研孔子思想，是孔子思想和政治主张的继承者、发扬者，也是孔子之后儒家学派的大师和代表人物。

为了推行自己的政治主张，孟子曾经游说齐国、宋国、滕国、魏国等国家，但他的主张始终没有被采纳。于是他回到故国，聚众讲学、著书立说，与万章、公孙丑等门徒为《诗》、《书》等经书作序，传达孔子的思想，并完成了《孟子》七章。

1083年，孟子被宋神宗封为"邹国公"。1331年，又被元文宗加封为"邹国亚圣公"。孟子至今仍被世人尊称为"亚圣"。

公元前372年左右，孟子诞生在邹，因为生在马车里，所以父母为他取名为轲。孟家是鲁国贵族孟孙氏的后代，但到了孟子家这一脉系时早已经没落了，所以他们迁居到了邹国。孟子的父亲孟激在孟子三岁的时候就离开了人世，孟子的母亲仉氏是位贤淑明理、颇有远见的女性，因此孟子的成长与她有着很大的关系。在中国，"孟母三迁"、"孟母断机杼"的故事可谓家喻户晓。

"孟母三迁"说的是，孟轲从小就聪明异常，也十分顽皮。仉氏贫穷，只能租便宜的房屋居住，所以居处环境往往不好。最初，他们居住的地方靠近墓地，小孟轲经常带领一群邻家孩子在墓地里玩耍，学着大人做挖穴筑墓、葬礼扫墓一类的事。仉氏见了忧心如焚，对孟轲说："这里不是你应该住的地方，我们换个地方住吧！"他们搬家了，这次住在靠近集市的地方。集市上做买卖的人，你来我往，讨价还价，大声吆喝，弄虚作假。小孟轲整天到集市上玩耍，也学起了大人做买卖的游戏，还流露出一副世故的神态。仉氏见了，又是忧心不已，商人追求利益，在当时是很被人瞧不起的。长此下去，仉氏担心孩子的品格培养不好，于是对孟轲说："我们还得搬家，这里也不能住了。"经过慎重考虑和选择，他们搬到了一所学校的附近。这学校正是从前子思和他的弟子们经常教书讲学、演练礼仪的地方，那里整天乐音隐隐，书声琅琅，进进出出的读书人都是彬彬有礼的样子，张口说话也都是孔子的那一套学说。一到春秋两季的重要节日，还会举行隆重的典礼。小孟轲看得入迷，觉得很有意思，也跟着儒者们学习作揖打躬、礼仪祭祀，模仿学生们吟诵的样子。仉氏见了，终于放心了，对孩子说："这里才是你应该住的地方。"于是母子俩就定居下来，靠织布为生。

后来孟轲上学了，因为儒家的那套礼仪艰深繁琐，过了一段时间，小孟轲就有点厌倦了，常常逃学，一个人溜到外面去玩耍。仉氏知道了，又生气又难过地问他："干什么去了？"孟轲不敢隐瞒："自己玩去了。"仉氏满面悲伤，突然举起刀，狠狠地将织机上的经线全砍断了。小孟轲吓了一跳。不明白母亲什么意思。母亲说："你不学习，就和我砍断机线一样。线断了织不成布，变成了废物，你学习半途而废，就不能成人，更成不了仁人君子！"那个时候的布是用梭子一点一点织出来的，好不容易织成的布匹被一刀割断是非常可惜的。但孟母就是要用这个例子来说明坚持的重要性。孟子果然受到了教育，从此发愤读书，早起晚睡，十分勤奋，为将来的博学打下了基础。

当然，孟母教子的故事远不止这些。

孟子生活的时代，游学风气很浓厚。当时的青年都向往通过读书游说来获取荣华富贵。所以很多年轻人离开家乡，到其他国家去追求知识，投奔到自己尊敬的思想家的门下，接受文化知识的熏陶。

年轻的孟子长成了半大小伙子，附近的学校已不能满足他的求知需要，母亲便打发他到鲁国去，因为那里有许多孔子的后学，而且是周代文化保存最完好的地方。更重要的是，孔子学派的讲学团体还在鲁国，这是最令孟子向往的。于是他满怀憧憬来到鲁国，参观古迹，求教贤士。孟子在孔子的故乡不但可以学习书本知识，还能走访古迹，亲临孔子生活的环境，参观孔子的遗物，这使他的学问突飞猛进。不过，这一切并没有满足他的求知欲，他找来所有孔子的著作，精心地自学起来。这就是后来他说的"私淑于孔子"，意思是私底下从孔子那里学到了知识。

孔子的学生中最有名的，一个是被称为"传经之儒"的子夏，另一个是被称为"传道之儒"的曾子。曾子在孔子死后仍留在鲁国继续讲学，并把他的思想学术传给了孔子的孙子——子思。当年轻的孟子游学到鲁国时，子思已经去世了，所以他就受教于子思的门人。孟子特别佩服子思，虽然子思跟孟子并没有师生关系，但从思想上说，他们是一脉相传的。子思的门徒正是孟子的老师，子思的言行对孟子的影响并不亚于孔子，特别是他在尊重士人和重视气节方面的言行对孟子有着深刻的影响。孟子在宣扬仁政王道的时候从不畏惧君权，敢于直面批评君主的一身浩然正气，正是和子思的"忠臣就是要不断批评君主的错误并指出缺点"的主张相一致的。所以后世有"思孟学派"的说法。

在鲁国游学三年后，孟子回到了故乡，并开始了讲学授徒的生涯，准备将他奉行的思想继续传递下去。跟孔子一样，孟子首先是个教育家。他认为，人生三大乐事之一就是广招天下英才并教育他们。所以，在正式担任官职以前，他开设了私人讲学的课堂，吸纳各方人才进行教育，时间长达十几年之久。他坚信孔子的"有教无类"说，认为人人都有受教育的权利，并都可以通过教育完善自我。所以，他的招生原则也跟孔子一样，"来者不拒，往者不追"。就是说，招收学生不论背景、年龄、身份、贫富，而学成后的去向也不追究。孟子希望通过教育来培养圣君、贤臣和仁人志士，从而实现"仁政"的政治理想。孟子将自己的招生原则公布以后，世人纷纷慕名而来，先后达几百人之多，其中不乏造诣很深、闻名当时的佼佼者。孟子的教育方法丰富多样，从不拘泥于课堂上的宣讲，而是带领学生春游秋察，进行书本知识与实际生活相结合的教育。他还因材施教，让每一个学生都找到自己身上的闪光点和长处，并使之发扬光大。孟子春风化雨般的教育方法为他赢得了学生们的尊敬，更赢得了社会的普遍赞誉。人们都尊称他为"孟子"或"孟夫子"。

儒家思想主张参与现实，过问政治，帮助君主管理国家。而要实现这样的目标就要"出仕"，也就是出任官员。孟子最初大约是40岁左右在他的祖国邹国出仕为官的，但因为直言邹穆公的治国不当而不被重用。眼看着自己的远大目标无法实现，抱负无法施展，孟子决定远游他国，寻找展露才华的机会。

这个时候正是后世所说的战国七雄瓜分天下、相互竞争的时代,也是各种学术主张层出不穷、各种思想自由开放的时代。而游士集团又是这个时代的另一个显著的特征。游士是一个十分独特的群体,他们通常是一群知识分子,有着满肚子的学问和能力,一边从事教育活动,一边周游列国,寻找着从政的机会,实现平生的理想和抱负。春秋时代的孔子和他的门人就是这样的游士集团。到了孟子所处的战国时代,这种游士集团的活动更加活跃了,他们游走于各国之间,阐述自己的主张,有的为了获取利益,有的为了追求理想,目的不一。孟子身处这个时代,当然也不免于时代风气的影响。所不同的是,孟子和他的弟子们是为了实现王道仁政的理想而奔走各国的。

孟子大约从43岁开始以士的身份游说诸侯,先后到过梁(魏)国、齐国、宋国、滕国、鲁国,致力于推行自己的政治主张。孟子师生一行最先来到齐国。当时的齐国正是齐威王当政之时,稷下学宫办得很热闹。稷下学宫广招贤人学士,任他们议论国政、讲学论道。只是当时的孟子尚无名气,不被重视,而且他的"仁政"思想与齐威王的心思相去甚远。齐威王当时正是兵强马壮、雄心勃勃、一心称霸诸侯之时,对孟子虽以礼相待,却并不采纳孟子的主张。不过稷下学宫的学者们都有着很优厚的生活待遇,孟子也不例外。他带来了十几名学生,一同住在宽敞的宅第里,继续他的讲学交游生活。

公元前327年,孟子的母亲仉氏去世。孟子以厚礼将母亲葬于鲁国,守孝三年后返回齐国。但此时的齐国早已风云突变,战乱不断。稷下学宫也已经衰落,学者们纷纷离开。就在这时,孟子听说魏国的梁惠王因为不甘心国家沉沦,正在广纳贤士帮助理政。孟子觉得自己离开的时机也到了。于是他告别了年迈的齐威王,准备去魏国。

　　前往魏国之前，孟子听说宋王偃想实行仁政，便临时决定去宋国看看。宋国是个小国，饱受强大邻国的侵扰，内政又有权臣干涉。宋王在位十几年，实在不甘心宋国就这样破败落后下去，很想有一番振兴国家的作为。无奈他虽然贵为国君，却并无自主权，其实只是个受奸臣挟持的傀儡，欲行仁政却什么都不能做。孟子眼见此景，只得动身离去。

　　此时，孟子的祖国邹国忽然传来消息，说邹穆公急招孟子回国商量国事。故乡来人召唤，孟子自然不能推辞，他急忙领着众弟子北上。没想到在薛城遇到连雨天，河水暴涨，师徒一行只好暂住在这里。等他们赶到邹国时，邹国已经在跟鲁国的冲突中大败。邹穆公不满于当邹国被鲁国围困时邹国百姓的无动于衷，向孟子讨教。孟子坦率指出邹穆公不施仁政，使百姓饱受官吏之苦，正是产生这一切后果的原因。孟子的态度让邹穆公大感意外，他根本接受不了孟子的仁政学说。两人话不投机，自然没法继续相处。

　　孟子的优秀弟子乐正克那时正在鲁国做官，便向鲁平公极力推荐孟子。鲁平公早已听说了孟子的才能，也正想采用他。孟子觉得自己的学术主张终于可以有用武之地了，十分高兴。然而，就在鲁平公沐浴更衣，准备去拜访孟子的时候，却遇到了一个名叫臧仓的宠臣的阻挠。臧仓在鲁平公面前搬弄是非，说了孟子的很多坏话，使得鲁平公最终放弃了拜访孟子的念头。乐正克愤愤不平，孟子却很看得开。他说，我见不成鲁平公并不是因为臧仓这样的一个小人，而是天意啊。

　　孟子想起了自己跟滕文公的交情，便决定去滕国看看。滕文公对孟子厚礼相待，常常与他一起商讨治国之道。孟子也乘机向滕文公灌输了仁政爱民、减轻百姓税负、办学施教等治国良策。这些政策自然受到百姓的欢呼拥护，但却侵犯了官僚贵族的权益。他们十分恼恨孟子，不断上书给滕文公编排孟子的种种不是，甚至造谣中伤他。孟子在滕国呆了三年，终于还是决意离开。

孟子最终来到了魏国首都大梁，此时他已经53岁了。魏国的梁惠王（即魏惠王）因为在军事上连续失败，正想奋发图强，所以不惜重金来招贤纳才。但他一心只想着如何能让那些贤士们提供智慧和谋略，以便满足他富国强兵的愿望。在朝廷上第一次召见孟子的时候，梁惠王张口就问孟子能为他带来什么好处。孟子心里明白，这个梁惠王也未必能够接受他的政治主张。但"知其不可为而为之"正是儒家的精神，孟子仍然对梁惠王抱有一些希望和幻想。经过几次接触和谈话，梁惠王对孟子的态度也确实有了一些改变。他渐渐能听得进孟子的话了，也常常主动请教孟子一些问题。四五次的见面畅谈之后，梁惠王跟孟子已经比较融洽了。可惜天意不给孟子施展抱负的机会。梁惠王不久就死了，他的儿子梁襄王继位。这是一个毫无礼貌，也毫无君主气派的国君。与他接触不久，孟子就断定自己在这里将毫无作为。他再次决定离魏赴齐。此时的齐国已是宣王即位。齐宣王很想有一番作为，他重振稷下学宫，招纳天下贤士，孟子来得正是时候。齐宣王盛迎孟子师徒，封孟子为客卿，并在孟子到达齐国的第四天就登门拜访，对孟子表现出了君主中少有的尊重。而孟子与齐宣王的几次谈话也成了《孟子》一书中的名篇。

就在此时，燕国发生内乱。作为邻国的齐国乘机讨伐燕国，短短一个多月就攻下了燕国。齐宣王兴高采烈地去见孟子，想征求孟子对于进一步吞并燕国的意见。孟子并不反对战争，只要战争是正义的。比如燕国的国王不义，让老百姓处于水深火热之中，讨伐它是没错的。但必须是正义之师才有讨伐的资格。齐国的政治比燕国好不了多少，担当不了正义之师的使命，伐燕当然就不可取。可是，齐宣王并没有理解孟子的意思，仍然进一步讨伐燕国，甚至在燕国烧杀劫掠，招致燕国百姓的愤恨，同时也打破了各国之间的平衡，引起了其他邻近国家的不满。其他邻国本来就惧怕齐国的强大，这时候正好利用燕国百姓的不满联合起来对付齐国。

　　这件事以后，齐宣王对孟子怀有很深的愧意。而孟子也觉得自己在齐国实现政治理想的希望彻底破灭了。他决定辞去卿位，离开齐国。齐宣王极力挽留，还许诺要给孟子一幢大房子，用厚禄供养他。可是，孟子坚决地推辞不受，并决心离开齐国。离开齐国对孟子来说是不容易的。他原本对于在齐国实行仁政抱有很大的希望，如今希望破灭了，内心是无比的痛苦和无奈。所以离开齐国的路程，孟子走得很慢，他甚至在齐国边境的小城停留了三个晚上，只是希望齐宣王能来挽留他，一起回去实行王道仁政。但这一切是不可能的了。

　　公元前312年，孟子终于离开了他居住了多年的齐国。

　　游说诸侯的生涯结束了，孟子的学说主张没有得到任何一个诸侯国的采纳，这对孟子立志拯救天下百姓的理想来说，是个很大的打击。但是孟子不甘心自己的政治主张和思想观点就这样消失而不能流传于世，便决心仿效《论语》，著成一书，阐明自己的主张，记述自己的一生。公孙丑、万章等弟子一起参与了这项工程量很大的工作。他们一起追记了老师孟子一生的主要活动，孟子也不断回答弟子们提出的一些新的问题。著书工作一直持续到孟子逝世，书终于写成，名为《孟子》。

　　公元前289年，孟子逝世，享年83岁。

Mencius, with the family name of Meng, the given name of Ke and the style name of Ziyu, was born in the State of Zou (the present-day Zou County of Shandong Province). Though views are widely divided regarding the exact year of his birth and death, it is generally believed that the version that he was born in the fourth year during the reign of King Lie of Zhou (372 BC) and deceased in the twenty-sixth year during the reign of King Nan of Zhou (289 BC) is relatively convincing. Mencius roughly lived during the mid Warring States Period (403–221 BC).

Mencius was a great thinker, statesman and educator of ancient China. When he was young, he studied under the disciples of Zisi, the grandson of Confucius. Confucius' teachings, thoughts, and life attitude exerted a great influence on him. He devoted himself to the study of Confucian thoughts and was the inheritor and developer of Confucius' thoughts and political philosophy, as well as a master and representative of the Confucian school after Confucius.

In order to promote his political philosophy, Mencius sought audiences with his proposals in the states of Qi, Song, Teng, Wei, etc., but his efforts were unsuccessful all along. So he went back to his home state, giving lectures to the assembled crowd, writing books to expound his doctrines, making prefaces for the classics of *Book of Poetry* and *Book of History* with his disciples such as Wan Zhang and Gongsun Chou to promote the Confucian thought, and completing the seven chapters of *Mencius*.

In the year of 1083, Mencius was awarded the title of "Duke of the State of Zou" by Emperor Shenzong of the Song

Dynasty and was accorded the additional title of "Junior Sage Duke of the State of Zou" by Emperor Wenzong of the Yuan Dynasty in 1331. Until now, people still respectfully address Mencius as "Junior Sage".

Mencius (Meng Ke) was born in the State of Zou in 372 BC and was named Ke (meaning "ornament on a horse's halter") as he was born in a cart. The family of Meng was the offspring of the aristocratic clan of Meng Sun of the State of Lu, but Mencius' faction of the family declined in the earlier generations, and moved to the State of Zou. Mencius owed his growth largely to his mother Lady Zhang, a woman of virtue and vision, as he lost his father Meng Ji at the age of three. The stories of "Mencius' Mother moved three times" and "Mencius' Mother broke the shuttle from the loom" are known to every household.

According to the former story, Meng Ke was an extraordinarily bright boy but very naughty. Lady Zhang was so poor that she could only afford to rent cheap abodes, very often in less desirable places. When they at first lived near a graveyard, young Meng Ke led the children from the neighborhood to caper about in the graveyard and act various scenes which he had witnessed, such as digging holes in the ground to build tombs, and imitating burial and tomb-sweeping services. Upon seeing this, Lady Zhang was laden with anxieties and said to Meng Ke, "This is not the place for you to live in and let's move to another place!" So they moved to a place near a market. The merchants in the market were hustling, bustling, haggling, hawking noisily and employing trickery. Young Meng Ke spent whole days hanging about in the market and mimicked the adults selling wares with an air of slyness. Upon noticing this, Lady Zhang again became anxiety-ridden because at that time the profiteering by the merchants was despised by the general public. She was worried that her child would be harmed as time went by. Hereupon she once again said to Meng Ke, "We can't stay here either and have to move again." After prudent consideration and selection, they ended up moving to the neighborhood of a school. The school, where Zisi and his disciples taught lessons, gave lectures and practiced rituals, was filled with the sound of music and recitals, and frequented by intellectuals in civil and refined manners proclaiming the philosophy of Confucius. Grand ceremonies would be held on festival occasions in spring and autumn. Attracted by the scenes, young Meng Ke began to learn the etiquettes and rituals and to mimic the recitals. At the sight of this, Lady Zhang finally felt relieved and said to her child, "This is the neighborhood for you." Hereafter the mother and son settled down there and lived on weaving.

Not long afterwards, Meng Ke went to school but was soon tired of the difficult and sophisticated Confucian rituals. He often played truant and hung around by himself. After knowing this, Lady Zhang asked him in anger and sorrow, "Where have you been?" Meng Ke did not dare to tell a lie and said, "I hang around by myself." After hearing his answer, Lady Zhang was so sad that she took a knife and cut off the threads on the loom. Young Meng Ke was startled but did not understand why his mother had behaved like this. His mother said, "Dropping your studies is like cutting off the threads. Just as threads that are broken will not make cloth, a person who gives up studies will not make a gentleman." At that time, cloth was weaved little by little with the shuttles and it was a great pity for a piece of cloth to be cut off by a knife. But Mencius' mother used this example to stress on the importance of perseverance. Mencius was enlightened and began to immerse himself in studies. Rising early and retiring late, he studied so hard that he laid a solid foundation for his future erudite scholarship.

Of course, there were far more stories about the instruction of Mencius by his mother.

In Mencius' days, the young people eager to achieve wealth and positions through scholarship and lobbying, tended to leave their homes and study in other countries as disciples under their respected thinkers to obtain knowledge.

When Mencius reached his adolescence, the schools nearby could no longer live up to his eagerness for learning. His mother urged him to go to the State of Lu, where many of Confucius' disciples lived and the culture of the Zhou Dynasty was best preserved. More importantly, many schools of Confucian thought, which inspired Mencius more than anything else, were still in Lu. He went to Lu, visited historic sites, and consulted learned scholars. Mencius could not only learn knowledge from books, but also visited historic sites, lived in the environments Confucius had lived, and saw things Confucius had used, which greatly enriched his knowledge. However, this did not satisfy his desire for knowledge. So he collected all the works of Confucius and studied by himself, and later he was considered to be a disciple of Confucius, though never actually studied under him.

Confucius had two outstanding disciples, Zixia, who was renowned for spreading the Confucian classics, and Zengzi, who was renowned for promoting the Confucian doctrines. Zengzi remained in Lu to give lectures after the death of Confucius, and passed on his thinking to Zisi, the grandson of Confucius. When Mencius arrived in Lu, Zisi had already passed away, so he became a pupil of Zisi' disciples. Mencius particularly admired Zisi. Their relationship was not one of pupil and mentor, but Mencius was a direct successor of Zisi in philosophy. Through his disciples, Zisi had no less influence on Mencius than Confucius. In particular, what Zisi said and did in respecting scholars and stressing integrity had a profound impact on Mencius. For example, Mencius was fearless before the powerful kings when he promoted the idea of benevolent governance, and was undaunted in criticizing the lords in their face. This fitted neatly with Zisi's argument that loyal officials should keep criticizing kings for their mistakes and faults. Therefore, Zisi and Mencius have been regarded as Zisi-Mencius school of thought by the later generations.

Mencius wandered and studied in Lu for three years before he returned to his hometown and began his education career to spread his philosophy. Like Confucius, Mencius was first and foremost a teacher. He believed one of the three happiest things in life was to recruit talented people and educate them. Therefore, he set up a private school and taught the pupils from all walks of life for more than a decade before he took public office. He believed in Confucius' idea that in education there should be no class distinction and everyone was entitled to education and could achieve self-improvement through education. Therefore, he had the same principle as Confucius that "you should never inquire about anyone who has left nor refuse anyone who comes". In other words, he admitted pupils regardless of their background, age, status or wealth, and did not care about what pupils did after graduation. Mencius strived to cultivate enlightened lords, virtuous and capable officials and people with high aspirations so as to realize his political vision of "benevolent governance". Hundreds of aspirant pupils applied for admission once Mencius publicized his recruitment principle. Some of them were already social elites with accomplishments and fame. Mencius had diversified teaching methods, rather than confined himself to the classroom. He led the pupils to travel in spring and autumn and gave instructions that combined knowledge in books with that in real life. He taught the pupils according to their aptitudes so that every pupil could identify his strengths and had them fully tapped. His encouragement practices in education won high respect from his pupils and wide recognition in the general public. Hence came his title "Mencius", a respectful form of address.

The Confucian thought claims the participation in real life and politics, and the assistance of the lords in running the state. To achieve this objective, one should take public office, i.e. becoming an official. Mencius became an official when he was around 40 in his home state of Zou. However, he was marginalized in the court for being outspoken about the mistakes of Duke Mu of Zou in running the state. He realized that his vision and aspiration could not be realized there and decided to travel to other states to seek opportunities.

In an era of heptarchy (475–221 BC) and contending thoughts, there were unique groups of lobbyists, learned and capable intellectuals, who were engaged in teaching while they traveled across the states to seek political positions in order to realize their ideals and aspirations. Among them were Confucius and his disciples during the Spring and Autumn Period (770–476 BC). Such lobbying groups became even more active in Mencius' era. They shuttled between the states and put forward their propositions for diversified purposes of seeking personal interests or pursuing their ideals. Mencius was no exception. What made Mencius and his disciples stand out was their pursuit for the ideal of benevolent governance.

Mencius began to lobby the dukes and princes as a scholar when he was about forty-three. He visited the states of Liang (Wei), Qi, Song, Teng, and Lu, sparing no efforts in promoting his political proposals. He and his disciples first visited the State of Qi, where King Wei was in power and his Jixia Academy was at its prime time. This academy extensively recruited virtuous and capable scholars to remark on ways of state governance, give lectures and air academic views. Mencius was not so famous at that time and was not taken seriously. His idea of benevolent governance contrasted sharply with King Wei's idea. The ambitious King Wei raised a strong army and was determined to seek hegemony. He treated Mencius well, but did not accept his proposals. Scholars in the academy led a decent and comfortable life. Mencius was no exception. He and a dozen of his disciples lived in a big house and continued to teach and travel.

When his mother Lady Zhang died in 327 BC, Mencius buried her in full honors in the State of Lu and observed three years of mourning before he returned to the State of Qi. Things had changed in Qi as war broke out among the states. The Jixia

Academy was in decline and many scholars had left. At that time, Mencius heard that King Hui of Liang did not reconcile himself to his declining state and invited virtuous and capable scholars to assist him in the governance. Mencius thought that it was time for him to leave. Therefore, he bid farewell to the senile King Wei and left for the State of Wei.

Mencius had learnt that King Yan of Song was considering the implementation of benevolent governance before he left for Wei. So he decided to go there by the way. The State of Song, a small country, had suffered invasions from its strong neighbours and interference from its own powerful officials. The King of Song, who had enthroned for more than a decade, did not reconcile himself to the decline of his state and was aspirant to strengthen it. However, as a powerless king, he was no more than a figurehead under the sway of the treacherous court officials. He wanted to put in place benevolent governance but could do nothing. Under these circumstances, Mencius had to leave.

At this time, a message came from his home state of Zou that Duke Mu extended an urgent invitation to Mencius to discuss the state affairs. Mencius could not turn down the invitation from his home state, and led his disciples to go north. However, they were delayed in the City of Xue by the overflowing river for days of heavy rain. When they arrived, the State of Zou was routed in the battle against the State of Lu. Duke Mu, who was resentful of the people in Zou who stood idle when his state was besieged by Lu, consulted Mencius over this issue. Mencius was outspoken in criticizing Duke Mu's failure in implementing benevolent governance. He pointed out that people's suffering from the officials was the cause. Duke Mu was surprised by Mencius' ideas, but could not accept Mencius' vision of benevolent governance. As the two had nothing in common, Mencius had to leave.

Yue Zhengke, an outstanding disciple of Mencius and an official in the State of Lu, tried hard to recommend Mencius to Duke Ping, who had heard about Mencius' talents and wanted to give him an official position. Mencius was glad that his ideas were about to be implemented in the end. However, when he was about to visit Mencius after taking a bath and changing his clothes, Duke Ping was stopped by his favoured official Zang Cang, who sowed seeds of discord before the Duke and made many negative comments on Mencius. When the Duke cancelled his visit, Yue Zhengke was indignant, but Mencius just shrugged his shoulders, saying that it was not because of Zang Cang but because of the Heaven's will that he could not meet Duke Ping.

Mencius decided to visit the State of Teng when he recalled his friendship with Duke Wen. Duke Wen treated him well and often discussed with him over how to run the state. Mencius grasped this opportunity and recommended policies of benevolent governance, tax reduction for the people, and promoting education. These policies were well-received among the people, but offended the vested interests of the officials and the noblemen. Annoyed at Mencius, they kept writing to Duke Wen about his wrong-doings and even slandered him. After three years in the State of Teng, Mencius decided to leave.

Mencius was fifty-three when he arrived at Daliang, capital of the State of Wei. King Hui of Liang (also known as King Hui of Wei), after successive military defeats, lavished money on recruiting talented people so as to solicit wisdom and strategies from them to make his country strong and powerful. At the beginning of their first meeting in the court, King Hui asked Mencius what he could do to profit his state. Mencius knew that King Hui might not accept his political proposals, but, still cherished some illusions about him in the light of the Confucian conception of doing the impossible. After a few meetings, King Hui changed his attitude toward Mencius, began to accept his ideas and consult him voluntarily. After they talked for four or five times, they established a cordial relationship. However, it was the Heaven's will that Mencius could not realize his aspirations as King Hui died very soon. King Xiang, his successor, was impolite and had no royal manners at all. Some initial contact with him made Mencius realize that he could achieve nothing there. He decided to leave and to visit the State of Qi again. King Xuan who was in power was aspiring. He revitalized the Jixia Academy and recruited the talented people from all walks of life. So, Mencius arrived at a right moment. After holding a grand ceremony to welcome him and his disciples, King Xuan appointed him the guest official and visited Mencius' residence on the fourth day of his arrival, showing a rare respect for him from the kings. Conversations between Mencius and King Xuan have become famous chapters of *Mencius*.

At this time, civilian strife broke out in the neighboring state of Yan while the State of Qi took this opportunity to invade it and conquered it in a month. The glowing King Xuan visited Mencius and consulted him on how to annex it. Mencius did not oppose war so long as it was for a just cause. For example, if the King of Yan was unjust and his people lived in the abyss of misery, an attack on it would be justified, but only by an army dedicated to a just cause. As Qi was no better than Yan, it was in an unjustified position to attack Yan. Failing to get the message from Mencius, King Xuan continued to invade Yan, burning, slaughtering and looting wherever his army went. All this made the people of Yan resentful, and so did its neighboring states as the invasion had broken the balance of power. In abhorrence of a powerful Qi, the neighboring states took advantage of this opportunity to enter into an alliance against Qi.

After that, King Xuan felt sorry about this, but Mencius, realizing that he could by no means achieve his political ideal there, decided to give up his position and to leave Qi. King Xuan tried his best to detain him, promising to give Mencius a big house and a handsome salary. However, Mencius flatly turned it down and decided to leave. It was not easy for Mencius, who had placed great hope in practicing benevolent governance in Qi. His hope was broken. He was deeply painful but he had no alternative. Mencius moved slowly on his way and even stayed for three nights in a border town of Qi in the hope that King Xuan might persuade him to come back and implement benevolent governance. All this was impossible.

In 312 BC, Mencius finally left Qi where he had stayed for many years.

Mencius' philosophy was not adopted by any state until the end of his lobbying career. This was a heavy blow to his aspiration of saving the people under the Heaven. However, he did not resign himself to this, but was determined to spread his political vision and philosophy. He decided to write a book like *The Analects* to expound his views and narrate his life. Gongsun Chou, Wan Zhang and other disciples were involved in this big project. They wrote about the major events of their mentor while Mencius continued to answer their questions one after another. The project lasted to the death of Mencius and the book was entitled *Mencius*.

Mencius died at the age of eighty-three in 289 BC.

孟子智慧故事
Wisdom of Mencius

何必一定要谈利

  梁国（即魏国）在战国初年本是一个强国。到了梁惠王统治的时候，与东面齐国的一场战争中，损失了大将庞涓，太子也被俘虏。与西边秦国一战，又损失了公子卯，割让了河西七百里的土地，只好迁都到大梁。此外，南面也遭受楚国欺辱。所以这个时候的梁惠王心里最难过，求强之心也十分迫切。他一心想着如何网罗人才，振作图强，恢复魏国曾经的霸业，以至于不惜用重金厚礼来招纳天下有才能的人，以帮助魏国振兴。所以当孟子第一次觐见梁惠王时，惠王开口便问："老先生不远千里而来，将能给我国带来利益吧？"

  孟子知道梁惠王关心的只有利益，但他认为，导致各国战争不断和一切混乱、争斗、罪恶、不幸的根源就在于这个"利"字上，"利"打破了延续几百年的社会秩序和统治体制。因此孟子一心只想阐述自己心中深埋已久的政治主张——仁义。于是孟子朗声回答道："大王何必一定要说利呢？只要有仁义就足够解决所有的问题了。假如大王问：'怎样才有利于我的国家？'下面的大夫问：'怎样才有利于我的封地？'士人平民问：'怎样才能有利于我自己？'那么上上下下的人都只知道争夺私利，这样国家就危险了。在拥有万乘兵车的国家，谋害君主的一定是拥有千乘兵车的大夫，在拥有千乘兵车的国家，谋害君主的必定是拥有百乘兵车的大夫。一万辆兵车中拥有一千辆，一千辆兵车中拥有一百辆，这不能算少了。可是假如君臣都不顾道义而只重利益，那大夫们不夺取全部的兵车是不会满足的。反过来说，从来没有一个看重仁义的人会遗弃他的父母，也从来没有一个看重仁义的人会怠慢他的君主。大王还是听我讲讲仁义吧，何必要说利呢？"

看得出来，孟子与梁惠王的第一次谈话就不是很愉快。在战国时代，"好利"是流行的心态，孟子所说的仁义对梁惠王来说实在是远水解不了近渴的。但孟子明明知道梁惠王所说的利是什么，却并不迎合梁惠王，而是直言不讳地告诉梁惠王不要谈利，只谈仁义就够了，唯有把好利之心转化为仁义之心，使人们重新获得纯净的心灵，才能恢复尧舜时代的和谐秩序，使人们安居乐业，和平相处。

不管自身的利害，毫无保留地阐释自己的思想，这正是孟子一贯的精神。假如他想讨好国君，为自己谋个一官半职的，那他就不会说这些令国君不愉快的话了。而孟子知道梁惠王很难接受自己的观点，却仍然抱着"知其不可为而为之"的态度竭力劝说他施行仁义，这就更是难得的勇气和精神。

WHY SHOULD YOU MENTION PROFITS?

The State of Liang (also known as the State of Wei) was a strong power at the beginning of the Warring States Period (475–221 BC). When King Hui was in reign, Liang fought with Qi, its neighbor to the east. His general Pang Juan was killed and his heir apparent was captured in the battle. Liang also fought with Qin, its neighbor to the west. It lost Prince Mao, the king's younger brother, and 700 *li* of territory to Qin, and was forced to move its capital to Daliang. In addition, it was bullied by Chu, its neighbor to the south. King Hui felt extremely bitter at this moment and was very eager to make his state stronger. He was bent on recruiting talented people so as to revitalize his country and resume the status of hegemony. Therefore, he lavished money on recruiting talented people to strengthen his country. When Mencius met him for the first time, his first question was "Venerable sir, since you have traveled a thousand *li* to come here, you surely have some way to profit my state, haven't you?"

Mencius realized that King Hui was only interested in profits, but believed that profits were the root cause of war, chaos, contention, evils and misery, for profits had broken up the social order and ruling system of several centuries. Mencius was determined to advocate his political vision — benevolence and righteousness. So Mencius answered loudly, "Why should Your Highness mention profits? What matters is benevolence and righteousness. If Your Highness asks, 'How can I profit my state?' the high officials will ask, 'How can we profit our fiefs' and the intellectuals and the commoners will ask, 'How can we profit ourselves?' If those above and those below strive to snatch profits from one another, the state will be endangered. In a state of ten thousand chariots, the murderer of the ruler must be the minister with a thousand chariots; in a state of a thousand chariots, the murderer must be the minister with a hundred chariots. A thousand chariots in a state of ten thousand or a hundred chariots in a state of a thousand is not a small portion. The ministers' desires will be insatiable if profits come first and righteousness comes second. No benevolent man will ever forsake his parents, and no righteous man will ever neglect his sovereign. Your Highness should discuss only benevolence and righteousness with me, but why should you mention profits?"

It was obvious that the first conversation between Mencius and King Hui did not go on smoothly. Profit-seeking was a vogue in the Warring States Period. The benevolence and righteousness advocated by Mencius could not meet King Hui's immediate needs. Mencius fully understood what profits meant in King Hui's eyes, but did not cater to him. Rather, he was straightforward in telling King Hui that he should talk about benevolence and righteousness instead of profits. Only when profiteering is transformed into eagerness for benevolence and righteousness, could the purity of soul and the harmonious order in the era of sage kings of Yao and Shun be regained while people live and work in peace and contentment.

It was an unswerving principle of Mencius to be outspoken about his ideas regardless of his personal interests. He would not say unpleasant things to the kings if he wanted to pander to them so as to land some political appointment. Mencius understood that King Hui could hardly accept his viewpoints, but still tried to persuade him into promoting benevolence and righteousness even though he knew that his mission was impossible. This was the remarkable courage and spirit of Mencius.

与民同乐

　　孟子第二次觐见梁惠王的时候，惠王正站在池边，观赏着飞雁驯鹿。他心情舒畅愉快地问孟子："你们这些贤者也喜欢这样的快乐吗？"

　　尽管梁惠王的问话里包含了一些轻蔑的意思，但孟子还是很有修养地回答："贤能者才有这样的快乐，不贤者虽有这些却并不感到快乐。就像《诗》里说的，'灵台刚刚奠基，正在规划之中。百姓闻讯赶来帮忙建造，没几天功夫就完工了。本来文王还说建台不急，可是百姓都像子女为父母出力一样踊跃，所以灵台很快就建好了。后来文王来到灵囿，也享受了母鹿安卧鱼儿游来游去的快乐。'文王虽然是用了百姓来建高台挖池沼，但百姓却个个欢欢喜喜的，称文王的台为灵台，称文王的池为灵沼，并且很高兴有麋鹿鱼鳖可以玩赏。古时候的贤君就因为能与百姓一起快乐，所以才能够感到快乐啊。"

孟子接着又讲了一个相反的故事。《汤誓》里记载，夏朝的暴君夏桀在位时，自夸自己的政权像太阳一样永恒，结果老百姓都恨透了他，满怀怨恨地说："你这个暴君什么时候才会没落呢？我们宁愿与你一起灭亡，也不愿受你的残害了。"一个做君王的，百姓恨他到了宁愿跟他同归于尽的地步，他即使有高台池沼、飞禽走兽，难道能独自安享这一切快乐吗？

孟子列举了两个历史上的史实，他的用心正是想说明：作君王的要与民同乐，才是真正的快乐。这种君民同乐、共有共享的政治思想在我们今天看来是没有什么稀奇的，但在孟子所处的那个君王家天下的时代却显得十分可贵。

SHARING HAPPINESS WITH THE PEOPLE

In his second meeting with Mencius, King Hui stood by a pond, looking about at his swans and reindeer, and said, "Do virtuous men like you also enjoy these things?"

For all the contemptuous tone in King Hui's question, Mencius answered politely, "Only virtuous men can enjoy these things. Those who are not virtuous can not, though they have these things. According to *The Book of Poetry*,

'Lord Wen the Magic Tower decreed;

He planned and worked on it indeed.

Construction of it did proceed

And all completed at high speed.

No hurry did Lord Wen demand,

But people flocked to give a hand.

Lord Wen surveyed the Magic Park,

Where does and stags lay in the dark.

The does and stags were fat and meek;

The snow-white cranes were big and sleek.

Lord Wen surveyed the Magic Pool,

Where fish sprang and leapt in shoals.'

King Wen built his tower and pool with the labor of the people, and the people enjoyed doing the work for him, calling the tower the 'Magic Tower' and the pool the 'Magic Pool', and were rejoiced that he had his does, stags and cranes. The ancient kings enjoyed these things with the people, and so they could have real joy."

Mencius went further and gave a contrary instance, "According to *The Declaration of King Tang*, King Jie, the tyrant of the Xia Dynasty, boasted that his rule would be everlasting so long as the sun shined. The people were so resentful that they said, 'You tyrant, when would you meet your doom? We would rather perish with you than suffer from your cruelty.' Even though the king had towers, ponds, birds and beasts, how could he enjoy them alone when his own subjects hated him so much that they would rather perish with him?"

Mencius gave two historical instances to drive home the message that a king could experience real happiness if he enjoyed things with his subjects. This political vision was common in today's world, but highly remarkable in Mencius' era of the supreme power of the king.

仁者无敌

梁惠王最初对孟子的态度是有一点轻慢的,但后来慢慢能够听得进孟子的话了,甚至说:"我愿意接受您的教诲。"这跟孟子的谈话技巧是有很大关系的。有一回,他以当时各国社会中的病态、乱象为例,从反面激发梁惠王实行王道政治。孟子首先问:"用刀子杀人和用棍棒杀人有什么不同吗?"梁惠王说:"没什么不同。"孟子接着问:"那用刀子杀人和用暴政杀人有什么不同呢?"梁惠王回答:"也没什么不同。""那现在您的厨房有肥美的肉食,马圈里有膘肥体壮的马匹,可是老百姓却面黄肌瘦,甚至饿死在路边,这难道不是统治者在率领着兽类吃人吗?为民父母的人能够做这样的事吗?"

孟子是非常尊崇孔子的学说的,所以他最后又引用了孔子的话说道:"孔子说:'最开始作木偶土偶陪葬的人,大概要断子绝孙吧。'孔子连'始作俑者'这样的事都感到愤慨,做君王的又怎能让老百姓因饥饿而死亡呢？"

此时的梁惠王正为魏国的衰落而烦恼，整日想着要重振国业，报仇雪耻。孟子趁此机会劝说梁惠王对百姓施行仁政，去除酷刑，减轻赋税，让百姓农闲时得到教养，孝顺父母，尊敬兄长，尽忠国君。到了这个时候，国君即使让他的百姓拿着木棒去征伐秦、楚这样的强国，他们也会勇敢地上前去的。有这样的百姓，那些让自己百姓处于水深火热之中的国家哪一个会是对手呢？所以施行仁政才能天下无敌。

推行仁政，教化百姓，最后达到国富民强、天下太平，这是孟子一贯主张的仁政、王道学说，也是孔子所代表的儒家思想的精华。孟子在惠王面前毫不留情地谴责统治者"率兽食人"、"杀人以政"，公然地为备受欺凌的百姓说话，表现出了知识分子的良心和勇气，是现代社会人道主义精神的体现。

A BENEVOLENT RULER NEVER MEETS HIS MATCH

King Hui was a little bit arrogant when he first met Mencius, but gradually accepted Mencius' words and even said, "I would like to seek your advice." This was attributed to Mencius' communication skills. Once he took social anomalies and chaos in the states as an example to stimulate King Hui to implement benevolent governance. Mencius asked, "Is there any difference between killing a man with a club and with a sword?" The king said, "There is no difference." Mencius then asked, "Is there any difference between killing a man with a sword and with tyranny?" "There is no difference, either." was the king's reply. Mencius then said, "In your kitchen there is fat meat; in your stables there are strong horses. But your people look thin and pale, about to be starved to death at the roadside. As this amounts to leading the beasts to devour men, how can he serve as the parent of his people?"

Mencius had high respect for the teachings of Confucius, so he concluded his words with the words of Confucius, "Confucius said, 'He who first made wooden or clay figurines to bury with the dead will have no posterity.' Now that Confucius was so indignant about the initial employment of figurines, how can a ruler let his own subjects die of hunger?"

King Hui was deeply worried about his declining state. How to strengthen it and to make revenges figured prominently in his mind. Mencius took this opportunity to persuade him to run a benevolent government, abolish cruel punishments, reduce taxes and levies, and educate the people during the slack seasons on filial and fraternal duties so that they would provide loyal service to the king. They will fight in great courage against the powerful armies of Qin and Chu even if they only have wooden clubs. A ruler who puts his people in the abyss of misery will be no match to a benevolent ruler. Therefore, only a benevolent ruler will have no match under the Heaven.

To practice benevolent governance and inculcate the people in order to achieve prosperity and peace was the quintessence of the political vision of Mencius as well as that of Confucius. Mencius criticized the rulers without reservation for "leading beasts out to devour men" and "killing a man with bad governance" in the face of King Hui and spoke on behalf of the miserable people. This was the conscience and courage of an intellectual, as well as a forerunner of modern humanitarianism.

望之不似人君

　　正当孟子与梁惠王慢慢开始谈得来的时候,不幸得很,梁惠王却死了。即位的是他的儿子——梁襄王。新王执政,形势发生了变化。梁襄王第一次召见孟子,孟子也去了,出来后孟子就对别人说了他对这位新王的第一印象:"望之不似人君。"意思是说,这位梁襄王一眼看过去就不像个君王。而走近他仔细看时,又一点谦虚之德、戒惧之心也没有。这样的一位君王一开口向孟子问政,果然也是不着边际的:"怎么定天下?"孟子也只好简略地答复:"定于一。"

　　"一"是什么孟子说得并不明确。可是没等他解释,梁襄王就以为这里的"一"指的是一个人,所以马上接着又问:"哪一个人可以定天下呢?"孟子也就顺着他的话说:"只有那个不喜欢杀人的人才能定天下。"

　　战国时期各国君主几乎都靠杀人征战来扩充领土,建立自己的霸业。梁襄王听了孟子的理论自然是很意外,于是问孟子:"一个君主不杀人,那谁还能和他一起合作并拥护他呢?"

孟子心里明白这个梁襄王必定不是块能够施行仁政的料,但他还是一如既往地宣讲自己的学说。他给梁襄王打了一个比方:禾苗到了七八月份,如果久不下雨,稻子很快就要枯萎。这时候突然乌云密布,大雨如注,那些本来就要枯萎的禾苗马上又有了生气,重新生机勃勃地生长起来了。这种自然的力量谁能阻挡呢?如今的君主没有不喜好杀人的,这时候如果有一位体恤百姓、不好杀伐的君主出现,那么百姓都会伸长脖子仰望着,期盼他的到来,像水往低处奔流一样地归附他,这样的力量同样是不可阻挡的。那么这个君主当然就可以统一天下了。可惜,孟子的理论对于这位"不似人君"的梁襄王来说,实在是对牛弹琴。所以孟子不久就离开了魏国。

是君而不似君正好印证了孔子的"君君、臣臣、父父、子子"的思想,也就是说,君王就要有君王的样子,臣子也应有臣子的样子。如果君不像君,臣不像臣,那就天下大乱了。先秦时代思想家热烈讨论的名实问题,就是在这样的背景下展开的。

NOT THE PROPER MANNERS OF A KING

Unfortunately, King Hui died shortly after he began to get along well with Mencius. King Xiang, his son, was the successor. Things changed after the new king was enthroned. Mencius went to see him when he was summoned. After the audience with the king, he told others about his impression of the king. A look at him from a distance did not reveal the manners of a king; a closer look at him did not inspire any respect for the king. The king consulted him with state affairs abruptly with a far-fetched question, "How can the world be unified?"

Mencius replied in brief accordingly, "By one."

Mencius' answer about "one" was not explicit. But instead of seeking further explanations, King Xiang asked, "Who could unify it?" assuming "one" for one person. Mencius followed his logic and replied, "He who finds no pleasure in killing people can unify it."

Almost all the kings in the Warring States Period achieved expansion and hegemony by waging wars and killing people. Therefore, the king was naturally surprised at Mencius' argument and asked, "Who will be the ruler's followers, if he does not kill people?"

Mencius realized that King Xiang was definitely not the one to practice benevolent governance, but still went on expounding his doctrine by citing an example. In the seventh and eighth months of the year when drought reigns, the plants begin to wither. When the clouds gather densely in the sky and torrents of rain come down, the crops thrive luxuriantly. Who can keep the crops back when they thrive? Now that all the rulers are fond of killing, the people will turn to one who really cares for his subjects and is not fond of killing. They will flock to him as the water flows downwards irresistibly at top speed. Such a ruler is bound to unify the world. It is a pity that Mencius was playing the lute before a cow, a king without the proper manners of a king. Not long afterwards, Mencius left the State of Wei.

Mencius' words of "without the proper manners of a king" echoed Confucius' argument that a king should behave as a king, a minister should behave as a minister, a father behave as a father, and a son behave as a son. If they do not behave in the proper way, the world will fall into chaos. The heated debate about the name and the substance by the pre-Qin scholars was conducted against such a background.

见牛未见羊

有一次,齐宣王坐在王宫里,有人牵着一头牛从殿堂下走过。齐宣王问:"牵牛干什么?"那人说:"杀了它用血来祭钟。"齐宣王说:"放了它吧!我实在不忍心看着它害怕发抖的可怜模样,像是一个无罪的人被推向刑场一样。"那个牵牛的人问:"那祭钟这样的大事就不进行了吗?"齐宣王想了想说:"那怎么可以呢?要不,就换只羊代替吧。"于是便换用了一只羊。

后来孟子见到齐宣王,宣王问到怎样才能够统一天下,孟子便提起了这件事:"听说您曾经不忍心杀牛而用羊代替祭钟,有这回事吗?"宣王说:"有。"孟子说:"大王有这样的仁心就足以施行王道了。百姓可能会以为大王是舍不得一头牛,所以用一只小点的羊取代牛祭钟。但我知道这是因为大王您不忍心啊。"齐宣王忙不迭地说:"就是啊!我们齐国虽小,我也不至于舍不得一头牛吧。我实在是不忍心看见它发抖的样子，所以才用一只羊取代它。"

孟子终于抓住了齐宣王话中的漏洞，毫不留情地说："大王也不必觉得百姓的想法不合理。您以小换大，他们怎么不会以为是大王您小气呢？大王既然是不忍心看见牛无辜被杀，那么羊又何尝不是呢？您是只见牛而不见羊啊！不过，大王既然有这样的仁心，那施行王道还是有希望的。"

齐宣王喜欢有学问的游说之士，因此，他当政时，齐国政府设立的稷下学宫正是鼎盛时期，先后到这里讲学的多达近千人。孟子离开魏国来到齐国也正是这个时候。

齐国的稷下学宫有一个传统，就是"不治而议论"，即学者们虽不参政，但可以自由议政。孟子也就是在这样的情况下表达了自己对于称王天下的看法。孟子的着眼点其实就是一个"不忍之心"，他认为，只要把这种"不忍之心"由动物推广到天下百姓的身上，就可以恢复以往的社会秩序，建立美好和谐的社会。孟子把称王天下、创造美好社会的理想都建立在这个"不忍之心"上，不能不说是脱离了现实的想法，但也反映了儒家思想中"仁政王道"的基本精神。

SEEING THE OX BUT NOT THE SHEEP

One day King Xuan of Qi was sitting in the palace when a man appeared, leading an ox across the hall. The king asked, "Where is the ox going?" The man said, "We are going to consecrate a bell with its blood." The king said, "Let it go. I cannot bear to see it trembling, as if it were an innocent man going to the execution ground." The man said, "Shall we cancel the important event of the consecration of the bell?" The king thought for a while and said, "How can it be cancelled? Change it for a sheep." Then, the ox was replaced by a sheep.

King Xuan met Mencius later and asked him about how to unify the world. Mencius mentioned this incident and asked, "I heard that Your Highness did not bear to see the consecration of an ox as the sacrificial offering to the bell and replaced it with a sheep. Is that true?" The king said, "Yes." Mencius said, "Since Your Highness has such a kind heart, you can implement benevolent governance. All your people think that Your Highness grudged an ox, and replaced it with a sheep for the consecration of a bell. But I know it was because Your Highness could not bear the sight." The king replied immediately, "You are right. There are indeed people who think that I grudged the ox. But how can I grudge an ox though the State of Qi is small? It was because I could not bear to see it trembling that I changed it for a sheep."

Mencius seized the loophole in the king's words and pointed out directly, "Do not think it strange that the people should think you were grudging the ox. How could they know the reason why you changed a large animal for a small one? And what was there to choose between an ox and a sheep if you felt grieved when an innocent creature was led to death? Your Highness only saw the ox but not the sheep. Nevertheless, Your Highness has such a kind heart that it is possible for you to practice benevolent governance."

King Xuan admired learned lobbyists. The Jixia Academy established by the Qi government was at its prime when he was in power. Nearly one thousand scholars offered teachings at this academy. Mencius arrived at the academy at this time.

This academy had a tradition for scholars to have free discussion of politics without participating in it. In this context, Mencius put forward his views on ruling the whole country. His key point was the "sense of compassion". He believed that a proper social order and a harmonious society could be restored by spreading this "sense of compassion" for the beasts to the people of the country. His vision for hegemony and a good society is based on this "sense of compassion". Though it was divorced from the reality, it nevertheless reflected the essence of benevolent governance of Confucianism.

不为与不能

齐宣王听见孟子夸自己有仁心、能行王道以后十分高兴。他说:"还是老先生您能够揣摩我的心思。回过头来想,我自己也不明白我舍不得杀牛的心理。为什么有这样的心理就能够施行王道呢?"孟子并没有直接回答齐宣王的问题,而是反过来问他:"假如有人禀报大王说:'我的力量可以举起三千斤的重量,但却举不起一根羽毛;我的眼力可以看清秋天鸟兽毫毛的末端,但却看不见一车柴火',大王您能相信这样的话吗?"齐宣王说:"不相信。"孟子说:"大王您的恩惠可以施与一头牛,却不肯推及百姓。这是什么原因呢?一根羽毛举不起,是因为不肯用力气;一车柴火看不见,是因为不肯用眼力。所以,百姓没有得到大王的恩惠,是因为您没有施与他们啊。所以大王没能一统天下,是因为您不为,而不是不能啊。"

齐宣王一听这话就有兴趣了:"那么,不为和不能有什么区别呢？"这正是孟子接下来要阐述的重点，所以他不假思索地回答说，"假如叫一个人用胳膊挟着泰山跳过北海，这个人说我办不到，那这是不能，是能力不够。假如叫一个人去为一个老人折一根树枝，这人回答说我办不到，那这是不为，是他不肯做，而不是没有能力。所以凭大王的国力和所处的环境，并不是没有推行仁政的能力，就像不肯为老人折树枝一样，是不为，是您不肯施行，而不是没有施行的能力。"

说到这里，孟子稍稍停顿了一下，继续宣传他的仁政，他说"您施行仁政，就要从自身做起，然后推广到百姓身上。让每一个人先敬重自己的父母长辈，然后再推广到别人的父母长辈。每一个人都爱护自己的子弟，然后再把这种爱护之心推广到别人的子弟身上。这样下去，就能保护四海百姓，最终保有天下。否则，只顾自己的权势、利益，到头来，恐怕连自己的妻子儿女都保不住呢。"

孟子以前历史上的圣贤之所以能够建立伟大的功业，其实也没有什么特别的地方，主要是因为他们怀有一颗仁心，并能推己及人。这就是所谓的仁政。如今齐宣王能够对一头牛发善心，证明他是有施行仁政的基础的。可是，他却没有把自己对牛的仁心推广到老百姓的身上去，老百姓得不到君王给予的任何恩惠，他凭什么拥护你呢？齐宣王自己都不清楚自己放掉一头牛是什么心理，说明他这君王实在缺乏反省精神。而孟子的分析正好击中了齐宣王的要害。

LACK OF WILLINGNESS VS. LACK OF CAPACITY

King Xuan of Qi was very pleased after Mencius paid him some compliments on his benevolence as well as his competence of being a ruler. He said, "Only you, master, can figure out what I am thinking. In retrospect, even I myself am not so clear about why I was reluctant to kill the ox. How does it relate to being able to rule a state?" Mencius did not answer the king's question directly but threw a question on him, "If someone reports to you that he has the strength to lift up the weight of three thousand kilograms but fails to pick up a feather; that he has the perfect vision to see the tips of hair vellus of animals and birds in the autumn but failed to see a cartload of firewood, would you believe his words?" The king replied, "No." Then Mencius went on, "Your Highness, your benevolence can reach an ox, but you don't want to benefit your own subjects. Why? The man cannot pick up a feather because he is not willing to do so; he cannot see a cartload of fireworks just because he is not willing to see it. By analogy, the very reason why your subjects are yet to be benefited by your benevolence is just because you have not granted them. Therefore, the reason why you have not yet unified the country is your lack of willingness rather than your lack of capacity."

Intrigued by his words, King Xuan asked, "So what's the difference between the lack of willingness and the lack of capacity?" As that is the point to be elaborated on, Mencius replied without thinking, "Suppose you ask someone to cross the North Sea while carrying Mount Tai between his arms and he tells you that he could not do it. That is a case of lack of capacity or beyond his capacity. Suppose you ask someone to pluck a tree twig for an elderly person and he tells you that he could not do it. That is a case of lack of willingness, because he has the capacity but is not willing to do so. Therefore, given the strength and the current situation, the reason why your subjects are not yet benefited is not because you are not able to rule benevolently, but not willing to promote benevolence like the man who refuses to pluck a twig for an elderly man. That is considered lack of willingness instead of lack of capacity."

After a short pause, Mencius continued to promote his political vision of benevolent governance to the king, "If you want to adopt benevolent governance, you have to take the initiative and then roll out to your subjects. You should first let each and every person respect their parents and the elder members of their own clan and then respect the others; take care of younger members of one's own family and then take care of the others. By doing so, we can protect all the people in the world and protect the sovereignty. Otherwise, if one only looks after his own power and interests, he might even not be able to protect his own family in the end."

Actually, there is nothing special about the sages before Mencius who scored great achievements. Their accomplishments are mainly attributed to their hearts of benevolence and willingness to spread their own thoughts to others. That is what we call benevolent governance. King Xuan's kindness to an ox is proof of his potential to practice benevolent governance, but he failed to extend it to others. As his subjects have not enjoyed the benefits of benevolent governance, why should they support the king? The king's bewilderment about why he freed the ox showed his lack of self-reflection while Mencius' analysis hit the nail on the head.

独乐乐不如众乐乐

有一次,孟子从他的学生——齐国的大夫庄暴那里得知齐宣王喜欢音乐,就在跟齐宣王见面的时候提出此事。齐宣王很不好意思地说,他喜欢的音乐是一般民间的流行音乐,不是什么古代圣王的高尚音乐。没想到孟子却说没关系,喜欢流行音乐和喜欢古典音乐是一样的。只要齐宣王喜欢音乐,那齐国就有希望了。齐宣王不理解地问:"那是为什么呢?"

孟子不失时机地开导齐宣王:"是一个人独自欣赏音乐快乐呢?还是和别人一起分享更快乐呢?"宣王回答:"当然是和别人一起分享更快乐。"孟子又问:"是和少数人一起欣赏音乐快乐呢?还是和多数人一起欣赏音乐更快乐?"宣王仍然回答:"当然是和多数人一起分享更快乐。""那如果你的百姓听见你在宫里击鼓鸣钟,吹笛奏乐,却个个愁眉苦脸、彼此诉苦:'我们的国王这么爱好音乐,为什么却让我们流落到父子不相见、兄弟妻子离散的地步？'相反，假如陛下在此奏乐，百姓听见以后奔走相告：'我们的国王身体一定健康吧？不然，怎么会奏乐呢？'这说明什么呢？没有别的，看陛下是否与民同乐了。陛下如果与民同乐的话，就可以王天下了。"

我们从这个故事里可以看到，齐宣王算得上是一个坦率的君主，他能够接受孟子的劝告，但又总是不自信自己能够做得到。于是孟子就一次又一次地启发、劝说他，表现出一种坚定的信念。此外，孟子的思想观念跟历史上其他许多儒学大家比起来也要开放、自由得多。爱好流行音乐，这在当时推崇古代礼乐的环境里并不是什么光彩的事。然而孟子却说爱好流行音乐没有什么不好，关键是要把这种好乐的精神推广开来，让百姓也可以和君王一起感受到音乐的快乐。这一方面说明了孟子善于诱导的说话技巧，另一方面也表现出了孟子所追求的与民同乐、共享共存的理想社会。这在那个专制的封建时代显然是很先进的。

ENJOYING THE MUSIC WITH THE PEOPLE IS BETTER THAN ENJOYING IT BY HIMSELF

On hearing from his disciple Zhuang Bao, a minister of the State of Qi, that King Xuan of Qi was very fond of music, Mencius mentioned this when he met the king. King Xuan told Mencius in embarrassment that he enjoyed the popular music rather than the refined classical music. Much to his surprise, Mencius said that it did not matter whether he was fond of the popular or the classical music. As long as the king enjoyed music, there was hope for the State of Qi. King Xuan was puzzled and asked why.

Mencius took the opportunity to enlighten the king, "In which way will you have more fun? Enjoying the music by yourself or with other people?" The king replied, "Of course, enjoying the music with other people will bring me more fun." Mencius went on asking, "In which way will you have more fun? Enjoying music with a small or large crowd of people?" The king replied, "Of course with a large crowd." "Suppose the scenario that your subjects, after hearing the drum-beating, bell-ringing and flute-and-music-playing in your palace, would look worried and complain to each other that their music-loving king brings them a sorrowful life and broken-up families; or suppose the other scenario that after hearing the music from your palace, they would rush to tell each other that their king must be healthy enough to enjoy the music. What do these two scenarios tell us? They tell us nothing more than whether you would like to share happiness with the people. If you would, you can lord it over the world."

Through this story we know that King Xuan of Qi could be regarded as a candid ruler, but while he was willing to accept Mencius' advices, he was not confident whether he could translate these advices into practice. Therefore, Mencius continued to enlighten and reason with him with a staunch faith. Also, Mencius held a broader and more liberal view compared with the other Confucian masters in history. In an age when the popular music was regarded as inferior to the refined classical music, Mencius insisted that there was nothing wrong in enjoying the popular music. He claimed that the key point was to promote a music-loving atmosphere, so that men on the street could enjoy the music as well. On the one hand, this reflected Mencius' exceptional persuasive techniques; on the other hand, it depicted Mencius' ideal society in which all the people are interdependent on each other and share the happiness and the benefits together. Obviously, his thoughts were very progressive in the autocratic feudal society.

大勇与小勇

齐宣王向孟子请教,与邻国的邦交有什么好办法、好策略。孟子说,大致有两种原则。一是"以大事小",即虽然自己的国土大,国力强,但是仍愿意配合领土比自己小、国力比自己弱的国家,这是仁者的策略。第二个原则是"以小事大",这属于明智之举,即为了在安定中求进步,采取退让的态度,不去和大国争斗。以大国之尊去配合小国,这是一种乐天的心理。以弱小的国力不去得罪大国,这是畏天的心理。乐天的原则具有博爱精神,一定可以使四海的百姓都归顺自己,所以可以保有天下;弱小的国家不跟强敌对抗,那么也能保住自己的国家。所以时刻怀着谨慎的心理,把握好环境发展的大趋势,才能维护自己的生存。

孟子说到这里,齐宣王突然插话了。他说:"你讲的这些理论太高深、太宏大了,我们还是谈点现实的问题吧。我这人有一个毛病,就是好勇。"

　　孟子顺着齐宣王的话头一转，继续宣传自己的仁政学说。他说，好勇也不是坏事，只要您好的勇不是小勇——即动不动就拔刀相向、舞枪弄棒的那种个人勇武。您齐宣王爱好的应该是像文王那样的大勇。当文王听说密国无故攻打阮国时，怒不可遏，立刻出兵阻挡密国的进攻，同时也巩固了周国的边界，让人民更加安居乐业。这样的大勇使百姓得到了安定。

　　孟子最后说，大王您好勇有什么关系呢？只要您好的不是匹夫之勇，而是文王一样能够一怒而使天下安定的大勇，那么哪个百姓不欢迎这样的大勇呢？

　　孟子每一次与齐宣王的谈话都少不了这种诱导的方式。不管齐宣王提出什么样的问题来为难他，他都能够顺势而上，最后把中心引向"仁政"。好乐也好，好勇也好，宣王后来说到的好货、好色也好，都不是什么坏事，只要能把自己的爱好推广开来，让百姓也能享受到同样的快乐和安定，这就是一个好的政治，好的君王。由此也可以看出，孟子教化君王的方式其实一点也不迂腐，他是很能变通的。不管话题从哪里开始，他总能使中心思想朝着自己预定的方向走，这又是他的高明之处。

VALOR VS. BRUTE COURAGE

　　King Xuan of Qi consulted Mencius about the methods and strategies of dealing with the neighboring states. Mencius suggested two major principles, "One is called 'He who rules a bigger state serves the smaller ones', i.e., although one's own state is bigger and stronger than the other states, he is still willing to coordinate with them, which is the strategy of a benevolent ruler.

Another principle is called, 'He who rules a smaller state serves the bigger ones', i.e., in order to seek development in stability and avoid conflicts with the bigger states, one adopts the attitude of taking concessions, which is a judicious move. That he who has the dignity of a bigger state serves smaller ones delights the Heaven. That he who rules a weaker state avoids offending the bigger ones comes from awe for the Heaven. The principle of delighting the Heaven is philanthropic, which will surely win the hearts of the people in the world and ensure the rule of the country, while a smaller state by avoiding conflicts with the stronger enemies can safeguard its own country. So only those with a prudent mentality and a good command of the general trends can sustain their survival.

At this point, King Xuan suddenly chipped in, saying, "Your theories are all too sophisticated and profound, but I'd rather talk about some practical issues. My infirmity lies in the fact that I love valor."

Mencius continued to sell his ideas about benevolent governance by following the issue the king just picked and said, "It is not necessarily a bad thing to be fond of gallantry as long as what you love is valor rather than brute courage — that kind of individual gallantry featuring brandishing one's swords and spears at every turn. Your Highness, what you love must be the valor displayed by King Wen. He was filled with fury after learning that the State of Mi was planning to attack the State of Ruan without any justification, and so he immediately sent troops to block the attacks by Mi. By doing so, he also provided safer environments for the life and work of his own people with a consolidated border. This kind of valor ensured the security and stability of his people."

In the end, Mencius said, "There is nothing wrong about loving valor. As long as you share the valor with King Wen who, with a fit of rage, ensured the security and stability of his state, none of your people will turn against it."

Mencius used reasoning in every conversation with King Xuan, taking advantage of every issue picked by the king, regardless how thorny the issue was, and finally leading the conversation to "benevolent governance". No matter whether the king was fond of music or valor or even goods and beauties, Mencius would not regard it as something bad. As long as the king could expand his hobby to the people and share the joy and stability with them, it was defined as successful governance of a judicious ruler. We can also see that Mencius was rather flexible than pedantic — no matter where the conversation started, he was able to redirect it in his own way.

胡服骑射

　　为了激励齐宣王勇于改革,大胆地施行仁政,孟子较为详尽地给他讲述了赵武灵王胡服骑射的故事。

　　赵武灵王是一个好武的国君。赵国北部边境与胡人接邻,胡人是游牧民族,为了生活方便,也为了打仗御敌方便,他们的服装都是短衣窄袖的式样。而汉民族的服装向来是宽袍阔袖,虽然美观,却不利于耕作与征战。赵武灵王为了使赵国强盛,便下令废除原来的服饰,改穿胡人的那一套装扮,希望通过这个来改革赵国的政治、民风,达到富国强兵的目的。此外,他还将赵国战车都改为骑兵,教导训练百姓们每天骑马打猎。

　　可是赵武灵王的这一改革措施遭到了国内很多人的反对。他们认为服装的式样是礼制的一个部分,改革服装就是违背礼制,破坏传统。赵武灵王辩论说,古代和现代的习俗各不相同,历代帝王的礼法也不是一成不变的。如果一定要遵循先王的礼法的话，我们究竟要遵循哪一个朝代的礼法呢？时代不同，礼制就要适应环境而有所变化，衣服、器具也是这样。所以你们就不要反对了吧。

后来，赵武灵王的改革措施确实收到了成效。不久，赵国的军队强壮起来了，赵武灵王便亲自率领部队攻打胡、翟的边境，扩展了几百里的疆土，接着就打算进攻西边强大的秦国。

孟子给齐宣王讲这个故事的目的在于，赵武灵王能成为诸侯之中第一个立志改革、胡服骑射的人，你齐宣王也可以成为诸侯中首先实行仁政的国君啊。胡服骑射本无先例，而古代圣贤施行仁政、统一天下的例子很多，并因此流芳百世。宣王为什么不去实行这样能使大家都得到利益的改革呢？

WEARING THE TARTAR ATTIRES AND TRAINING THE CAVALRIES

In order to encourage King Xuan of Qi to pursue reforms and implement benevolent governance boldly and resolutely, Mencius expounded the story about the adoption of the Tartar attires and the training of cavalries by King Wuling of Zhao.

King Wuling was a bellicose ruler of the State of Zhao, which bordered the nomad Tartar tribes to the north. The Tartars wore short coats with narrow sleeves for the convenience of daily life and military battles, while the Hans wore long robes with wide sleeves, handsome but not convenient for farming or military battles. To strengthen his state, King Wuling abandoned the traditional costumes and adopted the Tartar attires. He saw this as a way to reform the politics and folk customs so as to build his state into a prosperous one with a powerful army. Furthermore, he replaced the chariots with the cavalries and gave his subjects riding and hunting trainings.

However, those reforms met with a lot of opponents, who claimed that the style of clothing was part of the rites and the changing of clothing style violated the rites and traditions. King Wuling retorted, "The present customs differ from those of the ancients, and the rites have also evolved during the history of different rulers. If we have to follow the ancient rites, which dynasty's rites should we follow as a model? The ritual system itself has evolved with the change of environments and times, and the same is true for clothing and tools. Therefore, please get over your oppositions."

The reforms turned out to be a great success. When his army became stronger after some time, King Wuling headed his army to fight against the Tartars along the border and expanded the frontier of his state by hundreds of *li* and even planned to attack the strong state of Qin to its west.

Mencius told this story to King Xuan to inspire him that if King Wuling of Zhao established himself as the first king among his peers to carry out reforms to wear the Tartar attires and to train the cavalries, King Xuan could also become the pioneer in practicing benevolent governance. There was no precedence in wearing the Tartar attires and training the cavalries, but there were many extolled examples of practising benevolent governance to unify the whole country by great kings in the ancient times. So why not implement reforms which would be of great benefits to the people?

流连忘返

　　有一次齐宣王在雪宫接见孟子,孟子继续向他宣讲与民同乐的道理,并给齐宣王讲了齐景公和相国晏婴的故事来启发他。
　　齐景公是姜太公的后人。有一天他对晏婴说:"我想去看看转附和朝儛这两座名山,然后沿着海再到南方去,一直要到琅琊为止。你看,这一路要怎样才能够比得上先王那样的壮观呢?"晏婴不愧是名相,他不动声色地回答,"这问题问得好啊。"接着就说,依照礼法,天子去诸侯的领土巡视叫巡狩,意思是巡视诸侯所守护的地方;诸侯到中央政府去朝见天子叫述职,意思是报告自己职务以内的事。他们都是有很多事情要做的,春天要视察耕田播种的情况,设法救助那些不能度过春荒的人;秋天要视察收获的情况,帮助那些有困难的人。所以老百姓都希望天子出来巡视,自己能得到些帮助和好处。可是现在就不一样了啊,诸侯们只要一出动就要带领大批军队,这些军队都要消耗大量的粮食，别说饥饿者没有食物可得，就是劳动者也得不到休息。因此百姓就有了怨恨之心。此外，诸侯们和部下每到一地，吃喝无度，残害百姓。顺着河流朝下游走，忘了回来，这叫流；溯流而上忘了回来，这叫连；毫无节制地追捕野兽，这叫荒；大量饮酒而不知足，这叫亡。先王没有这些流连荒亡的行为。现在就看大王您怎么做了。"

晏婴的一番话让齐景公听了非常振奋，立即下命令改革政治。他还马上将部队驻扎郊外，拿出钱粮救济穷苦的人。处理完国事后，景公还把乐官请来，要他在国史上记下这件事，并把他和晏婴君臣相得的美事谱写成乐章。

孟子针对齐宣王喜欢享受的心理，用鉴古观今的手法启发他与民同乐的精神。

"流连忘返"这个成语就是来自于齐景公与晏婴相得相知的故事。不过，现在的意思是指对某个地方的美景迷恋、欣赏不已，以至忘了回去的时间。这与本意已经相差很远了。

RELUCTANT TO LEAVE IN INDULGENCE OF PLEASURES

During an audience with King Xuan of Qi in the Snow Palace, Mencius continued to expound his ideas of sharing joys with the people by telling the story which happened between Duke Jing of Qi and his prime minister Yan Ying.

Duke Jing of Qi, the offspring of Grand Duke Jiang, once said to Yan Ying, "I wish to go on an inspection tour to Mount Zhuanfu and Mount Chaowu, and then bend my course southward along the shore, till I reach Mount Langya. What shall I do to make my tour comparable to the inspection tours made by the ancient kings?" Yan Ying, a renowned minister worthy of his reputation, replied calmly, "That's a good question." Then he went on, "According to the rituals, when the Son of the Heaven made an inspection tour to the territories of the lords, he was surveying the states under their care; when the lords attended the court of the Son of the Heaven, they were reporting their duties in office. They all had lots of things to do. In the spring, they would inspect the ploughing and sowing, and help those in the spring famine; in the autumn, they would inspect the harvesting and help those in difficulties. Therefore, all the people wished that the Son of the Heaven would make inspection tours, so that they could get some help and benefit. But now things are different. Whenever the lords are touring around, a large troop will attend to them and consume large provisions. As the hungry will not get food and the toilers will get no rest, the people will naturally bear grudges. Furthermore, the lords and their subordinates make extravagant consumptions of food and drinks and bully the local people wherever they go. Walking down the river and forgetting to return is what I call yielding to it; pressing up against the current and forgetting to return is what I call lingering on it; hunting wild animals without inhibition is what I call being wild; binge drinking without satiety is what I call being lost. The late king has conducted none of those acts, now it is time for you, my king, to pursue your own course. The sage kings in the ancient times never acted like this, and now it is time for you to pursue your own course."

Greatly inspired by Yan Ying's words, Duke Jing immediately issued a proclamation to implement reforms in his state. Then he stationed his troops in the suburbs and provided the needy with food and subsidies. After he finished the state affairs, he called the grand music-master to enter this story in the annals and to compose a piece of music about it.

In the light of King Xuan's preference for leisure and pleasure, Mencius inspired him with the spirit of sharing joys with the subjects by making an inference from the past.

The Chinese idiom of "reluctant to leave in indulgence of pleasures (*liu lian wang fan*)" originates from the story between Duke Jing and his minister Yan Ying, but is a far cry from its original denotation.

鳏寡孤独

齐宣王问孟子:"有人建议我把明堂拆掉,您说我到底是拆还是保留呢?"孟子回答说:"明堂是有德行的天子举行教化活动的庙堂。您如果想实行王政,就不要拆掉吧。"齐宣王接着这话就问:"那你能给我讲讲王政吗?"

孟子想了一下,然后就举出周文王的例子来答复齐宣王。文王在岐山发祥之初就实行了王道政治。他对农民只收取九分之一的赋税,对做官的人给予世代承袭的俸禄,关卡和市场上只追查违法活动,不收税。任何人想要去河流湖泊里捕鱼都不禁止,对犯罪的人,刑罚不会牵连到他的妻子儿女。那时候,年纪大而没有妻子的人叫鳏,失去丈夫的老妇人叫寡,没有子女的老人叫独,从小就失去父亲的人叫孤。这四种无依无靠的人,文王最先照顾到他们。这就是文王的仁政。

听到这里,齐宣王就说了一句"这话讲得好",马上把话锋一转,说自己有个毛病，就是爱财。孟子紧逼不放地说，身为一国之君，喜欢财富是应该的。周朝的先祖公刘就是个爱财的人，他因此而积极创业，富国强民，让百姓得到了实惠，这不是好事吗？

齐宣王又说，可我还有个更不好的毛病，我很好色。孟子又说，这不要紧啊。文王的祖父古公亶父也很好色，不管走到哪里，都带着他喜爱的夫人姜女。可是那个时候，亶父的国境之内，没有找不到丈夫的怨女，也没有娶不到妻子的旷男，每一个家庭都幸福美满。所以好色没有什么关系，只要把您的好色之心推广开来，使百姓都能有幸福美满的家庭，这不是好事吗？

齐宣王与孟子每次谈到王道仁政，总是以自己好勇、好色、好财等缺点为借口来推托。但孟子总能因势利导。他举那些先王圣贤为例，目的是为了让齐宣王努力向他们靠近。只是，屡次的交谈似乎并没有起到很大的作用。也许对齐宣王来说，孟子的仁政学说虽然是正理，但在战国诸侯争霸的时代却并不合时宜。倘若齐国实行仁政，别的国家却在厉兵秣马，富国强兵，实行霸权，这就等于是一只羔羊与群虎相争啊，不是等着受气挨打吗？孟子的道理虽好，却有点远水解不了近渴。

THE WIDOWERS, WIDOWS, ORPHANS AND CHILDLESS

"Some suggested me to pull down the Hall of Distinction. Shall I follow his advice or preserve the Hall?" The King Xuan of Qi asked. Mencius replied by saying, "The Hall of Distinction is the temple for the virtuous kings to give teachings. So if you want to practice the true royal ruling, then do not pull it down." The king continued to ask, "Could you tell me more about the true royal ruling?"

Mencius thought for a while and replied with the example of King Wen of Zhou. King Wen started the true royal ruling as early as his initial rise to power in Mount Qi. He only collected one ninth of the harvest as taxation from the farmers; provided salaries to the descendents of the officials; inspected the illegal activities at the passes and in the markets without levying taxes on the goods. There were no prohibitions on fishing in the rivers and the ponds, and the family members of the criminals would not be involved in the punishment for their guilt. At that time, the elders without wives were called widowers; the old women without husbands were called widows; the elders without children were called the childless; the young without father were called orphans. The above four categories of helpless people enjoyed the utmost care from King Wen. All this constituted his benevolent ruling.

"Oh, well said!" said King Xuan and switched the topic of the conversation, "I have the infirmity of being fond of wealth." Mencius pressed on and told him, "It is unimpeachable for a head of state to love wealth. Formerly, King Liu of Zhou was so fond of wealth that he devoted himself to enriching the state and benefiting the people. Wasn't that good?"

King Xuan went on, "But I have another more serious infirmity — my fondness of beauties." "That doesn't matter," Mencius replied, "Grand Duke Danfu, the grandfather of King Wen also loved beauties. Wherever he went, he had the company of his beloved wife Lady Jiang. During his reign, there were no grieving spinsters or desolate men who could not find their spouses, and every family enjoyed a happy life. So fondness of beauties itself is not a bad thing. As long as you can expand its benefits to your subjects and bring happiness to every family, isn't it a good thing?"

While discussing royal ruling and benevolent governance with Mencius, King Xuan always dodged about under the excuses of his fondness of valour, beauties and wealth. Mencius, on the other hand, could always guide him by finding a way to make the best use of the situations. He cited the examples of the ancient sage kings to encourage King Xuan to emulate them. However, these conservations did not seem to be of much use. In the eyes of King Xuan, for all the benefits of benevolent governance put forward by Mencius, it would not be appropriate to practice it during the Warring States Period when states were incessantly fighting against each other for supremacy. Had the State of Qi practiced benevolent governance while the other states were grooming the horses, drilling the troops and strengthening their states to seek hegemony, it would be like a lamb competing against a herd of tigers, whose fate would be nothing but being bullied and humiliated. Therefore, like distant water that cannot quench the present thirst, Mencius' ideas, brilliant as they were, could hardly be put into practice.

如何识才

孟子觐见齐宣王，对他说："所谓历史悠久的国家，并不是指年代的久远，而是指文化根基的深厚。因此参天的古木并不能代表国家的古老雄厚，功勋卓著、德行优越的老臣才是一个古老国家的代表。如今齐国别说没有这样的大臣，就连亲近您、值得您信任的臣子都没有了。"

齐宣王听孟子这么说，连忙辩解说："我下面有那么多人，我怎么知道谁没有才能而罢免他呢？没法考察啊。"孟子说，用人本应该照规章制度办。但如果真的遇到人才的话，就不要拘泥于成规，而应该越级提拔，使他的才能发挥作用。接着，孟子就对齐宣王解说了用人的几个原则。如果有一个人，左右的人都认为他好，您还不可以任用他；朝中大夫都说他好，还是不能用；全国人民都说他好，您也还是要慎重；只有亲自考察，结果发现他是真的好，这时才能用他。相反，如果有个人，左右近臣都说他不好，不要轻信；朝中大夫都说他不好，也不要轻易相信；国人都说他不行，就要考察一下实际情况，真的不行才罢免。如果有个罪人，大家都说他该杀，您同样要去考察，真的该杀才杀，这样即使是您下命令杀了他，那也等于是全国的人杀了他，谁也不会怨恨您。能够做到这样，才能够说是为民父母。"

孟子在这里其实谈的是一个如何选用人才的问题。国家依靠的是贤才做支柱，而一个人贤不贤及该不该杀，这都不能仅仅听信左右近臣或诸大夫之言。只有广泛听取国人的意见，加上自己的慎重考察，才能得到真正的贤才，去掉不贤者。孟子的这一用人和选拔人才的标准即使是在我们今天强调民主法治的时代也不一定执行得很好，而他能在两千多年前的战国时代就提出来，不能不说是很有远见的。

HOW TO SPOT THE TALENTS

During an audience with King Xuan of Qi, Mencius said, "A state with a long history is not defined in the sense of time, rather in the richness of its culture. Similarly, the towering old trees cannot stand for the history of a state, but the meritorious and virtuous old ministers can. Now in the State of Qi, there are no trustworthy officials who are close to you, let alone the above-mentioned ones."

Hearing this, King Xuan argued, "I have so many officials and how is it possible for me to tell who is incompetent and should be dismissed?" Mencius replied, "We should follow the rules and regulations in appointing the officials. If you have spotted a true talent, however, don't be restricted by those set rules. You should give full play to his talents and promote him by overstepping his rank." Mencius added by expounding several principles of appointing officials, saying, "If a person who has won acclaim from those close to him, it is justified for you not to appoint him yet; if he has won acclaim from all the officials in the court, you still cannot appoint him on that account; if he has won the acclaim from the people, you still have to be cautious and can only appoint him according to your own investigations into him. On the other side, you should not listen indiscriminately to criticism of an official from your close circle or from other officials in the court. You should only dismiss him according to your investigations after you hear criticisms of him from the people. If all the people think that a certain criminal deserves the death sentence, you still have to make your decision according to your investigations. When you kill a criminal who deserves the death sentence, you have killed him in the name of the people and no one will hold any grudge against you. If you can act like this, you can indeed be regarded as the guardian of the people."

Here Mencius raised the issue of how to select the talents. As the talents of virtue are the pillars of a state, the criteria of judging the virtuousness, the non-virtuousness and those who deserve death are not to be judged according to the words of the king's close ministers or the officials in the court. Only by hearing the people's voices extensively and doing his own prudent investigations, can the king spot the genuine virtuous and dismiss the non-virtuous. Even in today's world with the hallmark of democracy and government by law, Mencius' criteria for appointing and promoting the talents are yet to be fully implemented. Mencius is far-sighted in that he put forward these ideas as early as over two thousand years ago in the Warring States Period.

何谓一夫

齐宣王有一次向孟子询问汤武革命的事:"商汤把夏桀放逐到南巢去,周武王出兵讨伐纣王,有这回事吗?"

儒家思想中关于君臣之间的关系有严格的规定,臣子谋杀君主,犯上作乱,这叫做"弑",是大逆不道的行为。以前孟子在齐宣王面前屡屡夸赞商汤、周武王的丰功伟绩,如今齐宣王拿出这个问题来问孟子,其实是有点为难孟子的意思。然而,孟子的回答也很巧妙。他首先说,在古书上是这么记载的。齐宣王马上接话说:"那这不是叛逆行为吗?为臣子的怎么可以弑君呢?"孟子的回答是对儒家这一传统思想的相对性的解释。他说,一个国家的领导者违背了仁义,那就叫做"贼";违反了道义的领导者叫做"残"。这种害仁残义的人就是"独夫",所以商汤、武王的革命除掉的是一个"独夫",并不是"弑君",不算叛逆行为。孟子还说,君王若犯了重大错误,那同宗的贵族公卿就应该加以劝阻。如果反复劝阻还不听，那就可以把他废掉，另立别人为王。听了孟子这番义正词严的议论，齐宣王连脸色都变了。

孟子在这里并没有把一国之君看做是神圣不可侵犯的，只要他毁坏了仁义道理，他就是独夫民贼，根本不配称为君，谁都可以推翻他的统治，甚至除掉他，这是人民的基本权利。难怪作为一国之君的朱元璋会对这一章节如此敏感了。据说明代开国皇帝朱元璋读到《孟子》这一段对君王"不敬"的言论时，曾大为震怒。还说："这老儿要是活到今天，非严办不可！"朱元璋于1394年组织人重新编写《孟子》，删去了其中八十五章他认为不敬的言论，孟子的这番话自然也是其中之一。

孟子这个观点正反映了他的"民为贵，君为轻"的民主思想。而后世历次推翻暴君的"革命"行为也从孟子的话里得到了合理的解释。当然，这些革命有些的确是合理的，有些却只是假借革命的名义图谋不轨而已。所以，以民意为中心，推翻暴政的，那就是革命；如果是出于野心篡位，那就是造反。孟子很清楚地区别了这两者之间的不同，再次表现出了他不畏权贵的道德勇气。

WHAT IS AN AUTOCRAT

Once King Xuan of Qi enquired Mencius about the Tang and Wu Revolutions, "Is it true that King Jie of Xia was exiled by King Tang of Shang and King Zhou of Shang was dethroned by the army of King Wu of Zhou?"

According to the strict stipulations about the relationship between the king and his vassals, regicide and rebellion against the king were regarded as treason and heresy. King Xuan put forward this question deliberately to give a hard time to Mencius who frequently spoke highly of the great achievements of King Tang and King Wu. Mencius gave a clever answer by first replying that it was recorded in the ancient books. The king pressed on immediately, "Wasn't that treacherous? How come vassals could murder their king?" Mencius replied by interpreting the relativity of the traditional Confucian ideology. He said, "The head of a state that violates benevolence is regarded as a 'robber'; the one who violates righteousness is regarded as a 'wrecker'. Thus, the one who violates both of benevolence and righteousness is deemed as 'a brutal ruler'. Therefore, the Tang and Wu Revolutions were not acts of regicide or rebellion since those to be punished were brutal rulers." Mencius added, "When the ruler makes a serious mistake, the noble family and the vassals should admonish him. If after repeated admonishments he still refused to listen, they are entitled to depose him and find another king." The face of King Xuan became stern after hearing these blunt words from Mencius.

Mencius did not regard the king of a state as sacred and inviolable, and once the king violated the principles of benevolence and righteousness, he became an autocrat and betrayer to the people, unworthy of the throne. Thus, it is the people's fundamental rights to dethrone him. No wonder that Emperor Zhu Yuanzhang found this chapter so repulsive. It is said that he, as the founder of the Ming Dynasty, got infuriated after reading these "subversive" lines, and said, "If that old man were alive today, he would be given a harsh punishment." The version of *Mencius* compiled in the year of 1394 under his instruction deleted the eighty-five chapters which he deemed as containing subversive ideas, among which this chapter was of course one of them.

Those words of Mencius, which reflected his democratic idea of "people are of greater importance than the monarch", justified the revolutions to dethrone autocrats later in history from the moral point of view. Of course, some revolutions did have their rationale while others might only have ulterior motives under justified disguise. Therefore, dethroning autocrats according to the public opinions was deemed as revolutions while usurping the throne with a wicked ambition as rebellions. Mencius made a clear distinction between the two categories, which demonstrated his moral force of defying the power and the authority.

孟子婉拒齐王

　　孟子在齐国呆了许多年,遗憾的是,齐宣王始终没有采纳他的仁政主张。放眼望去,四周仍是战火遍地,血流漂杵,生灵涂炭。孟子的心情是悲愤、失望、感慨交集的,人类的互相残杀何时才能停止?人类的贪婪、愚蠢、残忍什么时候才能改变?孟子一边思考着这些问题,一边也在考虑着自己的去向。

　　而齐宣王也很遗憾,那就是自己想实行霸权,与孟子的王道思想有很大差距。但孟子知识渊博,才能超凡,如果能改变观点,支持自己的霸业,那就跟当年的管仲、晏婴一样,齐国还怕不能强大、不能称霸吗?为此,宣王曾经专门召见孟子,向他表白了自己的这番心意。

　　可是,孟子怎么可能放弃自己的信仰和追求,改变自己的立场呢?他耐心地对宣王解释自己的心意:大王要造宫殿,必定要命令工匠去寻找大木材。工匠寻到了大木材,大王一定很开心,以为这工匠定能胜任。如果工匠把木材锯短砍小，大王就很生气，认为工匠不胜任这项工作。其实这些工匠自幼学习建筑技术，在实践中运用了无数次。可大王一来就想迫使他们放弃所学，服从自己的需要，那样能造出好房子来吗？再比如，有人得到一块璞玉，虽然价值连城，但不经雕琢，还是一块粗糙的石头。于是就请玉工到家里来，强迫他按照自己的意图来雕琢，结果因为主人不懂雕琢技术，最终毁了这块美玉。如今大王治理国家，强令别人放弃自己所学的技术，服从大王的意志来行事，这跟对待工匠和玉工的态度有什么不同呢？

孟子宣讲、辩论向来喜欢以形象的事物作比喻，从中说明自己的道理。齐宣王也不迟钝，他听出了孟子的意思，人各有志，孟子一心要推行仁政，怎么能强迫他辅佐自己实行霸道呢？

MENCIUS POLITELY REJECTING THE REQUESTS OF KING XUAN

Mencius stayed in the State of Qi for many years, but much to his regret, his ideas of benevolent governance were not put into practice all along by King Xuan. Blood was being shed in those war-ridden states and the people were plunged into misery and sufferings. With mixed feelings of sadness, anger and disappointment, Mencius pondered over his future while considering questions such as when the states could stop the brutal slaughters against each other and when they could get rid of the greed, stupidity and brutality in human nature.

At the same time, King Xuan also felt quite regretful, because his plans of seeking hegemony were way far from Mencius' ideas of benevolent governance. However, if Mencius could change his positions and support his ambition for hegemony as the former ministers Guan Zhong and Yan Ying did, with his erudite scholarship and exceptional talents, he could ensure his quest for hegemony. Therefore, the king once called in Mencius to bare his intensions on this.

However, how is it possible for Mencius to give up his belief and pursuit and change his positions? He explained his own intensions patiently to the king, "If Your Highness wants to build a palace, you will command the craftsmen to search for huge timbers and will certainly be pleased if they can find the big ones and believe that they will do a good job. On the contrary, you will be irritated if the craftsmen cut the huge limbers into small pieces and think that they cannot do a satisfactory job. The truth is that the craftsmen began to learn their skills from a tender age and have already gathered sufficient experience. However, if Your Highness forces them to obey your order and abandon what they have learned, how can they build a magnificent palace? Take another instance. A person got an uncut jade, which was still a rough stone despite its worth. So he invited a jade craftsman to his home to cut the jade according to his instructions. The result was that the precious jade was ruined due to the reckless instruction. Now if Your Highness forces others to abandon what they have learned to obey your ideas in ruling the state, what is the difference between your behavior and the two cases above?"

Mencius tended to illustrate his ideas through concrete examples in his teachings and arguments while King Xuan was smart enough to understand Mencius' dream of implementing benevolent governance. As everyone had his own ambitions, how could the king force Mencius to assist him in seeking for hegemony?

齐人伐燕

燕国的国君易王在位十二年后死了,他的儿子燕哙继位。燕哙即位三年,曾经与楚、韩、赵、魏等国联合攻秦,结果大败。燕哙遭受这次挫折,声誉下降,而宰相子之的权势却提高了。这时纵横家苏代正被齐宣王重用,同时他跟燕国宰相子之的交情也很好,于是就为齐国出使到燕国,劝说燕王哙向尧舜禅让的做法学习,把王位让给子之。燕王果然听信了苏代的话,将政权交给了子之。

三年之后,燕国大乱,百姓恐惧,将军市被和太子密谋讨伐子之。这时候有人劝齐宣王趁着燕国大乱去攻伐燕国,肯定能成功。齐宣王接受建议,以讨伐子之的名义出兵燕国,并很快就把燕国打败了,还占领了燕国的十个城池。

这个时候,齐宣王又来征求孟子的意见。他问道:"有人建议我到此为止,也有人建议我继续攻伐,把燕国吞并下来。你说说看,我们齐国跟燕国的国力相等,但齐国在两个月不到的时间里就把燕国打败了,人力应该是达不到的,应该是天意吧。如果不去把燕国攻下来,是不是违背了天意呢?上天会不会降灾于齐国呢?我看还是把燕国攻下来为好。先生以为呢?"

孟子回答齐宣王说,假如你去攻打燕国,而燕国的老百姓很高兴、很愿意的话,那你就去攻打它。假如你占领了燕国,可是燕国的老百姓不高兴的话,那你就不要去占领。齐国以万乘之国打败同是万乘之国的燕国,没有别的原因,只因为燕国的老百姓一心要逃避水深火热一般的暴政,所以欢迎你们去解救他们。如果你去了,而燕国的百姓反而过得更苦,那怎么行呢?

可惜,齐宣王并没有领会孟子这番话的含义。齐国把燕国攻下来后,破坏了诸侯间的平衡,诸侯们计划组织一个联合集团去讨伐齐国。齐宣王着急了,又来请教孟子。孟子说,商汤本来只有方圆七十里的领土,最后却领导了天下。齐国是方圆千里的大国,有什么可惧怕的呢?商汤那时候的百姓盼望商汤的部队前来解救他们,就像久旱的农民对着晴空,盼望雨云出现一样。现在燕国内政一片混乱,你发兵攻打他们,老百姓以为他们要逃离水深火热了,高高兴兴地招待齐国的部队。结果你们却杀他们的子弟,拆毁他们的宗庙,抢走他们的宝物,使他们的痛苦更深,这怎么行呢?其他诸侯对齐国的强大本来就畏惧三分,现在你从燕国那里得到了加倍的土地,又不行仁政,各国诸侯为了自己的安全,同时又有了借口,自然要联合起来攻打你齐国。你现在只有赶快发布命令,释放俘虏,停止抢掠,召集燕国臣民选出一个新国君来,然后就班师回国。这样才能制止各国对齐国的攻击。

在这里,孟子始终强调战争是为了救民,而不是为了占领土地的意义。占领土地只能招致百姓的怨恨,并为自己四周树敌。这个道理即使在现代社会也是积极的。只不过,现代历史上的许多战争往往是借着救民的名义,而企图实现占领别国土地的真正目的。这样的战争发动者还不如齐宣王,齐宣王至少是坦率的。而孟子不反对齐宣王攻伐燕国,也没有违背他一贯主张的仁义,因为燕国百姓处于水深火热之中，战争的手段可以达到更崇高的目的，是为天下除害，也就是伸张正义。只不过齐宣王军队的所作所为违背了施行仁义、为民造福的原则，这就不能称为正义之师了。因此，讨伐燕国的战争也就不是正义的战争了。

THE INCURSION OF THE STATE OF YAN BY THE QI ARMY

When King Yi of the State of Yan died after he reigned for twelve years, his son Yan Kuai succeeded the throne. After three years on the throne, King Yan Kuai was routed in his attack with allied forces including the states of Chu, Han, Zhao and Wei against the State of Qin. His reputations declined with this major setback while the power of his Prime Minister Zi Zhi was strengthened. At that time, the strategist-turned-diplomat Su Dai, who stood high in the favor of King Xuan of Qi and also stood on very good terms with Zi Zhi, was sent as an envoy of Qi to Yan to persuade King Yan Kuai to abdicate the throne to Zi Zhi following the examples of the sage kings in the ancient times such as Yao and Shun. King Yan Kuai listened to his advice and handed over the crown to his minister Zi Zhi.

Three years afterwards, general Shi Bei and the crown prince secretly planned to dethrone Zi Zhi because the state had sunk into great chaos and the people were panicked and terrified under his rule. Following the suggestions to attack the State of Yan under these circumstances, King Xuan of Qi attacked Yan in the name of suppressing Zi Zhi and won the war quickly, occupying ten cities of Yan.

King Xuan solicited suggestions from Mencius, saying, "Some people suggest me to stop there while others insist on furthering the attack until we annex the whole state of Yan. We defeated it in less than two months despite the fact that the two states are equally strong. This should be attributed to the will of the Heaven rather than to the efforts of men. Would it be to act against the will of Heaven if we do not further our attack on Yan? Would we suffer disasters because of our defiance of the Heaven's will? Therefore, I think it is better for us to press on. Master, what is your opinion on that?"

Mencius replied, "If the people of Yan are pleased and willing to see your incursion, then continue your attack. If you have occupied Yan but the people there are not pleased, then do not occupy it. The reason why Qi could defeat Yan when both states have ten thousand chariots is that the people there welcomed you to rescue them from the miseries of tyranny. Therefore, how disastrous it would be if your occupation were to plunge them into further miseries and sufferings?"

Unfortunately, King Xuan did not catch the full meaning of Mencius' words. After the occupation of Yan, the delicate balance of power among the states was broken; as a result, the other states planned to form an allied force to attack Qi. King Xuan was worried and resorted to Mencius, who replied, "Compared with Tang of Shang, who only had a land extending seventy *li* and occupied the whole country in the end, what should the State of Qi fear as a big country with a territory extending thousands of *li*? During that period, people were looking forward to Tang's troops to rescue them just as farmers affected by droughts wish for clouds of rain. Now that the State of Yan is in chaos, the people there are welcoming your army because they believe that your attack will lift them from miseries and sufferings. However, what would be the result if you were to make them suffer more by killing their people, demolishing their ancestral temples and robbing their valuables? The other states already dread the great strength of Qi and will get united to attack you under the guise of protecting their own security if you are to double your territory by annexing Yan and not to implement benevolent governance. What you should do now is to immediately issue orders to release the captives, stop looting, let the subjects of Yan to elect a new king for their own state, and finally withdraw your troops from Yan. Only by so doing can Qi be exempt from the attacks by the other states."

Mencius placed the focus of wars on rescuing the people instead of grabbing territories. The idea that occupation of land will only lead to the resentment of the people and the attacks by other states applies to the modern society as well. Many wars in modern history were waged under the guise of rescuing the people for the true purpose of occupying the land of other countries. The initiators of those wars were worse than King Xuan who was at least outspoken about his intentions. Mencius did not betray his belief of benevolent governance by not opposing to the war initiated by King Xuan because he believed that the war could achieve the lofty purpose of promoting justice by freeing the Yan people from miseries and sufferings. However, as they violated the principle of benevolent governance and of benefiting the people, the troops from Qi could not be regarded as justified and the war against Yan could not be regarded as justified, either.

终生奉母教

孟子一生的成就,除了他天生聪明圣贤的资质以外,还离不开他那位伟大的母亲。孟子的母亲不但在他年幼及青年时期的成长过程中给了他极大的指导与帮助,即使在孟子人过中年、壮志未酬、身心烦恼之时,也同样给了他很多的鼓励与支持。

孟子在齐国多年,尽管有着一份不错的俸禄,与齐宣王的交往也算得上融洽,但齐宣王也只是表面尊敬他,他的政治主张却始终得不到施展,这令他十分苦恼。天长日久,他渐渐意识到,自己只是齐王的一个调味品、装饰品,或者解答疑难的辞书而已,齐宣王并不会真的把他的学说主张当一回事。孟子心头笼罩着阴云,日渐心灰意冷,终于萌生了离开齐国的想法。

有一天,孟子把手搭在柱头上发呆,并轻轻地叹息,脸上露出愁苦的神色。孟母见了问道:"儿啊,你为什么在这里唉声叹气,愁眉不展的呢？"孟子听见母亲的问话，很后悔自己的失态，但他还是把自己的心思如实禀告了母亲。他说，一个君子，应该知道进退，他的一切行为应该名正言顺，不应该为了荣誉和俸禄委曲求全、勉强自己。如今他跟齐宣王话不投机，看起来齐宣王是绝对不会接受他的仁政建议了，这种情形之下，他觉得自己不该再在齐国待下去了。可是母亲年岁大了，不宜奔波劳累受苦，所以他觉得很为难。

孟母本来就是一个深明大义的女性，听了儿子的话，她坚定地说："我是个妇道人家，烧饭、缝补是我的本分。妇人的德行就是操持家务，不应该插手外务。何况自古以来的传统就是，女子在家从父，婚嫁后从夫，夫丧从子。儿子如今是我们的一家之主，我当然要以儿子的前途为中心，加以辅助。你现在所从事的是顶天立地的仁义之事，我理当跟随你、支持你。就算生活清苦，也是我分内的事。你果断地决定你自己的事，不要为了我而迟疑不决吧。"

孟子听了母亲的话，宽心了很多，他离开齐国的决心更大了。于是，他一边料理手边的事务，一边计划着离开的日程。

FOLLOWING HIS MOTHER'S GUIDANCE ALL HIS LIFE

Besides prominent talents, Mencius attributed his achievements to his great mother whose help and guidance not only contributed enormously to his growth during his childhood and youth, but also gave him encouragement and support when he was frustrated for failing to realize his ambitions in his adulthood.

After years of sojourn in Qi, Mencius was distressed because King Xuan never put his political ideas into practice, despite the apparent respect, the decent salary and the congenial relationship between them. It finally dawned on

Mencius that the king took him merely as a spice of life, a decoration or a reference book, but never took his teachings seriously. Downhearted, he was considering to leave the State of Qi.

Resting his hand on a pillar one day, Mencius let out a slight sigh with a worried look on his face. His mother noticed it and asked him what had happened. He confided everything to her although he was very regretful for having behaved like this in front of her. He said that a man with high morals should make the right decisions and do the right things without compromising his principle or being resigned to the circumstances for fame or a good salary. He thought that it was time for him to leave since he and King Xuan could not share agreeable conversations any more and the king would never adopt his suggestions of benevolent governance. But he was faced with a dilemma since the hard journeys would be too much for his old mother.

Upon these words, his mother, a lady with great visions, said determinedly, "I am a woman, whose duty is to cook the meals and do the needlework. Doing the housework without meddling in the worldly affairs is considered the virtues for women. According to the ancient tradition, a woman should submit to her father before she gets married; she should submit to her husband after she gets married; she should submit to her son after her husband dies. My son, you are now the head of our family; naturally, I should support you for your prospects. As you are pursuing the lofty cause of benevolence, I should follow you and support you. It is what I should do even if I am to lead an impoverished life. You should make up your mind and do not hesitate for my sake."

Feeling relieved after hearing his mother's words, Mencius strengthened his desire to leave Qi. While he handled the routine work, he was planning for departure.

邹鲁内讧

邹国和鲁国发生了冲突。鲁国强大,邹国弱小。邹国的文武大臣有的主张打,有的主张和。邹穆公举棋不定的时候,突然想起了孟子,于是急忙派人去请,想让孟子回来帮助自己重新整顿国家政治。可是,因为阴雨和洪水的阻碍,孟子耽搁了半个多月才回到邹国,这时,邹国已经被鲁国打败了。

孟子回国后就跟邹穆公见面了。谈到这场冲突,邹穆公愤愤不平地问孟子:"在这次战斗中,我的官员死了三十三人,可是普通百姓竟没有一个肯舍命营救长官的。把这些不效忠国家君主的百姓都杀了吧,又杀不了那么多人。不杀吧,这些人看着他们的长官被杀,却不去营救,实在太可恨,我该怎办呢?"

听了邹穆公这些话,孟子毫不客气地回答说:"堂堂一国之君,怎么竟然黑白不分呢?您看,闹灾荒的年头,您的老弱百姓在死亡线上挣扎，年轻力壮者则背井离乡、逃荒要饭，可是您的仓库里却堆满了粮食、财物，官员们花天酒地，挥金如土，却也不向大王您禀报，以便开仓赈济百姓，致使许多人在饥寒交迫中死去。这其实是当官的人怠慢失职，残害百姓。曾子说：'小心呀小心，你怎样对待人家，人家反过来也会这样对待你。'现在您的百姓终于得到了报复的机会，怎么可能去舍身营救您的官员呢？所以您就不要再过分责备老百姓了。您如果施行仁爱的政策，官员们能够善待百姓，那么您的百姓自然会敬爱他们的上级，并为他们拼命的。"

统治者怎样对待人民，人民就会怎样对待统治者。"出尔反尔"这个成语就来自于这段故事。不过现在的意义发生了变化，主要指的是人的言行反复无常，前后自相矛盾。在孟子生活的那个时代，这样的话不能不说是惊世骇俗的，同时也被以后的许多统治者作为一条重要的政治经验。

THE CONFLICT BETWEEN THE STATES OF ZOU AND LU

The State of Zou had a conflict with the State of Lu. As Lu was bigger and stronger than Zou, some officials in Zou were for war while others against it. Duke Mu of Zou was vacillating between the two opinions when he suddenly thought of Mencius and sent for him to help reform the politics of his state. But Mencius was delayed half a month by the rains and the flood, and by the time he arrived, Zou had already been defeated.

During the meeting between Mencius and Duke Mu afterwards, the Duke was indignant when talking about the conflict and said to Mencius, "Thirty-three officials died in the battle, but none of the subjects ever tried to rescue them. I really want to kill those disloyal subjects but there are too many of them. If I were to pardon them, I just could not vent my anger. What shall I do?"

Mencius answered bluntly, "How can you, as the king of a state, fail to distinguish right from wrong? During the famine years when the elderly and the weak struggled to stave off the starvation while the young and the strong left their hometown and resorted to begging for a living, your granaries were filled with grains and your treasury was filled with money. The officials lived a decadent and dissolute life and did not report the reality to you with the result that you did not open the granaries to relieve the affected, thus leading to the deaths of a multitude in hunger and cold. The sufferings of your subjects were caused by the neglect of duty on the part of the officials. As Zengzi once said, 'Be on the alert, since you will be treated the same way as you treat others!' Now that your subjects got their chance to take revenge, how could you expect them to save your officials at the cost of their lives? So do not blame your subjects too much. If you practice benevolent governance and your officials treat the people well, they will naturally support the officials and protect them with their own lives."

People will treat the ruler the same way as the ruler treats them. The Chinese idiom of "you will reap what you have sowed (*chu er fan er*)" originated from this story. Now its meaning has evolved and mainly refers to the self-contradiction of one's words and deeds. These words, which did shock the ears in Mencius' era, have been taken as an important political experience by the later generations.

从者如归市

　　滕国是一个小国,东北面是强大的齐国,南面又和强大的楚国接壤。夹在两个大国之间的滕国该怎么办,是向齐国靠拢还是向楚国靠拢呢? 滕文公把这个难题提出来,向孟子请教。

　　孟子的回答让滕文公很失望。他说,你的问题我也没有办法解决。一定要说办法的话,那就只有一个。你把自己的内政理好,把老百姓团结起来。然后加强国防设施,把护城河挖得深深的,把城墙加高加厚,与全国百姓团结一心,誓死保卫自己的国土。这样才能有所作为。

　　滕文公进一步向孟子请教说,薛也是和滕国一样的小国,现在齐国居然要在薛国建筑城池。我很害怕这样的事也会落到我们滕国身上,到底该怎么办才好呢? 孟子又拿出历史上周太王的事迹来说服滕文公:周太王从前住在邠地,狄人侵犯他,他只好搬迁到岐山下去住。并非因为岐山的土地更肥美,而是太王被凶猛的狄人欺凌得没有办法,不得已才搬走的。虽然如此,但太王却忍辱负重,自强自立。而他的百姓也放弃了原来在邠的土地,跟着太王到岐山脚下居住,重新开辟新的土地。这样跟着来的人很多,就像赶集一样涌进太王的基地,使得太王的基业得到巩固,这就是"从者如归市"的由来。后来太王的后代文王、武王强大起来,终于建立了周朝几百年的政权。您如果效仿太王为善、自立的行为,后代子孙就一定能够称王天下。

孟子接着说,还有一种观点就是,世代传下来的土地应该好好守着,不可以在自己的手里放弃。那么您就得宁肯战死,宁愿亡国,也要死守国土。这两种办法您可以选择其一,但千万不要在两者之间矛盾犹豫。

孟子的这一理论相当有见地。周围强国林立,弱小国家要想自强自立,的确是件很艰难的事。能自立的时候就自立,做不到的时候就要见机行事。无论国家,还是事业,或者是个人的人生,其实都有同样的启示。当环境有困难时,就要想办法改变环境。改变不了的时候,就要坚强自立,无论如何也不能向命运屈服。

FOLLOWING SOMEONE AS CROWDS HASTENING TO THE MARKET

The State of Teng was a small state, to its northeast was the strong Qi and to its south was another strong state Chu. Duke Wen of Teng consulted Mencius over the question of whether Teng, lying between two powers, should serve Qi or serve Chu.

Rather to his disappointment, Mencius replied, "The question is beyond me, either. If you want me to give you some counsels, my suggestion is dealing with the domestic affairs properly, uniting the people, and strengthening the defense facilities by digging deeper moat and building higher and thicker the city walls. To share the death-defying resolution with all the people in case of war is the proper way."

The duke continued to enquire Mencius, "Qi is going to build fortification within the boundary of Xue, a state as small as Teng. I'm afraid that the same thing will happen to Teng. What am I to do?" Mencius replied by citing the revealing example of the Grand King of Zhou, who moved to the foot of Mount Qi from his homeland of Bin to avoid the incursions by the Di people — barbarians from the north. He moved to Mount Qi not because there was fertile land there, but because he was bullied by the ferocious barbarians. He swallowed humiliation and strived to become stronger while his subjects followed him to give up their land in Bin, settle down and open up wasteland at the foot of Mount Qi. More and more people followed him just as crowds hastening to the market, which strengthened his power and influence. That was the source of the allusion of "following someone as crowds hastening to the market". Later on, with the growth of power, the offsprings of the Grand King, King Wen and King Wu established the Zhou Dynasty which lasted hundreds of years. If you can emulate the Grand King's benevolent acts and self-sustaining efforts, your offsprings are sure to rule the country.

According to another view, the land is to be kept from generation to generation and never to be disposed of. Therefore, you should defend it at the cost of your life or your power. You can choose either of the two, but not vacillate between them."

Mencius' words were very insightful. It was indeed difficult for a small and weak state to seek self-reliance among the surrounding powers. Keep self-reliance if you can, and act accordingly in adverse circumstances. Actually, this inspiration is true for the rule of a country, as well as for one's life and career. Try to change the environments under unfavorable conditions, and try to seek self-reliance while you cannot change the environments. Never submit yourself to the fate.

臧仓小人

　　孟子晚年回到了邹鲁,度过了修身养性明志的一段时期。当时的鲁平公身边有一个得宠的近臣叫臧仓,有一天,他看见鲁平公备好了车马,准备外出,就上前问道:"车辆人马都准备好了,可是下面的人还不知道您要去哪里,所以我来请示一下,您预备去什么地方?"鲁平公说他要去看孟子。臧仓马上抓住机会攻击孟子,说:"您身为一国之君,为什么要屈尊去看一个平民呢?而且您以为他是个贤人吗?所作所为合乎礼仪,才是贤人。可是这个孟子,父亲早死,葬礼办得简单草率。母亲后来去世,他办理母亲的丧礼,远比以前父亲的丧礼隆重得多。对于自己的父母,办丧礼竟有前后厚薄之差,这是不合礼制的。这样的人,您还去看他吗?"

　　孟子的学生乐正克此时正好在鲁国当大夫。有一次鲁平公与齐王会面,商谈国事的时候,乐正克曾经极力推荐过孟子。所以孟子回到鲁国，鲁平公便想亲自去看看他，没想到被臧仓阻挠了。乐正克听说了这个消息，急忙赶去问鲁平公为什么不去看孟子。鲁平公说，孟子对自己父母的丧事有厚薄之分，这样的人行为不合礼制，所以不去看他了。

乐正克听了这话，急忙为自己的老师辩解说，孟子父亲去世的时候，他是以士的身份行的丧礼。而他母亲去世时，他已经是大夫了，自然依照大夫的礼仪举行丧礼，这并不是他对父母的丧礼有厚薄之分，而是在依照礼制办事啊！

鲁平公明知道自己办错了事，可还是要继续为自己辩解。又提出孟子给父母买的棺材、寿衣用的料子不一样，父亲用的是便宜料子，母亲用的是价钱贵的好料子。乐正克说，这也不是违背礼制，这只是因为孟子的经济状况不一样而已。

但是，乐正克知道自己说这些也没用了，鲁平公看来是个喜欢听信小人谗言的国君。他又回头去见孟子，把这一切前因后果都告诉老师，并痛骂那个小人臧仓，但孟子倒是没有生气。他说，鲁平公来不来看我，这其实不是人力可以决定的，而是天命。臧仓不过是一个小人而已，他有什么能力来阻止我跟鲁平公见面呢？

孟子游历魏、齐两国多年，一直致力于推行他的政治理想，希望对天下、对社会有所贡献。此时已经是孟子游历生涯快要结束、已经进入晚年的时候，游走多国而政治主张不被采纳的经历已使他看透了很多世事的真相，也不会被外界的俗人俗事所困扰。用他以前说过的话来形容就是，"达则兼善天下，穷则独善其身"，有机会就去救天下、救百姓，没有机会就把自己管好。天下能得到挽救，他的理想自然会实现；天下动荡不安，他的力量也改变不了。这就是天意。

人必须顺势而为，时势才能造英雄。

ZANG CANG THE VILE MAN

Mencius returned to Zou (Lu) and spent years there cultivating his character, nurturing his nature and clarifying his ideals. One day, Duke Ping of Lu was about to leave his palace with his carriages ready. Upon seeing this, his favorite official Zang Cang asked, "You have the cart and four ready, but the officials do not yet know where you are going. May I venture to ask?" The duke said, "I am going to see Mencius." Zang Cang immediately made an accusation of Mencius by saying, "Why do you demean yourself as the head of a state to pay the honor of a visit to a common man? Do you really believe that he is a man of virtue? The rules of ritual proprieties are observed by men of virtue, but the mourning for his mother far exceeded that of his father who died earlier. Now that he is not consistent with the rituals, are you still going to visit him?"

Yue Zhengke, one of Mencius' disciples and an official in Lu, strongly recommended Mencius during a state-to-state negotiation between Duke Ping of Lu and King of Qi. Therefore, the duke planned to meet Mencius in person after he came back to Lu. Upon hearing that the duke's plan of visiting Mencius had been interrupted by Zang Cang, Yue Zhengke immediately went to see the duke and asked him why he was not going to see Mencius. The duke said, "Mencius' observances for his mother's mourning far exceeded those for his father's. This shows that he is not consistent with the rituals. It is on that account that I am not going to see him."

Yue Zhengke immediately defended his teacher by saying, "For the mourning of his father, he observed the rites appropriate to a scholar and, for that of his mother, appropriate to an official. Therefore, he has not treated the two occasions partially, but acted according to the rituals."

The Duke of Lu knew that he was wrong but tried to justify himself by referring to the differences in the coffins and the textures of shroud used for Mencius' parents. Yue Zhengke said that this could not be taken as a case of violating the rituals, but a case of different affordability.

Yue Zhengke knew his words were of no use since the duke seemed to lend a ready ear to the slanders. He told everything to his teacher Mencius and scolded Zang Cang the vile man, but Mencius was not ruffled and said, "Whether Duke Lu would visit me or not is really determined by the Heaven's will, which is beyond the power of any man. How can that vile man Zang Cang be able to stop the duke from visiting me?"

Mencius spent many years visiting the two States of Wei and Qi and kept promoting his political ideals which would benefit the country and the society. At that time, Mencius was in his old age and was near the end of his wandering life. From his experience of shuttling from one state to another with his political ideas being ignored all along, he had seen through the situation and was no longer troubled by the worldly affairs and troubles. In his own words, "In days of prosperity, I shall try to make the whole kingdom virtuous; in days of poverty, I shall attend to my own virtue in solitude." In other words, he would try to save the country and the state when opportunities avail and he would seek self-improvement when opportunities do not avail. If the land under the Heaven was saved, his ideals were realized; if the land under the Heaven was ferment and turbulent, he could not change it upon his own will. There exists the will of the Heaven. The human beings must conform to the course of nature, and a hero is nothing but the product of his times.

事半功倍

　　孟子与学生公孙丑谈论时事。公孙丑问:"先生如果能在齐国掌权,能建立像管仲、晏子那样显赫的功业吗?"孟子回答说:"你真是个齐国人,就知道管仲、晏子!曾有人问过曾西,他跟管仲比谁强?曾西很不高兴地说,管仲得到齐桓公那么大的信任,帮助治理齐国那么长时间,相比之下,他的功绩真是微不足道。你怎么竟然拿我和他比?管仲是连曾西都不屑的人,你难道想让我学他吗?"

　　公孙丑不解,他又接着问:"管仲辅佐齐桓公使他称霸天下,晏子辅佐齐景公使他名扬海内外。他们难道不值得效仿吗?"孟子说,凭齐国的实力,统一天下是易如反掌的事。有什么可效仿的呢?公孙丑说:"那像文王一样,活了一百岁,还要靠武王来继承他的事业,才实现了天下统一。照您这么说来,文王也不值得效仿吗?"

　　孟子答道,"谁能比得上文王呢?从汤到武丁,天下臣服殷朝的时间已经很久了，要改变是很难的。当时没有一寸土地不属于纣王，天下百姓没有谁不是他的属下，但文王却能凭借方圆百里的小国建功立业，举起反抗纣王的义旗，这是非常不容易的。现在的齐国，国土面积纵横千里，人口众多，这么强大的国家，不需要扩大疆土，也不需要增加人口，只要实行仁政，那统一天下的势头就没有谁能够阻挡得了。何况施行仁政统一天下的君主已经很久没有出现了，老百姓被暴政折磨得困苦不堪，也从没有像现在这样厉害过。饥饿的人不挑食，口渴的人不挑饮料。这个时候，齐国这样的万乘之国如果能施行仁政，老百姓欢欣鼓舞，一定像从倒悬之苦中解脱出来一样。所以付出的努力只有古人的一半，收获的功效却是古人的几倍，这只有现在这个时候能做到啊。"

孟子与公孙丑谈话的中心内容其实还是仁政。表面看来他没有明确回答公孙丑的问题，但其实他的意思很明白。齐宣王具备了统一天下、建功立业的最好时机，只要他愿意施行孟子主张的仁政，这一切都可以说是易如反掌的事。而跟文王那时候的辛苦相比，甚至能够达到事半功倍的效果。孟子是自视很高的，连管仲、晏子这样的名相都不怎么放在眼里，原因其实很简单，他自视很高，正因为他有仁政思想在手，他认为这是无往而不利的武器，放之四海皆有用。管仲、晏子那一套又怎么能够与此相比呢？所以，孟子在很多场合都表现出了对管仲、晏婴这两位名相不以为然的态度。

DOUBLING THE ACHIEVEMENTS WITH HALF THE EFFORTS

While discussing with his mentor Mencius over the current affairs, Gongsun Chou asked, "If you were to obtain the power to govern the State of Qi, would you score such grand accomplishments as Guan Zhong and Yanzi had done?" Mencius replied, "As a native of Qi, you know nothing more than Guan Zhong and Yanzi. Some one asked Zeng Xi, 'Who is more capable, you or Guan Zhong?' Zeng Xi was displeased and said, 'How dare you compare me with Guan Zhong? Considering how Guan Zhong enjoyed the whole confidence of the Duke Huan of Qi and the long period in which he governed the state, how little he had accomplished! How can you liken me to him?' Now that Guan Zhong is despised by Zeng Xi, how can you expect me to learn from him?"

Gongsun Chou was confused and continued to ask, "Guan Zhong helped Duke Huan gain hegemony while Yanzi helped Duke Jing gain fame. Do you think that they are not worthy of emulating?" "As Qi had strong military power, to help Qi gain hegemony was as easy as turning the hand," answered by Mencius. Gongsun Chou went on, "King Wen did not die till he was a hundred years old, but his influence had not penetrated throughout the kingdom. It was King Wu who continued his cause and unified the country. So is King Wen then not eligible for emulation?"

Mencius said, "How can I be in a position to match King Wen? From King Tang to King Wuding, the Yin Dynasty had lasted for a long time, and this length of time made a change difficult. King Zhou of Yin possessed every inch of land and every person in the kingdom. With a territory of a hundred *li* in the beginning, it was difficult for King Wen to revolt against King Zhou and found a new dynasty. With a territory of thousands of *li* and a large population, there is no need for the State of Qi to expand its territory and population. If the ruler can implement benevolent governance, no power will be able to prevent him from unifying the land. Moreover, a true sovereign is long in the waiting. The sufferings of the people from a tyrannical government are never more intense than in the present. The hungry are ready to partake of any food, and the thirsty are ready to partake of any drink. For a state of ten thousand chariots, let benevolent government be implemented and the people will be delighted when they are relieved from the sufferings. With half the efforts of the ancients, doubled achievements are sure to be made. It is only now that such could be the case."

The conversation between Mencius and Gongsun Chou mainly concerned benevolent governance. Mencius seemed to have not given an explicit answer but his intention was very clear. King Xuan of Qi was presented with the best opportunities of unifying the country and making great achievements as easily as turning a hand as long as he could adopt the benevolent governance advocated by Mencius. Compared with the pains and toils of King Wen, King Xuan could double the achievements with half the efforts. Mencius thought so highly of himself that those famous ministers like Guan Zhong and Yanzi were held in contempt by him. That was because he thought that his ideas of benevolent governance would be invincible and universally applicable and the political ideas of Guan Zhong and Yanzi were no match of his. For this reason, Mencius showed some contempt for them on many occasions.

四十不动心

公孙丑问孟子:"如果您做了齐国的卿相,从此可以实现自己的主张,成就王业也不足为奇了。如果真有这样的机会,您会动心吗?"

孟子答道:"不会。我四十岁以后遇事就不再会内心波动、意志动摇了。"公孙丑说:"这么看来,先生可比古代勇士孟贲强多了。"孟子说:"这并不难,告子做到这一点比我的年龄还小呢。"公孙丑接着问:"做到遇事不动心有什么窍门吗?"孟子说有,然后便给他举了两个例子。

北宫黝有一种锻炼勇气的窍门:肌肤被刺不躲闪,眼睛被戳不眨眼。既不受卑贱之人的侮辱,也不受大国之君的侮辱。刺杀一个国君就跟刺杀一个卑贱之人没什么两样。他心中没有值得畏惧的君王。另一个人是孟施舍,他把战胜不了的人看成是能够战胜的一样,从不害怕面对强大的敌人。这两个人的勇气很难说哪个更强,但孟施舍的方法比较简单。

公孙丑是个喜欢打破沙锅问到底的人。他接着又问老师:"您的不动心跟告子的不动心有什么不同呢?"面对学生的疑惑,孟子耐心地作了解答:"告子说过,言辞上无法取得成功,就不必求助于内心;不求助于内心,就不必求助于意气。后者我是赞成的,但如果言辞无法成功,又不求助于内心,这一点我就不赞成了。因为人的思想意志主导人的感情意气,思想意志到了哪里,感情意气也就在哪里表现出来。所以要坚定自己的意志,就不要随意扰乱感情意气。思想意志专一,也会促动感情意气的专一。反过来,感情意气专注于某一方面,就会影响思想意志,造成内心的波动。"

孟子的言下之意就是,自己是善于控制感情意气的,所以也就不会因外界事物而造成自己内心的波动、意志的动摇。常言道:不以物喜,不以己悲。这是一种很高的境界。孟子四十岁就能做到使自己的心境不受外界事物的干扰,这是需要很强的意志力和精神力量的。那么他是怎么做到的呢?这就是他后来所说的"善养浩然之气"。

ATTAINING AN UNPERTURBED MIND AT FORTY

Gongsun Chou asked Mencius, "Master, suppose you were to be appointed as the prime minister of Qi and thus be able to put your ideas into practice and it would be not surprising at all to raise the king of Qi to the royal dignity. If such an opportunity were to present itself, would your peaceful mind be perturbed?"

Mencius replied, "No. Since I reached forty years of age, I have acquired an unperturbed mind." Gongsun Chou said, "Thus we can say, Master, you are far superior to the ancient warrior Meng Bi." Mencius said, "That was not difficult to achieve. Gaozi achieved that at an earlier age than I do." Gongsun Chou went on, "How can you have achieved an unperturbed mind?" Mencius explained to him through two revealing examples.

With the knack of tempering his valor, Beigong You did not flinch from any strokes at his body and did not blink his eyes when they were thrust. He would neither bear any humiliation from the vile nor from the king of a big state. He viewed stabbing a king as stabbing a vile man. No king was to be awed in his eyes. Another example is Meng Shishe, who had his way of nourishing valour. He regarded the unconquerable the same way as the conquerable. It is hard to tell who had the superior valour to the other, but Meng Shishe's method was easier.

Gongsun Chou was inquisitive and went on to ask, "What's the difference between your unperturbed mind and Gaozi's?" Mencius replied patiently, "According to Gaozi, what could not be attained in words is not to be sought for in the mind; what could not be sought for in the mind is not to be helped by the passion. I agree to the second part of his view, but do not agree with the first part. The thought will decide the passion and the passion will follow the thought. Therefore, do not let the thought disturb the passion without any reason. A fixed thought will be conductive to passion, and vice versa."

The implication of Mencius was that as he was good at controlling his passion, he was able to exempt his mind from the disturbance of external influences. As the saying goes, "If you are not pleased with external gains, you will not be sad for personal losses." This is an ideal state of mind. It calls for tremendous willpower and moral force for Mencius to have reached the state of being undisturbed by external influences. Then how did he achieve it? It could be attributed to what he mentioned later in his life — "To be good at nourishing the vast and flowing nature."

何谓圣人

　　有一次，公孙丑向孟子请教何谓圣人的问题。公孙丑说："宰我、子贡擅长言谈，冉牛、闵子、颜渊善于阐述德行。孔子两方面都很擅长，可他却说：'我不善于辞令。'这么说来，老师您已经达到圣人的境界了吧？"

　　孟子正色道："你怎么能这么说呢？从前子贡曾经问孔子：'老师您已经达到圣人的境界了吗？'孔子回答：'圣人的境界我是达不到的，我只不过做到了学习不知满足，育人不知疲倦而已。'子贡又说：'学习不知满足，这是智的表现；育人不知疲倦，这是仁的表现。老师您这二者都具备了，就已经达到圣人的境界了。'但孔子仍不以为然。你看，连孔子都不敢以圣人自居，你却说我达到了圣人的境界，这是什么话呀？"

　　公孙丑还是想继续讨论什么是圣人这个话题。他提出了古代的贤人伯夷、伊尹来和孔子做比较。孟子也就一一做出分析：

"伯夷这个人,不是他的君主不侍奉,不是他的百姓不管理。国家太平就出仕,天下大乱就退隐。伊尹则不管谁的君主都侍奉,不论谁的百姓都管理。天下太平也出仕,天下大乱也出仕。孔子呢,可以出仕就出仕,想离开时便离开。时间可以长就长,可以短就短。他们都是古时的圣人,但我只愿学习孔子。"

再看看孔子的学生对于孔子的评价。宰我说:以我的观察,孔子比尧舜贤得多了;子贡说:看见一国的礼制就知道它的政治如何,听见它的音乐就知道它的德行如何。自有生民以来,没有出现过孔子这样的人;有若说:麒麟对于走兽,凤凰对于飞鸟,泰山对于丘陵,河海对于沟壑,都是同一类的事物。孔子对于一般人来说,也是同类。不同的是,圣人高出他的同类,而孔子又高出其他的圣人。这就叫出类拔萃。"

孟子说了这么多关于圣人的话题,其中心意思就是,自古至今,只有孔子真正算得上是圣人。我们知道,孟子一直是以孔子的嫡传弟子自居的,他在思想上也是一直推崇孔子的学说主张,并身体力行地加以贯彻,所以他以孔子为圣人的榜样其实是不足为奇的。

WHAT IS A SAGE?

When Gongsun Chou asked Mencius what a sage is, Mencius said, "Zai Wo and Zigong were good at speaking; Ran Niu, Minzi, and Yan Yuan were good at expounding the moral ethics. Confucius was good at both, but still said, 'I am not gifted with my tongue.' Therefore, Master, you have already attained sageness, haven't you?"

Mencius replied with a stern face, "How can you say that? When Zigong asked Confucius whether he had attained sageness, Confucius answered, 'I can never attain sageness. What I have attained is learning without satiety and instructing without tiredness.' Zigong went on, 'Learning without satiety shows your wisdom while instructing without tiredness shows your benevolence. With benevolence and wisdom, Master, you have already reached sageness.' However, Confucius did not agree. Now, even Confucius did not allow himself to be regarded as a sage, how can you say that I have attained sageness?"

Gongsun Chou wanted to further his enquiry on sageness and compared the ancient sages such as Bo Yi and Yi Yin with Confucius. Mencius made analysis one by one.

"Bo Yi would serve no other king than his own and govern no other subjects than his own. In times of peace and tranquility, he would take public office, but retire from public life in turbulent times. Yi Yin would serve any king and command any people. He would take office in times of peace and tranquility and in times of disorder. Confucius would take public office when it was proper to do so and retire from it when he desired to. When it was proper to serve for a long time, he made it long; when it was proper to serve for a short time, he made it short. They were all ancient sages, and among them I only wanted to emulate Confucius.

Let's look at the comments made by Confucius' disciples. Zai Wo said, 'According to my observation, Confucius was far more virtuous than King Yao and King Shun.' Zigong said, 'By looking at the ceremonial ordinances of a state, we can know its politics; by hearing its music, we know its social morality. From the birth of mankind till now, there has never been another one like Confucius.' You Ruo said, 'The unicorn is of the same nature as the quadrupeds, the phoenix as the birds, Mount Tai as the mounds, and rivers and seas as the rain-pools. Likewise, Confucius is of the same nature as the ordinary people. But sages stand out from their peers, while Confucius stands out from the other sages. That is what we call outstanding.'"

What Mencius really wanted to express here was that only Confucius could be crowned as a true sage from the ancient times to the present day. We know that since Mencius always claimed himself as a disciple of Confucius by the direct line, he held him in esteem and practiced his teachings and principles in person. Therefore, it is not at all surprising that he took Confucius as the model of sages.

心悦诚服

"心悦诚服"这个成语出自孟子的话。有一次他说,凭借武力强大,却假借"仁义"的名义称霸诸侯的,一定要有强大的国力。凭借德行来推行仁义的人才能称王,称王的人不必有很强的国力,比如商汤凭借的不过是方圆七十里的土地,文王凭借的也不过是方圆百里的土地。凭借武力而使别人臣服的,别人内心并不是真正的服气,只是力量不足不得已罢了。而凭借德行使人服从的,人家内心则会很高兴,就像孔子的七十二名弟子佩服孔子一样。

所谓"王道"与"霸道"的区别,孟子在这里说得很清楚。用武力征服别人的是霸道,凭德行让人顺服的是王道。行霸道不能使人真正臣服,只有王道才叫人心悦诚服。这是中国传统文化中最有代表性的政治理论。可惜,千百年来,哪一个统治者不是凭借武力征服他人?王道在哪一个朝代真正实现过?孟子推行仁政的道路如此艰难也就不奇怪了。

HEARTFELT ADMIRATION AND SINCERE CONVICTION

The idiom "heartfelt admiration and sincere conviction (*xin yue cheng fu*)" originated from Mencius' words. Mencius once said, "He who uses force to rule over the other lords under the guise of benevolence should have a strong state power while he who uses virtues to practice benevolence can become the sovereign. To become the sovereign does not necessarily need a strong state power. Tang of Shang did it with a land extending only seventy *li* while King Wen did it with only a land of a hundred *li*. When one subdues men by force, people do not submit to him from the bottom of their hearts but because they are not powerful enough to resist. When one subdues men by virtues, they would be pleased from the bottom of their hearts, as was the case with the seventy-two disciples in their submission to Confucius."

Mencius has explained clearly the distinction between "sovereign power" and "hegemony". Hegemony refers to the rule over others by force, while sovereign power refers to the submission of others by virtues. The practice of hegemony can never acquire admiration and conviction from the people, but the exercise of sovereign power can. That is the most representative political philosophy in traditional Chinese culture. Unfortunately, each and every ruler over the history of thousands of years has ruled others by force, haven't they? In which dynasty has sovereign power really been the reality? Therefore, it is not strange that Mencius suffered so many difficulties and resistances in his endeavor to practice benevolent governance.

未雨绸缪

  孟子说，国君要行仁政，才能得到荣耀；不行仁政，就必然招致屈辱。不愿受到屈辱却又不肯行仁政，就像讨厌潮湿却又住在低洼之地一样。如果不想受到屈辱，那就要重视道德，尊重士人，使贤能的人有职有权。国家没什么事的时候，及时修明政治，即使是大国也会敬畏你的。《诗经》上说："赶在天还没下雨的时候，修补我的巢，看树下的人谁敢欺负我？"说的就是这个道理。可是现在的国君哪里懂得这个道理呢？没事的时候就知道放纵享乐，不干正事，那是自求祸患啊！《太甲》说：天降祸，还可以躲；自己求祸，活不了。所以是福是祸，都是自找的。

  孟子在这里强调统治者要居安思危，防患于未然，不要等到大祸来临时再去寻找补救措施。其实，什么事情不是这样呢？所以，我们现在也还常常以"未雨绸缪"来提醒自己提前做好打算，以防备任何可能发生的意外情况。

SAVING FOR THE RAINY DAY

Mencius said, "Benevolence brings honor to a king, and its opposite brings disgrace. Those who hate disgrace and yet are not willing to practice benevolence are like those who hate moisture and yet are living on the low-lying land. If a king hates disgrace, the best course for him to pursue is to esteem virtue, to honor virtuous scholars and to give the worthy and capable among them places of dignity and offices of trust. When the state is free of troubles, make the government honest and enlightened and then even the great states will stand in awe of you. As is said in the *Book of Poetry*,

'Before it's rainy and dark,

I'll gather mulberry bark

To mend my house in the yard,

Lest the men below the tree

Might do some harm to me.'

But now the king knows nothing of these by abandoning himself to pleasure and idling away; he was in fact seeking for calamities by himself. This is illustrated in one passage from 'Taijia' in *The Book of History*, 'When Heaven sends down calamities, it is still possible to escape from them; when we occasion the calamities ourselves, it is not possible to live any longer. Therefore, calamity and blessing in all cases are men's own seeking.'"

Herein Mencius stressed that rulers should be vigilant in peace and be prepared for potential dangers, rather than hurriedly seek remedies in face of imminent calamities. Actually, it is true for all the cases, isn't it? Therefore, until now we still use the idiom "save for the rainy day (*wei yu chou mo*)" to remind ourselves of and get prepared for any unforeseen incidence.

天吏无敌

　　孟子不但提出了仁政的学说，同时也为如何实行仁政提出了一套自己的主张。他说：尊重有贤德的人，任用有才能的人，让才德兼备的人居于上位，这样天下的士人就会很高兴，都愿意到这里来做官。市场上为商人提供存放货物的场所，但不向他们征税，这样天下的商人就会很高兴，都愿意到这里来做买卖。关卡上只检查不收税，天下的旅行者就会很高兴，都愿意走在这里的大路上。农民只需耕种公田，不需要另外收税，天下的农民就都愿意到这里来耕种田地了。此外，住宅不收税，天下百姓也会很愿意做这里的臣民。如果做到了这五点，那邻国的老百姓也会像仰望父母一样看待这个君王。邻国要想攻打他，等于是让子弟们去攻打自己的父母，天下有这样的事吗？所以能做到以上五点，可以说天下没有对手了。没有对手，就等于说你是上天派来管理天下的，这叫天吏。天吏不能称王于天下，这是没有的事。

所以，只要能行仁政，关心百姓疾苦，国家就会强盛起来，也必定可以称王天下。

A HEAVEN-SENT MINISTER HAS NO RIVALS

Besides his principles of benevolent governance, Mencius also put forward his ideas on how to realize them. He said, "If a ruler gives honor to men of talents and virtue and employs men of competence, offices shall all be filled by individuals of talents and virtue, all the scholars of the land under the Heaven will be pleased and wish to serve in his court. If places in the markets are offered to store goods for the merchants without any tax levied on them, all the traders of the land under the Heaven will be pleased and wish to do business there. If there is only inspection at border passes but no taxes are charged, all the travelers of the land under the Heaven will be pleased and wish to travel on the roads there. If farmers only need to cultivate the public fields without any additional taxes, all the husbandmen on the land under the Heaven will be pleased and wish to plough there. Also, if no property tax is levied, all the people will be willing to come and be his subjects. If the ruler can truly deliver these five conveniences, the people in the neighboring states will look up to him as a parent. If a neighboring state plans to attack him, it is like asking them to attack their parents, which will never be possible. Thus, such a ruler will have no rival on the land under the Heaven, and he who has no rival is a minister sent by the Heaven to rule the land under it. Never has there been a case where a Heaven-sent minister cannot rule.

Therefore, as long as a king can practice benevolent governance and care for the well-being of the people, his state is bound to grow stronger and he is sure to become the sovereign of the land under the Heaven."

恻隐之心

孟子说,每个人都有不忍看别人处于痛苦之中的同情心。就好比看见一个小孩突然掉到井里去了,每个人都会产生恐惧同情的心理。会有这样的心理,并不是因为想跟孩子的父母套近乎,也不是想在四方乡里得到什么好名声,更不是讨厌孩子的哭声。这是因为同情心是天然的,没有同情心就不是人,没有羞耻之心也不是人,没有辞让之心也不是人,没有是非判断之心也不是人。这四心就是仁、义、礼、智,合称"四端"。这四端就像人的四肢,人有这四端却不能奉行仁义礼智之道的,等于自我作贱;说他们的君王不能做到,等于作贱他们的国君。凡是人都有这四端,都知道扩充、保养它们,就像水逐渐烧开,泉水越来越壮大一样。如果具备了四端,并加以扩充,那就足以保住四海之地;如果不扩充的话,那就连自己的父母都不能侍奉。

孟子认为,人人都有同情、羞耻、辞让、是非之心,这四心就是

"仁、义、礼、智"的开端,如果能把这四端好好培养,并加以扩充,那就上可以保住自己的天下,下可以侍奉好自己的父母。孟子就是在这个基础上建立了"性善论"的学说。这个观点对中国的伦理哲学产生了很大的影响,后世的一些儒家学者也在这一学说中找到了充分的理论依据。看起来,孟子是把仁义看成了无往不胜的利器了。一个值得思考的问题是,仅仅靠这四心四端来治理国家和自己的小家就可以高枕无忧了吗?

THE HEART OF SYMPATHY

Mencius said, "Each and every person has the heart of sympathy which cannot bear to see the sufferings of others. For example, if people suddenly see a child falling into a well, they would all experience a feeling of distress and sympathy. They will feel so not because in this way they may gain the favor of the child's parents, seek the praise from the neighborhood, or loathe the child's crying. It is because the heart of sympathy is inborn, and he who lacks it will be unworthy of a human being. The same is true for the heart of shame, the heart of deference and the heart of judgment. Those 'four hearts' are regarded as the 'four sprouts' of benevolence, righteousness, ritual propriety and wisdom. Men with those four sprouts are like men with four limbs. He demeans himself who has those four sprouts but claims that he cannot follow the four principles of benevolence, righteousness, ritual propriety and wisdom; he demeans the king who claims that his king cannot develop those principles. Each and every person has these four sprouts, and knows that they need to be expanded and nurtured just like bringing the water to the boil and accumulating the water of the spring. With possession and expansion of these four sprouts, the territory within the four seas will be guaranteed, while the denial of the expansion will lead to one's failure of serving even his own parents."

Mencius believed that all the people had the four hearts of compassion, shame, deference and judgment, which were the sprouts of benevolence, righteousness, ritual propriety and wisdom. If the four sprouts can be nurtured and expanded, then one's rule can be guaranteed and one's parents can also be well served. Mencius established his theory of "the human nature is good" on this ground. This theory has exerted great influence on China's philosophy of ethics and the later Confucian scholars have found a sufficient theoretical grounding. It seems that Mencius took benevolence as an unconquerable weapon. However, it is still worth asking ourselves whether we can really rest assured by solely resorting to the four hearts or the four sprouts in managing the country and the households.

反求诸己

　　孟子在谈到"仁"这个问题的时候曾经说：造箭的难道比造盔甲的更不仁吗？当然不是。可是那造箭的却唯恐自己的箭不能伤人，而造盔甲的却唯恐穿盔甲的人受伤。为什么呢？自然和他们选择的职业有关系，并不是他们的本性如此。因此，选择职业也得慎重考虑啊。孔子说，"与仁相处是完美的，能自由选择，却不与仁相处，这是不明智的。"仁，是上天给我们的尊贵爵位，是人们心灵的安逸居所。没有任何困难而不去行使仁，实在是不明智。不仁不智、无礼无义，就只能当别人的奴仆。但当了别人的奴仆却又感到羞耻，那就好比是造箭的人耻于造箭，造弓的人耻于造弓一样。既然感到羞耻，那还不如好好地做到"仁"呢。"仁"这种东西就如同射艺，射箭者时刻都要端正自己的姿势再发箭。如果箭发出去而不中，不要去埋怨别人的射艺比自己强，而应该反过来从自身寻求原因：我的姿势够端正吗？也就是说，我做到"仁"所规定的一切了吗?

孟子这番话说得挺拗口,他的意思其实就是:人的本性虽然是善良的,但是能否做到仁,还要看自己的努力。外在的环境是既定的,是不以人的意愿而客观存在的,但人具有自由选择的能力。能否做到仁,完全取决于一个人自身的选择。他希望每个人都能够反省自己,从自身找到原因,这就是成语"反求诸己"的由来。

REFLECTING AND TRYING TO FIND FAULT WITH ONESELF

In discussing the issue of "benevolence", Mencius said, "Are the arrow-makers less benevolent than the armour-makers? Of course not. Yet, the arrow-makers only fear that men would not be hurt, while the armour-makers only fear that men would be hurt. Why is that? Naturally, this is related to the choice of their profession, not to their inborn nature. Therefore, we should be careful and prudent in choosing our profession. Confucius said, 'It is ideal to find the company of benevolence; it is unwise not to choose benevolence when he has the discretion.' Benevolence is the most honorable dignity conferred by the Heaven, the quiet and comfortable home in which the heart dwells. It is unwise for one not to practice benevolence when he meets no difficulties. A man without benevolence, wisdom, propriety and righteousness is only fit to be a servant.

One who is a servant and feels ashamed of his servitude is like an arrow-maker or a bow-maker who feels ashamed of his vocation. If he feels ashamed, he'd best practice benevolence. Benevolence is like the art of archery. The archer must adjust himself before he shoots. If he misses the target, he should never put the blame on those who shoot better, but find fault with himself, checking whether his posture is correct or not, i.e., whether he has done everything in accordance with the requirements of benevolence."

Mencius' words may sound difficult to comprehend, but what he wanted to say is that though human nature is good, it depends on one's efforts to conform to benevolence. Though the external environments are fixed and not dependent on one's will, one still has the right to make his own choice. Therefore, whether one can conform to benevolence is entirely determined by his own decision. Mencius hoped that each and every person could examine himself and find faults with himself. That is the origin of the Chinese idiom "Reflecting and trying to find fault with oneself (*fan qiu zhu ji*)".

孟子装病

　　孟子正要去觐见齐宣王,而齐宣王也正好派人来传话:"我本来应该来看你,但我感冒了,不能受风寒。你如果能来上朝,我便临朝听政。不知道能否让我见到你?"听了这话,想不到孟子回答说:"不巧我也生病了,不能到宫廷里去。"

　　第二天,孟子出门到东郭氏家吊丧。公孙丑见状便问:"老师昨天以生病为由,拒绝了齐宣王的召见,今天却又出门去吊丧,恐怕不太好吧?"孟子说:"昨天生了病,今天病好了,为什么不能去吊丧呢?"

　　齐宣王听说孟子病了,派人来问候,连医生也带来了。孟子却说:"昨天有大王的诏令,但得了点小毛病,不能去朝见大王。今天病稍有好转,但我不知道能不能去。"宣王于是派人在孟子回家的路上拦截他,并对他说:"您千万不要回家了,赶紧去朝廷吧。"孟子没办法,就躲到齐国大夫景丑家过夜。

景丑对孟子的行为很看不惯，就说："在家有父子，在外有君臣，这是人与人之间最重要的关系。父子之间要慈爱，君臣之间要尊敬。但我好像只看见齐王尊敬你，没有看见你怎么恭敬齐王。"孟子不高兴地驳斥景丑："这是什么话！在齐国人中，没有一个拿仁义的道理向齐王进言的，难道他们认为仁义不好吗？他们只不过是觉得这个君王不配去跟他谈道理而已。还有比这个想法更不恭敬的吗？我呢？不是尧舜的道理我不敢拿来说给齐王听，所以齐国人中没有像我这么尊敬齐王的了。""可是按照礼制的规定，父亲叫你，不等答应就要前去；君主召见，不等车马驾好就要出发。你本来是要去朝见齐王的，可是听说齐王要见你，你倒反而不去了。这好像不合礼制吧？"景丑继续质问孟子。

孟子解释说："天下有三样东西最重要，就是爵位、年纪、道德。朝廷最重爵位，乡里最重年纪，辅佐君王最重道德。齐王不能靠着他的爵位而轻视我的德行和年纪吧。想要建立功业的君王都有召见而不去的大臣，有什么事要和他商量就应该主动去拜访。他对道德的尊敬如果没有达到这种程度，就不会有大的作为。商汤对于伊尹，桓公对于管仲，都是这样，所以他们不用费心就能称王天下、称霸诸侯。现在的几个大国，实力相当，道德相近，彼此之间都不服气，就因为他们都喜欢任用不如自己的人，而不喜欢任用比自己强的人。当年齐桓公是不敢召见管仲的，如果连管仲都不能召见，何况我这个看不起管仲的人呢？"

孟子认为，君臣的关系不应该只注重外在的礼节等形式，而应该建立在共同努力治理朝政的基础上。作为君主，应该崇尚美德，尊重贤士，才有可能建立伟大的功业。这些观点在强调礼制的儒家思想中可谓独树一帜。应该说，齐宣王给孟子的礼遇也算很高的了，在孟子游历过的国家里并不多见。君王亲自召见，孟子却称病不去，其实是想反对"君命一有传唤应该不等马车驾好就去"的古礼，他认为，评说政务、劝善行善才是最重要的。孟子的这种气节对现代读书人来说还是可以借鉴的。

MENCIUS FEIGNING ILLNESS

As Mencius was about to go to court, King Xuan of Qi sent a messenger to say, "I intended to call on you, but I have caught a cold and may not expose myself to the wind. I will hold the court if you can attend it. I do not know whether you will grant me the opportunity of seeing you then." Mencius answered with a rather unexpected reply, "Unfortunately, I am also unwell and will not be able to go to the court."

The next day, Mencius went out to pay a visit of condolence in the Dongguo family. Upon seeing him, Gongsun Chou said, "Master, yesterday you declined to go to the court on the ground that you were unwell, and today you are going out to pay a visit of condolence. Can it be regarded as improper?"

"Yesterday," said Mencius, "I was unwell; today, I feel better. Why should I not pay this visit?"

In the meantime, the king sent a messenger with a doctor to inquire about his illness, but Mencius said, "When the king's order came yesterday, I was feeling a little bit unwell and could not go to the court. I am a little bit better today, but not sure whether I am well enough to attend the court." After learning what Mencius said, the king sent people to stop him on the road and said to him, "Don't go back home now. Please go to the court at once." Mencius had no way out but to spend the night at Minister Jing Chou's residence.

Jing Chou held Mencius' behavior in detestation and said, "In the family, there is the relationship of father and son; outside the family, there is the relationship of king and ministers. These are the most important relationships. The ruling principle between father and son is kindness and affection; the ruling principle between king and ministers is respect. I have witnessed the king's respect to you, but I have not seen your respect to him."

Mencius was annoyed and retorted, "What do you mean by these words!

Among the people of Qi there is no one who speaks to the king about benevolence and righteousness. Is it because they do not think that benevolence and righteousness are admirable? No, rather because they think that it is not worth discussing about these principles with him. Thus, they manifest the greatest disrespect to him. I do not dare to speak anything before the king but the ways of King Yao and King Shun. Therefore, no one else in Qi respects the king so much as I do."

Jing Chou pressed on, "But according to the rituals, when one's father calls, one should set on the way without any hesitation; when the king's order comes, one must set out before the carriage is ready. You were going to the court, but when you heard the king's order, you deliberately refused. You seem to be not in accordance with the ritual propriety."

Mencius answered, "Three issues are of the utmost importance in the kingdom — nobility, age and virtue. In the court, nobility holds the first place of the three; in villages, age holds the first place; in assisting a ruler in running the state, virtue holds the first place. How can the king of Qi rely on his nobility to despise my virtue and age? Kings with the ambition to accomplish great feats all had ministers who might defy their orders to go to the court. When the king wishes to consult with a minister, he should pay a visit to him. The king who lacks such respect to virtues will not be able to make outstanding achievements. On the other hand, Tang of Shang's reverence for Yi Yin and Duke Huan's reverence for Guan Zhong facilitated them to reach the throne over the whole country and the sovereign power over other states. The powerful states nowadays are on a par in power and virtue, for the lords in these states tend to use those who are inferior to them instead of those who are superior. Duke Huan did not venture to call Guan Zhong to the court. If Guan Zhong could enjoy such reverence and I despise him, why should I accept the call?"

Mencius believed that the relations between the king and his ministers should not only focus on the superficial aspects such as rituals, but on the joint efforts to run the state. Only by valuing virtues and respecting virtuous talents can great achievements be scored by a king. Those ideas were quite distinct from the orthodox Confucianism which took rituals as a priority. Despite King Xuan's great reverence for him, which was rare in other states, Mencius feigned illness when the king called him. His intention was to oppose the ancient rituals of "When the king's order comes, one must set out before the carriage is ready". He held the view that the assistance and suggestions for running the state together with the advocacy and practice of benevolence should be of primary importance. Mencius' integrity and moral courage are still worth imitating by the present-day scholars.

该要的为何不要

孟子的弟子陈臻问:"当年您在齐国,齐王送您上好的黄金一百镒,您不接受。后来您到了宋国,宋王送您黄金七十镒,您却又接受了。在薛国的时候,薛君送您五十镒,您也接受了。如果先前不接受是对的,那后来接受就是错的;如果后来收下是对的,那先前不接受就是错的。这两种情况,老师您必定属于其中一种。"

孟子平静地回答说:"我接受和不接受都是对的。在宋国时,我将要远行,对远行者必定要送礼物。宋君说这是赠送给我的礼物,我为什么不接受呢?在薛地时,我需要警卫,薛君说这是给警卫士兵的给养,我为什么不接受呢?而在齐国,没有什么特别的事,没有原因地送我礼物,实际上是用钱收买我。君子怎么可以被金钱收买呢?"

有一句古话叫做:君子爱财,取之有道。君子对于礼物不以多少来确定接受不接受,而是以是否符合道理来决定该不该取。符合道理的话,虽然菲薄,也该接受;违背道义收取钱财,那是接受贿赂,君子也就不成为君子了。孟子所言所行，坦坦荡荡，率真可爱，正是他一贯的大丈夫精神。

WHY DECLINE WHAT OUGHT TO BE ACCEPTED

Chen Zhen once asked his teacher, Mencius, "During your stay in the State of Qi, you refused the king's gift of 2,400 taels of gold; during your stay in the State of Song, you accepted the king's gift of 1,680 taels; during your stay in the State of Xue, you accepted the king's gift of 1,200 taels. If your declining the gift in the first case was right, then your accepting it in the latter cases must be wrong; if your accepting it in the latter cases was right, then your declining it in the first case must be wrong. Master, your behavior must be in one or the other of these two scenarios."

Mencius replied calmly, "I was right in all the cases. When I was in Song, I was about to take a long journey and travelers are to be presented with gifts. The king's message with the gift was, 'A gift for the journey.' So why should I have declined the gift? When I was in Xue, I need protection and guards. The king's message was, 'Subsidies for the guards.' So why should I have declined that gift? But when I was in Qi, the gift was sent on no occasion and with no reasons, and it was meant to be bribery. How could a gentleman be bought over with money?"

As an old saying goes, "A gentleman loves wealth but will gain it in the proper way." A gentleman accepts or rejects a gift not according to its value, but according to its justification. The gift should be accepted if it is justified, no matter how humble it was. A gentleman who accepts an unjustified gift means that he accepts bribery and thus he is no longer a worthy gentleman. Mencius' candid and admirable words and deeds embodied his spirit of a real man.

孔距心知罪

　　孟子到平陆去，见到齐国大夫孔距心，就对他说："如果您的士兵一天之内三次掉队，那么您开除他吗？"孔距心说："不要等到三次我就会开除他。"孟子接着他的话说："那么您的失职行为也很多次了。灾荒年成，您的百姓，年老的倒毙在沟壑里，年轻力壮的四处逃荒，差不多有千余人了。"孔距心忙为自己辩解说，这种事情不是他一个地方官的力量能够改变的。于是，孟子就打了一个比方：有一个人接受了别人的委托替人家喂养牛羊，那这个人一定会为那些牛羊找到合适的牧场和充足的草料。如果找不到的话，那该怎么办？他是应该把这些牛羊还给主人，还是眼睁睁地看着这些牛羊饿死呢？孔距心听了孟子这话，一下子醒悟了，说："这的确是我的罪过。"

　　孟子后来见到齐宣王，就把这件事告诉了他，并说："您的地方官我认识五位，能够察知自己过失的，只有孔距心一个人。"齐王听了这话回答说:"那么这是我的过错了。"

孟子在这里通过两个类比推理,说明推行仁政的必要,严厉指责了地方官员对百姓生死的漠然和不负责任,并对齐王旁敲侧击地提出批评,迫使齐王也承认了自己的过失。

KONG JUXIN REALIZED HIS MISTAKE

Mencius went to Pinglu and met Minister Kong Juxin of Qi and said, "If one of your soldiers should lose his place in the ranks three times in one day, would you dismiss him?" "I would not wait for three times to dismiss him," replied Kong. Mencius went on, "Well then, you have also failed your duty for many times. In years of disaster and famine, the old and weak who have been found dead in the ditches and the young and strong who have been scattered about to the four quarters, have amounted to several thousand."

Kong Juxin argued, "These things are beyond a governor's capability." Mencius drew an analogy and said, "Here is a man who receives charge of the cattle and sheep of another, and undertakes to feed them for him. Of course he must search for pasture-ground and adequate grass for them. If, after searching for those, he cannot find them, should he return his charge to the owner or do nothing and just let them die from hunger?" After hearing Mencius' words, Kong Juxin suddenly realized his mistake and said, "Those are indeed my fault."

Later on, when Mencius met with King Xuan of Qi, he told this to him and said, "I know five of your governors, among whom, only Kong Juxin could perceive and realize his own fault." After hearing that, the king said, "Then I am the one to blame."

Herein, Mencius used two analogies to explain the necessity of practicing benevolent governance and harshly criticized the indifferent and irresponsible attitude of the governors towards the life and death of the people, and also his implied criticism has made the king realize his own fault.

绰绰有余

　　孟子刚到齐国的时候闲暇无事,于是四处访问齐国的名士,跟各界人士接触,宣传他的仁政思想。蚳蛙是齐威王的心腹,在灵丘当邑宰。灵丘是齐国的西北边城,军事要地。蚳蛙对孟子的仁政思想有着浓厚的兴趣,他在自己管辖的地方试行了孟子学说中一些简单易行的内容,结果很有成效。于是他就辞去了邑宰的职务,到朝廷去当办案的士师。因为这个职务跟齐威王接触比较频繁,很方便向威王进言,使他接受仁政思想。

　　然而蚳蛙多次进言,威王不但没有采纳,反而十分反感。于是蚳蛙就辞官走了。消息传开,有些齐国人就讽刺孟子说:"孟轲为蚳蛙考虑得倒挺周到的,但不知道他是怎么为自己着想的呢?"这话的意思是,孟轲到处宣传仁政,害得蚳蛙进言不成,只好辞官走了。你自己也经常向齐威王进言,也不被采纳,为什么还要赖在齐国不走呢?

孟子的学生公都子听到这些议论就告诉了孟子。孟子说:"并不是我脸皮厚不肯走,我的行为都是有根据的。有固定职务的人,如果无法尽责,那是应该辞官而走;有向君主进言责任的人,如果没有尽责,那也应该辞官离开。而我,既无官职,又无进言之责,进退自由,难道不是绰绰而有余地吗?"

"绰绰有余"这个成语由此而来。孟子认为,作为正式的官员,有自己的职责范围,应该尽到自己的责任。如果不能尽责,就应该离去。这也就是孔子说过的"不在其位,不谋其政"。孟子无职无位,就不能用这样的标准来要求自己。当然,这主要是从执政的角度来说的,孟子并不曾因为自己无职无位而推卸自己作为一名有良知的士人所应该具有的责任和使命。他行事磊落,不畏惧别人的非议,进退都掌握在自己的手里,显示出一种大无畏的丈夫本色。

ACT FREELY AND WITHOUT ANY CONSTRAINTS

When Mencius just arrived at Qi, free and not occupied as he was, he visited the famous scholars hither and thither, and contacted people from all circles within the state in order to promote his ideas of benevolent governance. At that time, Chi Wa enjoyed the trust and favor of King Wei of Qi and acted as governor of Ling Qiu, a fortified city located in the northwest. Chi Wa was very interested in Mencius' ideas of benevolent governance and implemented some of the simple principles within his jurisdiction which proved to be quite effective. Therefore, he quitted his post as governor and requested to be appointed as chief criminal judge because he thought this job might grant him with more opportunities of contacting with and offering suggestions to the king, through which he could make the king accept the principles of benevolent governance.

However, instead of taking Chi Wa's remonstration, the king showed a marked antipathy towards him. So Chi Wa resigned from his office and left. This news spread around and some people satirized Mencius and said, "In the course which he marked out for Chi Wa he did well, but we do not know as to the course which he pursues for himself." What they meant was Mencius' principles of benevolent governance led to Chi Wa's resignation and departure, and why Mencius himself, still lingered in Qi after his ideas had been constantly rejected by the king.

Gongduzi informed his master of those criticisms. Mencius said, "I am not thick-skinned, I have my reasons for why I still linger here. He who is in charge of an office, when being prevented from fulfilling his duties, ought to take his departure; he who bears the responsibility of making remonstration, when finding his words unattended to, ought to do the same. But I am in charge of no office, on me places no duty of remonstration — may not I therefore act freely and without any constraints either in going forward or in retiring?"

The idiom "There is enough room to spare (*chuo chuo you yu*)" originates from this story. Mencius held that he who, as an appointed official, having his own duties should fulfill his responsibilities. If he failed, then he had to leave. That was the idea of "Everyone should confine himself to his own duties" put forward by Mencius. Mencius has no office or post, so he should not apply this principle to himself. Of course, this idea was from the perspective of the execution of power. Mencius had never shrunk away from his due responsibilities and missions as a conscientious scholar under the excuse of not holding any post or office. He acted in an honest and candid manner, not afraid of being challenged by others, and able to control the advance and retreat freely, which showed his dauntless heroism as a true man.

孟子吊丧

　　滕文公去世,孟子听到这个消息,自然是很伤心。当年滕文公还是太子的时候,就曾经多次拜访孟子,并向他请教学问,两人性情相投,彼此结下了深厚的友谊。滕文公即位后,还把孟子请到滕国,尊他为师,请教国政。孟子还为滕文公详细制定了一套井田制、赋税制的仁政方针。虽然因为种种原因,滕国的仁政没有成功实现,但在孟子心目中,滕文公仍然是一位贤者。所以当齐宣王知道孟子精通礼数,便派孟子以卿相身份前去吊丧时,孟子自然很愿意奉使出吊滕文公。当时,齐宣王派孟子为正使,盖邑大夫王驩为副使同行。

　　孟子在滕国行了兄弟之礼、君臣之礼,又读了祭文赞颂滕文公的功德和彼此的友谊。最后伏地叩头,痛哭流涕,心情沉痛。在返回齐国首都临淄的途中,孟子、王驩一行人白天赶路,夜里住宿,朝夕相伴,却很少交流,更不谈论这次出行的公事。公孙丑见了很奇怪,问孟子:"齐国卿相的职位不小了,齐国和滕国之间的路途也不近啊,但是往返一趟,夫子竟不曾与王驩谈论过公事,这是为什么呢?"

孟子觉得公孙丑的头脑既简单又愚鲁可笑。他说:"他既然一人独断专行,我又何必多嘴说话呢?"

实际上,孟子在齐国的身份并不是正式的官员,只是被齐宣王拜为客卿,领有一份俸禄而已,职责范围是议政,而不执政。所以地位虽高,却并不被一些当权者重视。在去滕国吊丧的过程中,王驩虽为副使,但仗着自己是地方官员,根本不把孟子放在眼里,处处独断专行,很多事情都是由他一人说了算。孟子心中明白,所以不与他争执,但也用一种沉默的方式来表达自己对小人的一种抗议。公孙丑对这一切却看不明白,实在有点愚钝。

A CONDOLENCE VISIT PAID BY MENCIUS

Of course, Mencius was deeply grieved when he got the news that Duke Wen of Teng had passed away. Their friendship burgeoned when Duke Teng, then still the crown prince, paid several visits to Mencius and consulted him about learning, during which the two found each other congenial. After succeeding to the throne, Duke Wen invited Mencius to Teng and respected him as teacher, consulting him about how to rule the state. Mencius had made a detailed plan for King Wen on benevolent governance covering a nine-square land system and taxation system. Though his ideas of benevolent governance had not been materialized in Teng for various reasons, Mencius still esteemed Duke Wen as a man of virtue. Therefore, Mencius was very willing to accept the mission of paying a condolence visit to Teng when King Xuan of Qi, on account of his mastery of rituals, appointed him as an envoy with the status of a senior official of Qi. Besides appointing Mencius as commissioner, the king also sent Wang Huan, the governor of Gaiyi, as assistant-commissioner to Teng.

While in Teng, Mencius observed the etiquette appropriate for a man to his brother and that for a minister to his king; also, he read the funeral oration to sing the praises of the achievements and virtues of Duke Wen and their friendship. Finally, he fell down upon his knees, kowtowed and cried bitterly with sorrow. On their way back to Linzi, capital of Qi, Mencius, Wang Huan and their followers hurried on with their journey during the day and rested at night. Despite being together all the time, they seldom communicated, and never discussed about their mission.

Gongsun Chou was surprised after he learnt that and asked Mencius, "The position of a senior minister of Qi is not low; the distance between Qi and Teng is also not short. How was it that during all the way there and back, you never spoke to Wang Huan about your mission?"

While deeming his question naive, stupid, as well as funny, Mencius replied, "Since he always went his own way, why should I bother myself talking to him?"

Actually Mencius, instead of being a formal minister of Qi, was only serving in the court of Qi from another feudal state. He was salaried with the responsibility of discussing the politics, rather than at the helm of governance. So despite his high status, he was not respected by those who were in power. During their mission to Teng, Wang Huan as assistant commissioner, relying on his position as a local official, did not respect Mencius and went his own way, indulging in arbitrary decisions on many issues. Mencius was clear about that and did not want to argue with him, but he used silence as a way of protest against this vile man. It is really stupid for Gongsun Chou to have failed to realize all that.

孟子葬母

　　孟子因为重视孝道,将母亲的葬礼办得十分隆重,这曾经引起墨家信徒的质疑,也成为小人挑拨离间他与君主关系的一个话柄,甚至连他的弟子也产生过疑问。

　　就在孟子到鲁国安葬好母亲,返回齐国的时候,弟子充虞就来求教了:"前些日子承蒙您不嫌弃我,派我管理工匠。那时事务繁忙,我没敢打扰您,现在我有件事想私下里求教老师,我觉得老师给母亲做的棺木似乎太过华丽了。"

　　这个问题并没有让孟子感到尴尬,也没有让他恼火生气,他随时随地都能给弟子灌输儒家的学问知识。他回答说:"古时候的棺椁是没有一定尺寸的,中古以来的棺椁厚度大概七寸,这是在变化的。从天子到庶民,不仅是为了棺椁好看,更主要的是为了尽儿女孝心。达不到应有的标准不会称心,没有相当的财力也不会称心。古时候的人都这样做了，我现在既能达到标准又具备了财力，为什么就不能做呢？要知道，我们庇护死者最好的办法，就是不让他们的身体肌肤与泥土接触，这样做儿女的才能感到欣慰啊。我听说，君子是不会在天下人都做得到的事情上节省自己父母亲的所有费用的。"

　　孟子对于父母丧礼的态度一向坚持两条，一是是否尽到了做子女的孝心；二是与自己的能力是否相当。如果丧礼没有达到自己财力所能达到的程度，那就说不上是尽孝了。孟子对于父母丧礼的这种思想跟孔子是一脉相承的。而今天的中国人对于父母长辈的丧礼比较讲究，甚至流于铺张的传统，恐怕也跟儒家思想中对于丧礼的倡导不无关系。

THE FUNERAL OF MENCIUS' MOTHER

　　Mencius, who highly valued filial piety, held a grand funeral for his mother. However, some Mohists challenged this, also it became a meat for gossip capitalized by the vile to create alienation between Mencius and the king, and even cast doubts on his own disciples.

　　When the funeral was over and Mencius planned to go back to Qi from Lu, his disciple Chong Yu asked him, "Formerly, honored by your trust, I was assigned to superintend the making of the coffin. As you were then pressed by the urgency of the business, I did not venture to disturb you by inquiring you. Now, master, I wish to consult you in private, for it appeared to me that the coffin for your mother was too luxurious."

　　Mencius was neither embarrassed nor irritated by his words. Instead, he wasted no opportunity to instill the ideas of Confucianism into his disciples. He replied, "In ancient times, there was no set size for coffins. From middle antiquity onwards, the coffins were about seven inches thick, but that was changing all the time. That was done by all, from the sovereign to the common people, not simply for the beauty of the appearance, but more importantly for fulfilling their filial piety. If the coffins could not reach the expected standard, men would not be gratified, neither would they if they could not afford such coffins. The ancients all behaved like that. Why should I, despite being able to get the satisfying coffin and my adequate financial capabilities, be prevented from doing that? As you know, the best way to protect the deceased is to prevent their bodies from being exposed to the soil, and only by achieving that, can we as sons and daughters feel relieved. I have heard that a man with high morals would not be niggardly to his parents on the issue which all the people can offer to their parents."

On the funeral for one's parents, Mencius held two principles: one was whether they have fulfilled the filial piety as sons or daughters, the other was whether the funeral was appropriate to their affordability. One could not be reckoned as having fulfilled his filial piety if the funeral is too humble compared with one's financial capabilities. Mencius' ideas on the funerals for parents are of the same strain as those of Confucius. China's tradition of attaching great importance to the funerals for parents and other seniors in the family, or even making them extravagant, is perhaps related to the value put on funerals by Confucianism.

沈同问伐燕

当年齐国攻打燕国这件事,在齐国上下引起了很大的反响。齐国大臣沈同就曾经私下问过孟子:"可以讨伐燕国吗?"

孟子回答:"可以。因为燕王哙不可以随便按照自己的意志把燕国让给别人,他的相国子之也不可以就这样从燕王的手里接收燕国。这就好比有一个人,你很喜欢他,就不向君王请示而自作主张,把你自己的官位俸禄让给他。而他呢,也没有君王的任命就直接从你的手里接受官位俸禄,这样行得通吗?燕王、子之两人私自把燕国给来受去的,跟这个例子有什么两样呢?"

孟子批评燕国的让位事件,认为它并不符合古代禅让政治的本意。也就是说,王位或官位都不是私有的,不能私自转让接受。如果要转移政权的话,应该以民意为主导,得到百姓支持的人才能做天子。燕王哙私自将国家政权授予相国子之,没有得到百姓的支持,就是不尊重民意，所以从这一点出发，孟子认为讨伐燕国是正义的。但是有一点，只有同样是怀着正义愿望的军队才有资格去讨伐燕国，如果一心只想着霸占别国的领土，却假借正义之名，行不义之事，那么他就没有资格去讨伐燕国。

孟子也将他的这个想法说给齐宣王听过，可惜齐宣王听不进去，认为孟子又是老调重弹，不切实际，所以还是一意孤行地派兵攻打了燕国。

ENQUIRY OF SHEN TONG ON THE INCURSION OF YAN

The incursion of Yan by Qi caused quite a stir within the State of Qi. Shen Tong, one of Qi's ministers once asked Mencius, "Can Yan be attacked?"

Mencius replied, "Yes, it may. King Kuai of Yan had no right to give Yan to another man at will, neither should his minister Zi Zhi accept it. Suppose there is a man here, with whom you are so pleased that you are to give him your salary and rank without getting the permission from the king first; and suppose that man, also without the king's order is to accept them from you privately, would such behaviors be acceptable? And what is the difference between these two cases?"

Mencius criticized the abdication of the throne by King Kuai and held that was against the original purpose of the ancient political system of abdication. That was to say, neither the throne nor the rank was private, thus neither of them could be transferred to others in private. If one were to transfer the throne, that should be based on public opinion and only those who got support of the people could succeed the throne. By giving the throne to his minister Zi Zhi privately without the support of the people, King Kuai despised public opinion. Therefore Mencius believed that the incursion of Yan based on that was morally justified. However, only the troops with aspirations for serving justice were entitled to the incursion, but not those preoccupied with the purpose of occupying land and acted immorally under the guise of serving justice.

Mencius also told this to King Xuan of Qi, who turned a deaf ear to all these and thought Mencius was impractical and just striking up the same old tune. As a result, he still persisted in arbitrarily sending troops to attack Yan.

宣王愧对孟子

　　齐国攻伐燕国不久，燕国人又起来造反，很快就收复了失地，光复了国家，并拥戴燕太子平为王。这时，齐宣王才想起孟子曾经对他说过的话，心中十分惭愧，便感叹说："我真是愧对孟子啊！"齐国大夫陈贾在一旁听了，自作聪明地开导齐王："大王以为自己跟周公比，谁更仁德、智慧呢？"齐王嗔怪地说："这是什么话！我哪敢跟周公比呢！"陈贾没有理会，接着说："周公派管叔监管殷地遗民，管叔却率领殷朝遗民起义反抗周公。如果周公预见到管叔会反叛他，仍派他去监管殷地人，那他就是不仁义；如果周公没有预见到管叔会反叛他，那他就是不明智。连周公这样的先贤都没有做到完全的仁义与明智，您又何必自责呢？我去跟孟子解释清楚。"

　　陈贾跑到孟子那儿把这番话又说了一遍，满以为自己很有道理，不料却被孟子一一驳回：周公是弟弟，管叔是哥哥，难道弟弟会怀疑哥哥反叛自己吗？周公犯的错误是人之常情，没什么奇怪的。何况古代圣人知错就改，不像当今的一些君主，明明犯了错误，却不思悔改，还将错就错。古代圣人犯的错误好比日食月食，百姓看得很清楚，一旦改正，百姓也是高兴地仰望他。现在的君主呢？却要找一大堆的借口来掩饰自己的错误，为自己辩解。

陈贾满以为自己的一番说辞能为齐王讨点好处，却不料被孟子击中了要害。作为一国之君，犯了错误不足怪，只怕犯了错误还要掩饰，而且不肯改过。那所谓的"惭愧"又有什么意义呢？

KING XUAN IS ASHAMED BEFORE MENCIUS

Shortly after the invasion by Qi, the Yan people rebelled and recovered the lost territory and state as well as supported the crown prince of Yan to succeed the throne. At that time, King Xuan finally recalled what Mencius had told him and felt ashamed, "I am ashamed before Mencius." he sighed. His minister Chen Jia, after hearing this, said to him presumptuously, "Who does Your Highness consider is more benevolent and intelligent, yourself or Duke Zhou?" The king rebuked, "What words are these? How dare I compare myself with Duke Zhou?" Chen Jia went on, "Duke Zhou appointed Guan Shu to oversee the heir of Yin, but Guan Shu with the power of the Yin State rebelled. If having predicted that this would happen, he still appointed Guan Shu, he was deficient in benevolence; if he appointed him, not knowing that it would happen, he was deficient in wisdom. Since even ancient virtuous kings as Duke Zhou were not completely benevolent and wise, why should you blame yourself on that? I beg to visit Mencius and explain these to him."

Chen Jia repeated these words to Mencius and thought his words were well-founded. However, much to his surprise, Mencius retorted him back one by one: "Duke Zhou was Guan Shu's younger brother. How could one suspect his own elder brother of rebelling against him? So Duke Zhou's mistake was because of human nature, nothing to be surprised at. Moreover, when the ancient sages made a mistake, they would correct it immediately after recognizing it; while the sovereigns of the present time, persist in their own mistakes instead of correcting them. The errors of ancient sages, as eclipses of the sun and moon were seen clearly by all the people and when they were rectified, all the people looked up to their kings with joy. How about the current sovereigns? They try to cover and refuse to correct their mistakes with lots of excuses."

With the expectation of justifying for the king with his arguments, Chen Jia turned out to be retorted harshly by Mencius. As a sovereign, it is not at all strange to make mistakes. What is to be afraid of is that one tries to cover the mistakes rather than rectify them. Given all that, then why bother with feeling so-called "ashamed"?

孟子辞官

孟子向齐宣王提出了辞呈,准备回国。宣王亲自到孟子的寓所去见他,并说:"过去想见您却见不到,后来好不容易能够有幸跟您在一起,我一直很高兴。可是现在您又要离我而去,不知我们什么时候才能再见面呢?"孟子回答说:"这原本也是我的希望,只是我不敢勉强罢了。"

过了几天,齐王对大臣时子说:"我想在临淄城中给孟子一幢房屋,用万钟之粟来养活他和他的弟子,这样我们齐国的官民便能够向他学习。你替我去找孟子谈谈吧。"于是,时子便托人把这话转告给了孟子。孟子回答说:"这个时子也不想想这样的事情做得做不得。假如我是贪图富贵的人,我干么辞去十万钟俸禄的官位,而接受这万钟的赐予呢?"

孟子的意思是说,物质利益的大小并非是否出仕的标准。假如自己会为齐宣王承诺的这万钟俸禄而留在齐国，那自己又何必辞去十万钟俸禄的官职呢？既然我不是为了这官职俸禄而留在齐国，那我现在要离开了，又岂是多少钱财能留得住我的呢？齐宣王也有意思，他欣赏孟子，却又不接受孟子的政治主张，不采纳他的治国方针。如今孟子要走，他又舍不得孟子这个学问深厚、知识渊博的人才，想竭力挽留住他。他这种矛盾的心理，自然使得孟子在离开齐国的路途中仍然对他抱有一丝幻想。

RESIGNATION OF MENCIUS

Mencius submitted his letter of resignation to King Xuan of Qi and was going to return to his home state. King Xuan called at his residence and said to Mencius, "Formerly, I wished to see you, but I couldn't. Then, I got the opportunity of being by your side, and I was so delighted for your company. Now you would leave me, and I do not know if hereafter I may expect to have another opportunity of seeing you." Mencius replied, "I dare not request permission to visit you at any particular time, but, indeed, it is what I desire."

After a few days, the king said to his minister Shizi, "I wish to give Mencius a house, somewhere in the city of Linzi, and to support him and his disciples with an allowance of 10,000 zhong (a unit of measurement for grain) of millet. By that all the officers and the common people would be able to learn from him. Talk to Mencius about it for me." Thus, Shizi conveyed this message to Mencius through other people. Mencius said, "Shizi should have realized that he could not accept this mission. If I were a man hankering after wealth and fame, why did I formerly decline the office with a salary of a hundred thousand zhong of millet and now accept this gift of ten thousand zhong?

What Mencius meant was that the value of material benefits was not the principle for him to decide whether to take public office or not. If he would stay in Qi just for ten thousand zhong promised by King Xuan, then why did he formerly give up his post with a hundred thousand zhong of millet for salary? Since he stayed in Qi not on the account of the post and its accompanying salary, how was it possible that he would change his mind just for the amount of money? King Xuan was also quite interesting, because though he appreciated Mencius, he would not adopt Mencius' political ideas and his principles of governing the state. But now when Mencius was about to leave, he was loath to lose Mencius, such a learned and erudite talent, and tried his best to persuade him to stay. Of course, his ambivalence made Mencius still hold the slightest illusion on his journey away from Qi.

告别齐国之路

  孟子离开齐国,向西南方向走,准备返回故乡。走了一天,到了昼邑这个地方,便住下休息。有个想替齐王挽留孟子的人,恭恭敬敬地坐在那儿对孟子说话,孟子却不理不睬,自顾自地靠在桌子上睡觉。那人不高兴了,说:"我对您那么恭敬,斋戒了一宿,清净了身心,才敢坐在这里与您说话,您却装睡不理我,我不敢再来见您了。"孟子这才开口说话:"你坐好,我来明白告诉你从前鲁穆公是怎样对待贤士的。他如果见没有人在子思身边,就不能安心;如果泄柳、申详这些贤者没有人在鲁穆公的身边陪伴,鲁穆公自己也不能安心。你虽然是为我这个老头儿考虑,却比不上子思,因为你连鲁穆公怎样对待子思这一点都忘了。你不去劝说齐宣王改变主意,却在这里说些空话挽留我,你说,这到底是你跟我决绝,还是我跟你决绝呢?"

  孟子在昼邑住了三天三夜才离开齐国的边境。这时有个叫尹士的人听说了，就说起了牢骚怪话："不知道是齐王当不了商汤、周武，还是孟子太糊涂。如果是知道齐王不行还要来，那是他贪求富贵。如果是因为得不到齐王的信任而离去，那为什么在昼邑住了三天三夜，磨磨蹭蹭不肯离开呢？我很看不上他的行为。"

高子把尹士的话告诉给孟子听。孟子回答说："这个尹士哪里了解我呢？不远千里来见齐王自然是我所希望的；得不到信任而离去，难道也是我所希望的吗？我是不得已啊！我在昼邑歇息了三天，我还嫌快呢。我想，齐王也许会改变态度，召我回去。直到我离开昼邑，齐王也没派人来追，我才无所留恋地准备回家乡。即使是这样，我也不想抛弃齐王啊！齐王还可以好好干一番事业的。假如他肯用我，不只齐国百姓能得到安宁，天下百姓也能得到太平啊。齐王或许会改变态度的，我天天盼望着呢。我难道要像那些气量狭小的人一样，劝谏之言得不到采纳，就怨恨、生气；一旦离开，就非要走到精疲力竭不肯歇息吗？"尹士听到孟子这番话后惭愧地说："我真是个小人啊！"

在离开齐国的路上发生的这两件事，表明了孟子为官的态度。前者说的是，君主要挽留贤者，就要使贤者安心；反过来，贤者所顾虑的，也是能否以自己的主张来影响君主。想挽留孟子的齐王不能真正理解孟子，那孟子只好走了。后者表现了孟子以天下为己任的胸怀，对于有可能施行仁政的君主，哪怕有一丝希望，他也是不愿轻易放弃的。常言道：君子坦荡荡，小人长戚戚。以小人之心，度君子之腹，充分表现出了人性的卑琐。

JOURNEY AWAY FROM QI

After he left Qi, Mencius forwarded southwest on his journey back to his home state. After one day's journey, he arrived at Zhouyi and rested there.

There was a person sitting there and speaking to him in an attitude of respect with the intention of persuading Mencius to stay in Qi on behalf of the king. But Mencius totally ignored him, and leant upon his table and slept. The visitor was displeased, and said, "I respected you so much by having passed the night in careful vigil and cleaned my body and soul, before I would venture to come and speak to you, while you feigned sleep and ignored me. I would not dare to visit you again." By that time Mencius finally said, "Sit down, and I will explain to you how Duke Mu of Lu treated his men of virtues in the past. If Duke Mu had not kept a person by the side of Zisi, he would not be rest assured; if Duke Mu had not enjoyed the company of the virtuous such as Xie Liu or Shen Xiang, he would not feel relieved either. Though you were considerate for an old man like me, you have not treated me as Zisi had been treated because you even forgot how Zisi had been treated by Duke Mu. Instead of persuading King Xuan to change his mind, you said all those empty words to ask me not to leave. So, sir, is it you who break up with me or is it I who break up with you?"

Mencius stayed in Zhouyi for three days and nights before he left the border of Qi. After knowing that, one called Yin Shi grumbled, "I don't know whether it's because the king of Qi could not become a great king such as Shang Tang or Zhou Wu or because Mencius is too muddled. If he knew that the king could not be made such a great sovereign, and came notwithstanding, that showed he was just hankering after wealth and fame. If he took his leave because he could not win the trust of the king, then why did he dawdle and linger by spending three days and nights in Zhouyi before he quitted Zhouyi? I hold in contempt his behaviors."

Gao Zi informed Mencius of these remarks. Mencius said, "How could this Yin Shi know me! When I came a thousand li to wait on the king, it was what I desired to do; but when I took leave as a result of my failure to win his trust, was that still what I desired? It was because I have no other choice. Though I rested for three days in Zhouyi, in my own mind I still considered my departure rather speedy. I was hoping that the king might change his mind and send for me. Till I quitted Zhouyi and the king had not sent after me, then, was my mind resolutely bent on returning to my hometown. But, notwithstanding that, I am still not willing to give up the king. The king, after all, is the one who may accomplish some great causes. If he were to trust me, not only the Qi people would be blessed with peace, but also all the people on the land under Heaven. Every day, I am hoping that the king will change his mind some day. How can I act like those narrow-minded, who would be irritated and held a grudge against their king once their remonstration was not accepted or those who once decided to leave would press on until exhausted?" When Yin Shi heard those words of Mencius, he was ashamed and said, "I am indeed a vile man."

The two incidences which happened during Mencius' journey away from Qi manifested his attitude of how to be an official. The former case told us that if a king wanted to persuade a sage to stay, he had to make the sage be truly rest assured; on the other hand, what the sage worried about was whether he could influence the king with his own ideas. The king of Qi, though trying to let Mencius stay, could not really understand him, so he had to leave. The latter case showed Mencius' broad mind of shouldering the responsibility of ensuring the well-being of all the people. For those kings who might practice benevolent governance, he was not willing to desert them with the slimmest hope. As the saying goes, "A man with high morals is honest and poised while a vile man is full of anxiety." The vile think of the noble in terms of their own desires which fully exposes the sordidness of human nature.

此一时彼一时

孟子离开齐国返回故乡的途中,内心一直充满了矛盾,常常情不自禁地叹气。弟子充虞就问他:"老师您好像有点不太高兴的样子。记得以前您曾经说过,有德行的人既不抱怨上天,也不埋怨别人。"孟子回答说:"那时是那时,现在是现在。自古以来,每五百年必有一位贤明的君主出现,这期间还会有举世闻名的杰出人才出现。从周武王到现在已经七百多年了,早已超过五百年了。所以从时势上看,现在应该是贤明君王和杰出人才出现的时候了。看来上天不想使天下安定吧?如果想的话,普天之下,除了我还有谁做得到呢?我为什么要不愉快呢?"

孟子的自信在此表现得近于自负,五百年必有王者兴,而这辅助王者的贤才则是"当今之世,舍我其谁?"这并非是孟子聊以自慰的空话大话,而是孟子一心拯救天下的抱负和使命感的体现。这既显示出了他性格中自负的一面，也显示出了他救世济民的奉献精神。可惜他空有一腔抱负，却得不到施展。即使是如他一般的圣人，当遭遇现实挫折的时候，也难免会有失望沮丧的时候吧。所以就连孟子也说出了"此一时彼一时"这样的无奈之言。

THAT IS THEN AND THIS IS NOW

On the way back to his hometown from Qi, Mencius harbored ambivalent feelings and couldn't refrain from sighing. So his disciple Chong Yu asked him, "Master, you look like not so happy. I still remember you told us once that those with virtues do not murmur against Heaven, nor grudge against others." Mencius replied, "That was then and this is now. Ever since the ancient times, it has been a law that a true virtuous sovereign should arise in the course of every five hundred years, and should also emerge some extraordinary talents of universal renown among their peers. Over seven hundred years have elapsed since the period reigned by King Wu of Zhou, which is well over five hundred years. Therefore, judging from the time, it is high time that the virtuous sovereigns and extraordinary talents should emerge. But it seems Heaven does not yet wish that the land under Heaven should enjoy tranquility and good order. Had Heaven wished for that, who would be there besides me to bring it about? Why should I be unhappy then?"

Mencius' self-confidence displayed here almost equaled to conceit. Every five hundred years there should arise a true sovereign and he believed the talent to support such a sovereign of his era should be no other than himself. These were not empty boasts for Mencius to console himself, rather they manifested his ambitions and sense of mission to save the whole land under Heaven. On the one hand, it showed the conceit side of his character while, on the other hand, showed his dedication to saving the land under Heaven and all the people. It is a shame that his ambitions could not be realized. Even a sage like him would be disappointed and disheartened in front of all the frustrations of reality and uttered words as "That is then, and this is now."

滕文公问丧仪

滕定公去世了。太子对他的老师然友说:"过去我跟孟子在宋国曾经交谈过,至今念念不忘。现在不幸遇到了丧事,你去问问孟子,再举行丧礼。"然友来到邹国,向孟子请教。孟子说,父母去世了,是应该尽心尽力。父母在世时,好好侍奉他们,父母去世后,好好埋葬他们、祭祀他们,这样才是孝子。诸侯的礼节我没学过,但是我知道,三年的丧期里穿粗布衣服,喝稀粥,这是从夏商周以来,从天子到老百姓都一直遵守的规矩。

然友回去后就把孟子的话告诉了太子,于是太子决定滕国的丧期为三年。但是滕国与国君同姓的百官、大臣都不愿意,在下面议论纷纷:我们的宗主国鲁国的先王没行过三年的丧礼,我们自己的先王也没有。为什么到了你这儿就要违反这个规矩呢?

太子又对老师然友说:"过去我没有学过礼仪,只喜欢骑马和剑术。现在文武百官都反对三年丧礼，我担心完不成这个礼仪。你再帮我去问问孟子该怎么办。"然友又来到邹国去问孟子。孟子说，这样的事首先要靠自己。孔子以前说过：先君去世了，政权先由宰相掌管着，自己就喝着稀粥，一坐下来就哭，百官也没有一个不悲哀的，因为自己做出了表率。在上位的喜欢什么，下面的人也就喜欢什么。君子的德性就像风，小人的德性就像草，风吹在草上，草肯定就倒了。所以关键还是要看太子自己啊。后来太子就按照孟子的说法举行了葬礼，前来吊丧的人都很满意。

　　滕国太子就是后来的滕文公，他内心一直仰慕孟子的才学，当太子的时候就数次向孟子求教。即位成了国君以后，他也一度想请孟子来帮助滕国实行仁政。无奈滕文公性情优柔寡断，缺少魄力，遭到滕国那些身居高位的权臣贵族的反对以后，仁政之事也就不了了之。在孟子看来，能否行礼仪、行正道，关键要看自己有没有信心，他借风与草对德性的比喻是意味深长的。当然，孟子对丧仪的要求是按照周朝的礼制而来的，在战国时代以利益为先的氛围里显然是格格不入的。

DUKE WEN OF TENG INQUIRING ABOUT FUNERAL MANNERS

Duke Ding of Teng passed away. The crown prince said to his teacher Ran You, "I am impressed with the talk with Mencius in the State of Song. Now that I am bereaved of my father and confused with the funeral manners, please ask him for some suggestions concerning the burial." Ran You then went to Zou and consulted Mencius about relevant advices. Mencius replied, "After one's parent passed away, one should do his utmost to arrange for the funeral. A filial son should take good care of his parents while they are still alive, and bury and commemorate them in best possible manners after their death. I have not learnt about the aristocratic etiquette, but I am well aware that during the three dynasties before our era, both the king and the public obeyed the rules to wear coarsely-made clothes and drink plain porridge three years within the death of their parents."

Ran You told Mencius' word to the crown prince, who in turn decided to set three years as the national mourning period. All the officials and ordinary people shared the same family name with the king, however, were unwilling to observe that national mourning, and complained, "Neither the former dukes in our suzerain State of Lu or those in our own state have ever declared such mourning period. How could this young man violate the existing practices?"

The crown prince said to his teacher Ran You again, "I didn't learn about the etiquettes before and was only interested in horsemanship and fencing. Now that all the officials are against the national mourning, I'm afraid I can't implement it. Please ask Mencius for a feasible solution." Ran You went to Zou and consulted Mencius again. The latter answered, "The prince must rely on himself. Confucius once said that formerly when the former king passed away, the new King would cry and drink plain porridge only, having the prime minister temporarily in power, so all the lower-ranking officials followed suit to be sad. The higher ranking people set examples for their subordinates. Moral people are sure to prevail over the immoral in the way wind crushes grass. Therefore it all depends on the crown prince himself." The crown prince followed Mencius' advices and all the people attending the king's funeral were contented.

The prince became Duke Wen of Teng later. He was always filled with adoration for the talent and learning of Mencius. He had solicited advices from him for several times when he was crown prince and requested Mencius to assist him in implementing the benevolent governance after ascending to the throne. It was a pity that Duke Wen was weak in character and determination, and the benevolent governance saw little achievement due to the opposition of aristocrats. In

Mencius' opinion, the correct governing as well as the proper etiquette must be carried out with full confidence and power, and his analogy between wind, grass and morality was pregnant with meaning. His standards for burial ceremony took after that in Zhou Dynasty, which were doubtlessly at odds with the profit-oriented atmosphere in the Warring States Period.

滕文公问政

　　滕文公有意施行仁政，于是专程邀请孟子到滕国。在滕国，孟子受到了隆重的接待，被安排住在舒适的客舍里。滕文公就常到客舍来拜访孟子，向他请教为政之道。

　　孟子耐心指导滕文公：老百姓的生活得到保障是最要紧的。没有稳定的资产作为生活保证，却又保持良好的道德品质，恐怕只有贤人圣人才能做到。一般的百姓，假如没有稳定的资产收入，便会心神动摇。一旦心神动摇，便会放纵、奸诈、欺骗、胡作非为。等到这些人犯了罪，然后再用刑罚惩罚他们，这就等于是国家用罗网故意引诱百姓，而后抓捕他们。因此，贤明的君主应该为百姓创造稳定的产业，使他们上可以奉养父母，下可以养活妻子儿女。好年景终年丰衣足食，坏年景也能免于冻馁死亡。如果民众连基本生活都不能保证，天天在死亡的边缘挣扎，哪里会有功夫来奉行礼义呢？所以，贤君就应该认真办事，节省用度，对待臣下有礼，尤其是征收赋税要有一定的制度。

孟子对滕文公详细解释了古代的税收制度，并说，丰收年成多征收一点也不算苛政；但如果灾荒年成，每家的收成甚至还不够第二年肥田的开销，却还要收满规定的赋税，那就是不管百姓死活了。滕国做大官的人都有一定的田租收入，并且子孙相传，为什么老百姓不能有一定的田地收入呢？

等到百姓生活都有了着落了，就要兴办学校来教育他们。学校教育的目的在于阐明人伦的道理，百姓明白了道理，自然会相亲相敬。如果努力实行这些措施的话，国家一定会气象一新，而君王也一定能称王天下。

孟子跟滕文公的谈话集中体现了他的仁政方针，那就是首要解决百姓的生活问题，使他们有固定的收入，减轻赋税、恢复井田制，百姓生活稳定之后，再兴办学校教育他们。那样，称王天下就为时不远了。

DUKE WEN OF TENG INQUIRING ABOUT POLITICAL ADVICES

Duke Wen of Teng wanted to implement the benevolent governance, so he invited Mencius to his state. Mencius was grandly received and accommodated in a comfortable residence and the duke frequently visited Mencius there and consulted him about political advices.

Mencius instructed Duke Wen patiently, "The top priority is to ensure the well-being of your subjects. Only saints can preserve their morality without sufficient means to support an adequate living while most people would deviate from the moral rules by indulging themselves, committing frauds, treachery and other evil acts. If the government punishes those people after they have committed those crimes, it would be like trapping and tempting them to commit crimes so as to apprehend them. Therefore, a virtuous king must provide his people with assets which could bring them stable incomes so as to enable them to support their parents, wives and children. They will live with abundant clothing and food in bumper harvest years and be spared of death from starvation in bad years. If the people could barely survive, how can they have the luxury to follow the etiquette? Therefore, a virtuous king should be earnest in governing, practice economy in expenses, be polite to state officials and particularly, should institutionalize the collection of tax."

Mencius explained the details of ancient taxation system to Duke Wen, "Heavy tax is not excessive in bumper harvest years; but in famine years, usually the poor yield of each family is even not enough to cover the cost of fertilizing the soil for the following year. It would be cruel and ignoring the suffering of the people to levy the same amount of tax. The high-ranking officials in Teng all have the income from the rental of the land which is hereditary, so why can't the ordinary people enjoy a fair amount of income derived from the soil as well?

After the ordinary people are enabled to afford their living, the king should establish schools to educate them with the purpose of illustrating morality and ethics to them. Once the ordinary become enlightened, they will surely love and respect each other. Once efforts are made to implement these measures, the state will take on a new look and the king is sure to be the sovereign of the land under Heaven."

These words of Mencius reflected his ideas on benevolent governance, i.e. firstly guarantee the basic living needs of the people through providing them with fixed incomes. After their well-being is guaranteed with the light tax and the ancient land system, provide them with education. By doing all these, the day is not too distant when one can become the sovereign of the land under Heaven.

孟子舌战陈相

有一个叫陈相的人,听到农家许行的一番言论后,深受感动,立刻放弃了自己原来所学而改投许行的门下。

陈相学了一点农家的主张后就跑去见孟子,想跟孟子理论一番,炫耀一下自己的所学。他对孟子说:"滕国的国君确实是个贤明的君主。尽管如此,但他仍然没有通晓治国的大道理。真正的贤君应当与百姓一起耕作,一起吃饭。现在滕国还有仓库官府,这是剥削百姓来养活自己,怎么能算是贤君呢?"

孟子一开始并没有回答陈相的问题,而是向他发起了一连串的质问:"许行一定是自己种庄稼,收获以后再吃饭吗?"陈相答道:"对。""许行一定是自己织布,然后再穿衣吗?""不是。许行穿麻布做的短衣。""许行戴帽子吗?""戴。""戴什么帽子?""戴白色帽子。""自己织的吗?""不是,用谷物换来的。""许行为什么不自己织帽子?"

"那会影响耕作。""许行用锅罐做饭,用铁犁耕作吗?""对。""锅罐、铁犁都是自己做的吗?""不是,是用谷物换来的。""用谷物换器械,不算影响陶器的锻冶;那用器械换谷物,又怎能算影响耕作呢?许行为什么不自己去锻冶陶器,用自己制作的东西,而要去与百工交换呢?许行为什么不嫌麻烦呢?""百工各有各的产业,不可能既耕作又做自己本行的事。""那治理天下就可以同时耕作吗?有君主百官的事,有普通百姓的事。如果所有的东西都要自己制作后再用,这不是让君主率领天下人奔波于道路上吗?因此说:有人做脑力劳动,有人做体力劳动。做脑力劳动的人管理别人;做体力劳动的人被别人管理。被别人管理的人供养别人;管理别人的人被别人供养。这是千古不变的公理。"孟子抓住了陈相的好几个漏洞,步步紧逼地追问,令陈相无法自圆其说,被逼进了墙角。孟子的论辩到这里几乎是胜利在望了。

孟子接着又批评陈相:"你的老师陈良是楚国人,他喜欢周公、孔子的学说,北方的学者很多都比不上他,他是人们所说的豪杰啊。可他去世了,你就背叛他。这个许行来自落后地区,胡乱批评君主的政事,你倒拜他为师。我从没听说过高处的乔木要搬迁到低洼的山谷里去的。"

陈相被孟子抢白了一番,很是狼狈,但仍然强撑着为许行辩护:"如果按照许先生的主张做的话,市场上物价统一,布匹长短相同,麻线重量相同,粮食多少相同,鞋子大小相同,那么价格也相同。这样就没人作假,即使是孩子也不会被人欺骗了。"

孟子冷笑道:"事物间存在差别,这是再自然不过的事了,你却硬要它们统一。如果鞋子的尺寸相同,价格就相同的话,谁还会做质量好的鞋子呢?真要施行许先生的主张,那就天下大乱了,还怎么治理国家呢!"论辩到这里,陈相终于认输,哑口无言地回去了。

孟子反对农学家许行"君臣并耕"的主张,提出了"劳心者治人,劳力者治于人"的儒家学说。在今天的民主时代看来,这显然是具有封建色彩的。他还认为偏远地区文化落后,难免有歧视他族的嫌疑。不过,从这个故事里我们也能够欣赏到孟子强有力的雄辩口才。

MENCIUS' DEBATE WITH CHEN XIANG

A scholar named Chen Xiang was deeply impressed with some arguments of the agronomist Xu Xing, and immediately forfeited what he had learned before and decided to study under Xu Xing.

After having learned some principles held by the agronomists, Chen Xiang went to see Mencius. He wanted to debate with Mencius in order to show off his wisdom. Chen Xiang said, "The king of Teng is wise indeed, but he still fails to understand the principles of governing the state. A wise king must do the farming and eat together with his subjects. The king still exploits people to support his living since there are still warehouses and government offices in the State of Teng. So how can he be acclaimed as a wise king?"

At first Mencius didn't answer Chen's question. Instead he launched his own inquiries, "Is the crop taken by Xu Xing planted and harvested by himself?"

"Yes." said Chen Xiang.

"Is the cloth made for Xu Xing's clothes woven by himself?"

"No, he wears short clothes made from linen."

"Does Xu Xing wear hat?"

"Yes."

"What kind of hat?"

"White-colored."

"Woven by himself?"

"No, he traded crop for it."

"Why doesn't he weave hats himself?"

"Because weaving would affect farming."

"Xu Xing uses the pots to cook and the iron plough in farming?"

"Yes."

"Does he make the pots and iron ploughs by himself?"

"No, he traded crop for them."

"Trading crop for machinery, in your opinion, wouldn't affect the forging of pottery. Why do you think that the trading of machinery for crop would affect farming? Why doesn't Xu Xing forge the pottery himself rather than trade his own products with other workers? Why does he take all the troubles to do that?"

"Workers specialize in different fields. They can't possibly do their own job while farming the land by themselves."

"Then how can a king govern his state while handling the farming by himself? The king and the state officials have their own responsibilities, so do the ordinary people. If everything needs to be done by oneself, it is like asking the king to lead his subjects rushing on the road. Thus we say that some people are mental workers and some are manual workers; the mental workers govern others, while others are to be governed. The governed support others, while the governors are supported. This is timeless truth." Mencius caught many loopholes in Chen Xiang's words and bombarded him with loads of questions. Chen Xiang couldn't justify himself and was cornered. Till then, Mencius had almost won the debate.

Mencius then continued to criticize Chen Xiang, "Your teacher Chen Liang was from Chu, who followed the philosophy of Duke Zhou and Confucius. He stood out among the northern scholars. Now that he passed away, and you immediately betrayed him to follow Xu Xing, who is from a backward region and groundlessly criticizes the policies of the kings. I never heard that trees want to be planted onto low-lying valleys."

Being satirized, despite his great embarrassment, Chen Xiang still defended for Xu Xing, "If Xu Xing's ideas were to be adopted there would be uniformed price on the market. The cloth would be sold in the same length; the linen threads would be sold with same weight; the crop would be sold with the same quantity; the shoes would be sold in the same size and at the same price. In that case, there would be no cheating, and even children would not be cheated."

Mencius sniffed at that, "There are differences among things, and it is natural, but you ruthlessly want to unify everything. Who would make shoes with better quality, if all the shoes were to be sold in the same size and at the same price? The market would be thrown into chaos had Xu Xing's ideas been implemented, let alone the governance of the whole state." Chen Xiang was finally silenced and admitted his defeat.

Mencius was against the idea of "king doing farming together with his subjects" put forward by Xu Xing, and supported the Confucian idea of "Mental workers are superior to manual workers". From today's democratic viewpoint, that was feudalist. Furthermore, his idea that the culture of underdeveloped area should be inferior to that in developed area was also somewhat racist. Nevertheless, his talent in debating was fully displayed in this debate.

墨家治丧辩

　　战国时代,各家学派之间常常会就双方的某一个观点进行辩论。比如对于丧葬,儒家是主张厚葬的,墨家却主张薄葬,而道家则认为葬礼没有多大意义。有一次,墨家的信徒夷子通过孟子的弟子徐辟的关系拜会了孟子。孟子立刻就墨家"兼爱"、"薄葬"的观点进行批判。他说:我听说墨家办理丧事,主张节俭。可是夷子父母的丧事却办得很隆重,这不是跟墨家的主张相矛盾吗?夷子辩解说,人对人的爱不应该有亲疏之差,实行起来就要从自己的父母开始。我厚葬父母,不过是使爱从父母开始而已。

　　孟子反驳说,你真以为别人爱自己哥哥的孩子会跟爱邻居的孩子一样吗?你们的理论不过是抓住了这样一点:婴儿在地上爬,眼看着就要爬到井里,此时此刻,无论谁见了都会出手去救。你以为这是"爱无次等",其实这只不过是人的恻隐之心罢了。万物出生的根源只有一个，那就是父母，所以儒家主张"老吾老，以及人之老"。你们墨家却说自己的父母与别人家的父母没有什么区别，爱无差等。这不等于说万物的根源有两个了吗？

　　孟子接着举了个例子。很早以前，人们的父母去世以后都不埋葬。有一个人，父母死后，按习俗把他们的尸体丢弃在山沟里。过几天又经过那里时，发现狐狸在啃咬父母的尸体，蚊虫也在尸体上吸吮。这人不禁额头冒汗，心中悔恨得无地自容，眼睛也不敢正视父母尸体。为什么呢？心中愧疚啊。于是他赶忙回家拿来工具埋葬了父母。掩埋父母的尸体当然是对的，而仁人孝子厚葬双亲，就更是理所当然的了。你们说爱无差等，怎么可能呢？听了孟子这番议论，夷子沉思了好一会儿，然后叹了一口气说道："孟子教我明白了一个道理啊。"

　　墨家的"兼爱"主张虽然美好，但却显然不符合人性。而夷子厚葬自己父母的行为本身也违反了墨家所主张的"薄葬"原则。孟子所举的例子就是要说明，人对父母的爱是先天的，无可取代的，因为生养我们的只有父母这一个根源。儒家学说重视孝悌也是因为这个原因。爱自己的父母不等于不爱别人，正是因为爱自己的父母，才能由己及人，善待别人的父母。

MENCIUS' COMMENTS UPON MOHISTS' ATTITUDE FOR BURIAL MANNERS

　　In the Warring States Period, different philosophical schools always debated for certain topics. For example, as to the issue of funeral manners, Confucians supported luxurious funerals; Mohists supported simple funerals while Taoists didn't attach any importance to them. Once, Yizi the Mohist visited Mencius through Mencius' student Xu Pi. Mencius immediately criticized Mohist ideas of "universal love" and "simple funerals". He said, "I heard that Mohists prefer simple funerals; but you held grand burial ceremonies for your parents. Is it against the Mohists' idea?" Yizi explained, "There shouldn't be any difference in our love for people, and the love must begin from our parents. I held grand funerals because my love for all people begins from that for my parents."

Mencius retorted, "Do you really think people can love other people's children as their own brothers' children? Your theory is only based on a simple fact that everybody would rescue a baby who is crawling towards a well. You think it is because there is no difference in love for everybody, but actually it is only due to compassion. Everybody has only one root — their parents, and that's why we Confucians hold the idea that 'Respect our parents together with other old people'. You Mohists think no difference lies in your own parents and those of others, and does that mean that everything has two roots?"

Mencius continued to set an example, "Long ago people didn't bury their deceased parents. Once, a man discarded his parents' bodies in a waste valley. Some days later, he found fox and mosquitoes biting the bodies. The man sweated and felt extremely ashamed; he didn't dare to stare straight at his parents' bodies. Why? It is because of his guilty conscience. He hurried back home, fetched some tools and buried them. We ought to bury parents' bodies and it comes natural for the benevolent and filial sons to hold grand burials for their parents. You claim that people can love all equally, how can that be possible?" Yizi quietly ruminated over Mencius' word and sighed, "Mencius made me realize a truth!"

Though Mohist idea of "universal love" was ideal, it was in conflict with human nature. Yizi's grand burial for his own parents also violated Mohists' idea of "simple funeral". Mencius set that example to explain it was instinctive to love one's own parents and the love was irreplaceable because we only had one root — our parents. The focus of Confucianism on filial piety was for the very reason. Loving our own parents doesn't necessarily preclude our love for other people. On the contrary, because we love our parents, we know how to convey our love to other people and respect other senior citizens.

枉己者怎能直人

陈代是孟子的弟子,他对孟子坚持原则、不得到合乎礼仪的邀请就不去见诸侯的行为有点不太理解,觉得老师可以在礼仪的问题上暂且委屈一下。于是对孟子说:"不去见诸侯似乎显得太拘谨了吧,现今要是游说他们,弄得好可以称王天下,弄不好也可以称霸诸侯,古书上说'弯曲小的而伸展大的',游说诸侯似乎可以试一试。"

孟子说:"过去齐景公打猎,用旌旗去传唤管理山林的虞人,虞人没去,景公就要处死他。孔子得知后说:'志士不怕弃尸山沟,勇士不怕丧失头颅。'孔子这是赞赏什么呢?是赞赏虞人对不符合礼仪的传唤不回应啊。要是不等传唤而前去,那算什么呢?所谓'弯曲小的而伸展大的',是从利益上来说的。要说利益,如果为了追逐利益而弯曲大的、伸展小的,是否也能做呢?过去赵简子派王良为他宠幸的小臣奚驾车打猎,一整天也没打到一件猎物。奚就向赵简子汇报说:'王良是天下最差劲的驾车手。'有人把这话告诉了王良,王良说:'请让我再试一次。'反复请求之后才获准许再为奚驾车,结果一个早上就捕捉到了十只野兽。奚又向赵简子汇报说:'王良是天下最优秀的驾车手。'赵简子就说:'那我派他专门为你驾车吧。'然后就把这个决定告诉了王良。想不到王良坚决不同意,说:'我替他按规则驾车,一整天捕不到一只猎物;不按照规则驾车,一个早上就捕到了十只。我只想证明这一点才第二次请求为他驾车的。其实我不习惯替小人驾车,所以这个差事我不干。'你看,一个驾车手尚且耻于与奚这样的射手合作,即便合作所捕获的鸟兽堆得像山丘一样高,也不肯干。如果违背了自己的主张和原则去附和诸侯,那算什么呢?而且你还有一个错误:自己行为不正的人,是不可能让别人刚正的。"

陈代的想法有点像我们俗话所说的"吃小亏占大便宜",但孟子严肃地指出了陈代的错误之处。如果一开始就在礼仪这样的问题上让步,那又怎么能达到远大的目标呢?坚持原则是通往崇高理想必须具备的精神。所谓"以小见大",说的就是从小处做起。小事都不能循规蹈矩,大事上又怎能符合道义呢?很多时候人们都会觉得,只要能够成就大事,达到目的,过程中的一些小节就不必那么在意了。然而,不行正道、不择手段,真的就是一条成功之路吗?

HOW COULD THOSE WHO ACT IMPROPERLY MAKE OTHERS BEHAVE PROPERLY

Chen Dai was Mencius' student and couldn't understand Mencius' refusal to visit the dukes without proper invitation. He thought the teacher could condescend a little in formalities. Then he said to Mencius, "It was a bit rigid to be critical of dukes' invitation. If we go to lobby them, they might become the sovereign of the land under Heaven, or at least, rule over other dukes. Classic books tell us to be flexible in small details for more significant gains. Therefore, we can try to visit and deliver our opinions to them."

Mencius said, "Duke Jing of Qi once called upon Yu Ren, the forest ranger, with flags. Yu Ren didn't obey the call because of the improper invitation manners. Duke Jing nearly killed him for that. Confucius commented after hearing that, 'Courageous people are not scared to have their bodies deserted in wilderness or be killed.' What did Mencius appreciate? He appreciated Yu Ren's courage of disobeying inappropriate invitation. What if he went forward even without the invitation at all? If it might be profitable to bend insignificant principles in order to stretch the significant ones, then what if one in order to gain more profits, to bend significant ones in order to stretch insignificant ones? Once Zhao Jianzi sent for Wang Liang to drive for his minion Xi. After a whole day's hunting, Xi caught nothing. Then Xi complained to Zhao Jianzi, 'Wang Liang is the worst driver ever.' Someone told that to Wang Liang, who then repeatedly requested to try again and got the permission from Zhao Jianzi finally. This time, after one morning's hunting, Xi caught ten animals. Xi then reported to Zhao Jianzi, 'Wang Liang is the best driver ever.' Zhao Jianzi then designated Wang Liang as the exclusive driver for Xi. Wang Liang refused resolutely, 'If I were to drive for him according to the rules, nothing could be caught after a whole day's hunting; if I were to drive against the rules, ten animals could be caught in one morning. I requested to drive for the second time just to prove that. I am actually not used to driving for the despicable, so I don't want to take that position.' You see, a driver is ashamed of cooperating with Xi, the immoral hunter, despite that he could acquire considerable prey. So how can we go against our own opinions and principles to cater for the dukes? And you are mistaken to believe that those who act improperly can make others behave properly."

Chen Dai's idea was a bit like the idiom "suffering small losses for more gains", but Mencius pointed out the error in Chen Dai's logic. If one makes compromise in etiquette, how can he possibly achieve great ambitions? The adherence to basic principles is the prerequisite of the realization of lofty ideals. The saying of "from particulars to generals" means we must adhere to moral principles even in small issues. If we bend the basic principles in petty matters, how can we be upright in more serious issues? Many people think as long as we can score great achievements, the accomplishment will justify the means. However, is it really that accomplishments by hook or by crook could be regarded as success?

什么是大丈夫

魏国有一位名叫景春的纵横家,对公孙衍和张仪这两个出名的外交政客十分崇拜。有一次他就问孟子:"公孙衍、张仪难道不是大丈夫吗?一发怒,诸侯就害怕;一平静下来,天下就安宁。"

孟子回答说:"这怎能算是大丈夫呢?你没有学过礼吗?男子行冠礼时,父亲教导他;女子出嫁时,母亲教导她,亲自送到门口,告诫她到了丈夫家要恭敬、顺从,不要违背丈夫的意志,这是为人之妻的道理。居住在天下最宽广的房子里,站立在天下最正直的位置上,行走在天下最广阔的大道上,具备了仁义礼智,能实现志向的时候就与百姓一起去实现,不能实现志向时就独自固守自己的原则,走自己的路。不受富贵诱惑,不为贫贱动摇,不为权势屈服,这才叫大丈夫。"

"富贵不能淫,贫贱不能移,威武不能屈"因为孟子的这一段话而闻名。真正的大丈夫就要有这样顶天立地的品格和气势,所谓的孟子精神也就是指这个。在一个只崇拜英雄不注重道德的时代，孟子的这番话流露出来的大丈夫气概，令无数政客、纵横家们黯然失色。即使在两千年后的今天，仍能让我们感受到一种震撼力。

WHO CAN BE DEFINED AS GREAT MEN

Jing Chun, a famous strategist-turned-diplomat of the State of Wei really adored the two famous diplomats Gongsun Yan and Zhang Yi. Once he asked Mencius, "Aren't Gongsun Yan and Zhang Yi great men? The dukes are scared to see them annoyed; however, peace will set in if the two calm down."

Mencius replied, "How can they be defined as great men? Haven't you learnt anything about the etiquette? When a son attends the adulthood ceremony, his father must instruct him; while a girl is to be married, her mother must instruct her to obey her husband and parents-in-law. A real great man should live in the most spacious house, stand in the most upright positions, and walk on the broadest road, acquire benevolence, righteousness, etiquette and wisdom, make endeavors to realize his ideals with the people when the opportunities present themselves and adhere to his own principles and follow his own way if he is denied of such opportunities. He should also be able to reject the temptation of fame and fortune, to get through the ordeal of poverty, and not to yield to those with power and authority."

"One needs to reject the temptation of fame and fortune, get through the ordeal of poverty, and stand up to the oppression to become a great man." This is a famous saying by Mencius. A true great man must be gifted with such great character and heroic mettle. This is also the so-called spirit of Mencius. In the Warring States Period when people idolized heroes while neglecting their morality, these words of Mencius oozing with his wisdom and mettle, outshined numerous politicians and strategists-turned-diplomats at that time. Two thousand years later we are still overwhelmed by his words.

父母之命，媒妁之言

孟子在魏国的时候，是以宾客的身份和梁惠王交往的。他对于出任官职的事，并不像当时的许多游士一样热衷。所以有一个魏国人周霄就问他："古代的君子出去做官吗？"孟子回答说："做啊。古书上说，孔子如果赋闲三个月就会焦急不安。到国外去时，必定要带着礼物去觐见国君，希望能谋到官职。鲁国的贤人公明仪也说，古时候的人如果赋闲三个月，大家就要去慰问他。"

周霄又问："赋闲三个月就要去慰问他，是不是太急切了啊？"孟子回答他说："读书人失去官位就像诸侯失去国家一样啊！""既然读书人都迫切希望出任官职，那为什么有些道德学问很高的人却又不肯轻易接受官职呢？"周霄追问道。这话其实是针对孟子的。孟子一方面希望得到国君的任用，能够实现自己的理想抱负，另一方面又不愿意随便去谋取官职，这不是有点自相矛盾吗？

对于这样的疑问,孟子是这样回答的:"做父母的,都希望自己的儿子能娶到好妻子,女儿能嫁个好丈夫。这样的父母之心,人人都有。如果不等到父母之命、媒妁之言,就自己钻孔穴、趴门缝互相偷看,翻过墙头见面相好,那他们的父母及国人都会看不起他们。古人并不是不想出任官职,但又厌恶那种不走正当途径的行为。不走正当途径去达到目的的人,跟那些钻洞翻墙的人没有什么两样。"

人们一般把父母之命、媒妁之言与古代婚姻制度联系起来,但孟子在这里想说的是大丈夫精神。俗话说,"君子爱财,取之有道",这句话用在这里就可以说:"君子欲仕,由道而往",也就是说,真正的君子,并非是故作清高,不爱钱财,不愿做官的人,但一定要遵循礼制,谋取正道,通过正当的途径实现自己的理想。现代社会如果人们都能把自身的品德看得比钱财、官位重要的话,那官场一定会清廉许多,社会风气也一定会纯净许多。

THE ORDER OF PARENTS AND THE WORD OF MATCHMAKERS

When Mencius was in the State of Wei, he visited King Hui of Liang as a guest. He was not so passionate about seeking public offices as other wandering scholars. Zhou Xiao from Wei asked Mencius, "Did great scholars in ancient times go out to take official positions?" Mencius answered, "Yes, they did. The classics told us that Confucius would feel uneasy dallying for three months; he would visit the kings with gifts when he went to other states in order to secure public offices. Gongming Yi of Lu also said those who stayed at home for more than three months would receive sympathy and reassurance from family and friends."

Zhou asked, "Were those people too hasty to reassure the one who was not occupied for only three months?" Mencius answered, "For the scholars, the loss of their official positions is as serious as the loss for dukes of their states."

Zhou asked again, "Since all the scholars aspire to become state officials, why some people with great wisdom and high morals refuse to take public offices readily?" That actually alluded to Mencius, who on the one hand, wanted to be trusted and appointed by the king to realize his ideals, while on the other hand didn't want to take public offices in a slipshod manner. Was he being self-contradictory?

Mencius answered, "Parents want their son to marry a good wife, and their daughter to marry a good husband. All the parents bear this heart. If the children can't wait until getting their parents' order and matchmaker's introduction, dig holes and peek through the door to see their perspective lovers, or even climb over the walls to date with each other, they would be disdained by their parents and people in the same state. It was not that the ancient people did not want to take public offices, but that they disdained getting them through indecent means. There is no difference in realizing their aims through improper means and in the practices of digging holes and climbing the walls."

Usually people related parents' order and matchmaker's introduction of the children's marriage with the ancient matrimony system, but actually Mencius drew an analogy between that and the spirit of true man. The idiom has it that people with high morals love wealth but only obtain it through decent means. Likewise, we can say great men seek officialdom only through proper manners. Namely, great men don't pretend to be upright and hate wealth or officialdom, but they need to obey the ethics and achieve their goal in decent ways. In our modern society, if all the people can place their morals above wealth and their posts, our government would become much cleaner and more honest, and the social ethos would be purer.

食志与食功

　　孟子在齐国的身份是客卿，虽然不是实质性的官员，但也领取一份较高的俸禄，他出行的装备和阵容从滕文公开始就日益强大，以至于弟子彭更有些看不惯了，觉得老师这样太过奢侈。有一天，彭更就向孟子提出疑问："您一出门，后面就跟着几十辆车马，身边的随从也有几百人，走来走去都有诸侯供养着，您不觉得这样有些过分吗？"孟子回答说："如果不符合道德，一碗饭都不该接受别人的；合乎道德的话，舜连尧的天下都接受了也没觉得过分。你觉得我过分吗？"

　　彭更说："我看不对。士人没有任何成就，却白吃人家的，这是不可以的。"孟子反驳说："你如果不去跟人们的劳动成果互相交换，用你的多余来弥补他们的不足，那农夫就会有剩余的粟米，女子就会有剩余的布匹。相反，如果你跟他们互通有无的话，那么工匠都能从你这里得到吃的。这样你就觉得很自然。可是假如现在有那么一个人，是一个在家孝顺父母，出外友爱别人，处处恪守先王的准则，扶持后进的学者，但没有什么东西来和你交换，那他就不能从你这里得到吃的吗？你为什么那么看重工匠，而轻视实行仁义的人呢？"

彭更不甘示弱，继续质问："工匠们的愿望是靠手艺来谋取养活自己的食物，君子施行仁义道德，难道他们的愿望也是要靠这个来谋取食物吗？"孟子抓住了彭更话里的漏洞，紧接着问："你为什么要在乎他们的愿望呢？他们对你有功劳，值得酬劳，所以你才酬劳他们的，对吧？你到底是酬劳他们的愿望呢，还是酬劳他们的功劳啊？"

彭更不肯服输，回答说："酬劳他们的愿望吧。"

孟子紧逼不放："那假如现在有个人，干活时把瓦片毁坏了，又把墙壁弄脏了，可他的愿望也是要换碗饭吃，你会给他吗？"彭更只好回答说："不会。"孟子总结道："那你酬劳的就不是愿望，而是功绩了。"

孟子和彭更师徒的这段对话其实提出了一个物质产品与精神产品的问题。前者就是如粮食、布匹这类可以看见、摸到，具有实用性价值的物质；后者则是如知识、道理、学说这一类精神性的东西。两者都具有不可代替的价值，都应该得到相应的报酬。劳动者的志向是比较直接的，就是用自己的物质产品来换取食物，养活自己。知识分子一心传道授业解惑，可能志向更为高远，不是简单地为了换碗饭吃，但别人却不能因此就认为他不要吃饭、无需报酬。所以，孟子最后总结说，社会在给予不同行业的人报酬时，应该依据他们的功劳的大小（即"食功"），而不是他们具有怎样的志向、愿望（即"食志"）。

LIVING ON WISHES OR LIVING ON ACHIEVEMENTS

Mencius was a visiting scholar in Qi. Though his post was not a real official position, he received a decent salary and always went out with an increasingly large entourage since the reign of Duke Wen of Teng. His student Peng Geng couldn't stand the extravagant style of Mencius. One day he asked Mencius, "Sir, you go out with scores of carriages and hundreds of attendants. And whichever state you go to, you are always financially supported by the dukes. Don't you think it is a bit inappropriate?" Mencius answered, "If it is immoral, it would be inappropriate to even accept a bowl of rice, but if it is moral, it is justified even for Shun to have accepted the whole country from Yao. So do you think there is anything inappropriate of me?"

Peng Geng said, "I don't think so. It is inappropriate for scholars to accept foods from others gratis while producing nothing." Mencius retorted, "If you don't exchange products with other people, the farmers will be left with redundant crop and females with redundant fabric. On the contrary, you would accept the fact that if you were to exchange products with other people, the craftsmen might be able to get food from you. Suppose there is a person who supports his parents, behaves friendly to his friends, obeys the principles of the late king, helps young scholars, and has no substantial products to exchange with you, then do you think he is unworthy of any food from you? Why do you value those craftsmen and scorn benevolent scholars?"

Peng Geng said, "The workers want to earn their living by their craftsmanship. The scholars just behave benevolently, but can they wish to obtain food just for that?" Mencius asked through the loopholes of his words, "Why do you care their wishes? They do you favor and you reward them, right? What do you reward them for? Their wishes or their achievements?"

Peng Geng didn't want to admit he had lost the debate, and said, "Reward them for their wishes."

Mencius pressed on, "If a person destroys the tiles and smears the walls when he works for you, and he still wishes to get food from you, would you give him anything?" Peng Geng said, "No." Mencius concluded, "So you will reward people for their performance instead of their wishes."

The dialog between Mencius and his student actually centers on the issue of material products and spiritual ones. The former category covers many substantial and tangible matters, such as crop, fabric, etc.; while the latter category includes intangible things, such as knowledge, truth, philosophy, etc. Both categories boast irreplaceable value and are worthy of relevant reward. Manual workers' wish is more direct, that is to exchange their tangible products for food to feed themselves. Intellectuals, with loftier ideals, are preoccupied with disseminating knowledge and enlightening others, and their purpose is not merely to get food for survival. However, people can not ignore their need to feed themselves and to get rewarded just based on that. Therefore, Mencius concluded that the society should reward people from all walks of life according to their achievements instead of their wishes.

商汤复仇

孟子离开齐国后,听说宋国想实行仁政,于是决定去宋国看看情况。他的弟子们都表示反对,因为宋国是一个小国,就算实行仁政,也改变不了天下的局势。其中得意门生万章就直截了当地问孟子:"宋国是个小国,它若实行仁政,万一隔壁的强国齐楚因此而攻击它,那可怎么办呢?"孟子没有回答这个问题,而是给他讲了一段商汤的故事。

商汤住在亳都的时候,与葛国是邻居。葛国首领葛伯放纵无度,不守礼法,不祭鬼神。汤便派人去问他为什么不祭祀?葛伯回答说:"没有牛羊做祭品。"汤就派人给他送去牛羊。可是葛伯却将牛羊杀掉吃了。汤又派人去问:"为什么不祭祀?"葛伯回答说没有五谷做祭物。汤就又派亳地的强壮百姓去替他们耕种,年老体弱的人去给他们送饭。可是葛伯不但不感激,反而带人抢夺酒肉饭菜,不肯给的就把他杀掉。汤终于忍无可忍,就为了这些被杀的百姓而起兵讨伐葛国。

现在人们都知道汤不是因为贪图天下财富而征战，而是为他的百姓报仇。汤从讨伐葛国开始，一共出征十一次，天下无敌。他往东征战，西方的夷人抱怨；向南征伐，北方的狄人埋怨。他们说："汤为什么先征伐别国，后征伐我们呢？"原来他们都企盼着汤的军队早日到来，就像久旱的人们盼望下雨一样。汤的军队每到一处，做买卖的人安心，耕田的人不回避，杀死暴君，抚慰百姓，民众个个都欢欣鼓舞啊。

孟子讲完这段历史故事就总结说，可见行仁政的国君，四海之内的百姓都仰头盼望他。就算齐楚是大国，又有什么可怕的呢？所以说强弱之势是可以改变的，关键在于行仁政，得民心。如果这样做了，弱国有可能变成强国。反之，强国也可能因为失去民众拥护而衰弱。

THE REVENGE OF KING TANG IN THE SHANG DYNASTY

After he left Qi, Mencius heard that Song wanted to implement benevolent governance and decided to visit Song. All of his disciples were against his decision, because Song was a small state, and its benevolent governance, if there would be any, would not make much difference to the whole country. Wan Zhang, one of Mencius' favorite students asked Mencius straightforwardly, "Song is a small state, and what if its benevolent governance invites invasion from its strong neighboring states such as Qi and Chu?" Mencius didn't answer directly and told him a story of King Tang in the Shang Dynasty.

When Tang lived in Bo, the capital of the Shang Dynasty, Ge Bo, head of Tang's neighbor, the State of Ge, was indulging himself and did not obey any etiquette. He never sacrificed any votive offerings to the deceased and the

Heavens. Tang sent a messenger to ask him why he didn't offer sacrifices. Ge Bo answered he didn't have any cow or sheep as offerings. Tang sent him the live stock as offerings, but Ge Bo killed and ate them. Tang asked him again why he still didn't offer sacrifice to the Heavens. Ge Bo said he didn't have the crop as votive offerings, so Tang sent strong people from his own capital to Ge to plant crops for them, and sent weak-bodied people to deliver food for the laborers. However, Ge Bo was not grateful and instead, he and his subordinates grabbed the food and drinks from the laborers, and killed those who didn't give the food. Tang couldn't stand the atrocities any more and crusaded against that state to revenge for the murdered people.

Then all the people knew that Tang embarked on the incursion of Ge to revenge his subjects instead of lusting for wealth. Tang's expedition started from Ge and then became unconquerable with victories in all eleven wars he waged. He waged wars eastward, and Yi people in the west complained; while he went southward, Di people in the north complained. They said, "Why did Tang conquer other states before coming to ours?" They all aspired after the early arrival of Tang's army, just like people in a drought-stricken area wished for the rainfall. Wherever Tang's army went, the tradesmen were rest assured, the farmers didn't evade, and all the people were joyful because Tang killed the tyrants and reassured the people.

After telling the story, Mencius concluded, "People of all states look forward to kings who could practice benevolent governance. Even though Qi and Chu are strong states, why should we be afraid of them? The balance of power among states can be changed and the key is to practice benevolent governance and to win people's support. A weak state can grow into a stronger one by doing so. On the contrary, a strong state may lose momentum without people's support."

难道是我好辩吗？

在齐国的稷下学宫，孟子接待了许多前来拜访的学者，与当时农家、墨家、纵横家等派别的代表都有过思想交锋，他对其他学派的学说主张几乎都持反对意见。

有一次，孟子和弟子谈起了其他学派的学说。孟子评论说：杨朱主张"为我自己"，要他拔一根汗毛以利天下，他都不肯干。墨子主张兼爱，只要对天下有利，什么都可以干。子莫主张中道，缺乏弹性，固执于一，有害于仁义之道。听到孟子的评论，直率的公都子头脑中闪出了一个问题，禁不住就问老师："人家都说您好辩，请问为什么呢？"

孟子听了这话有点急了，说："我哪里是好辩啊，我是不得已啊！尧舜死了以后，圣人之道就逐渐衰落了，暴君不时出现，百姓不得衣食，无处安身。到商纣的时候，天下更是大乱。后来周公辅佐武王，把纣王杀了，百姓都非常高兴。但是从那以后，就再也没有出现圣人了。

诸侯无所忌惮，学者大发议论，杨朱、墨翟的学说到处散布，使得天下的言论也被他们左右。杨朱学说没有君臣观念，墨翟学说没有父子观念。无父无君，这是禽兽的行为。杨朱、墨翟的学说不停止，孔子的思想不发扬，就会阻塞仁义的道路。仁义的道路被阻塞了，就等于禽兽吃人、人与人互相残杀。我因此深感忧虑，所以要抗拒杨墨学说，驳斥错误言论，捍卫古代先贤的大道。像杨、墨这样目无君上父母的人，正是周公要惩罚的。我也要端正人心，消灭邪说，驳斥荒唐的言论。我难道真的是喜欢辩论吗？我是不得已啊！能够用言论来反对杨、墨的，也就只有我这圣人的徒弟了。"

听了孟子这一大段的辩解，让人突然对他产生了一点怜悯。多年游说失败的经历，已经使孟子渐渐感到了无望，但内心却又不甘心，因而涌现出一股强烈的卫道之情。孟子最担心的就是世道沦落，邪说害民。面对诸侯放纵，百家争鸣的现实，孟子禁不住以圣人的徒弟自居，一面缅怀先圣的功绩，一面批驳杨、墨，维护正统思想。但是，战国时代的可贵之处就在于它在思想上的自由开放，百家争鸣。孟子以正统思想的卫道士自居，把其他学说都看做是洪水猛兽，似乎有点过头了。

AM I REALLY ARGUMENTATIVE?

Mencius received many visiting scholars in Jixia Academy of Qi, and debated with many scholars from other schools of philosophy such as the School of Agriculture, Mohism and the School of Strategists-Turned-Diplomats. He opposed almost all the views of other schools of thoughts.

Once, Mencius talked with his disciples on other schools of thoughts. Mencius commented, "Yang Zhu holds the idea of 'Everything for oneself', and he doesn't want to sacrifice even a hair for the benefit of the people. Mo Tzu holds the idea of 'universal love' and he wishes to do everything as long as it is good for the people. Zi Mo supports the middle way and lacks flexibility and his stubbornness is against the principle of benevolence." After hearing Mencius' comments, the straightforward Gongduzi asked his teacher, "Many people say you are argumentative, and why is that?"

Mencius was a bit annoyed, and said, "Am I really argumentative? I have no other choice. The morality held by ancient saints has been gradually decaying after the death of such wise kings as Yao and Shun. Tyrants emerge from time to time, and the people are deprived of adequate clothing, food and shelter. Under the reign of King Zhou of the Shang Dynasty, the country was sunk into an absolute chaos. Later, Duke Zhou assisted King Wu and killed Zhou. The people were excited, but after Duke Zhou, no more virtuous people emerged. The dukes indulged themselves; various schools of scholars spread their ideas at their will. Yang Zhu doesn't stress the relationship between the king and his officials; Mo Tzu doesn't attach importance to the relationship between father and son. Without respect for the king and father, one would be barely human. If those ideas continue to be promoted, and the principles of Confucianism can't prevail, the practice of benevolence would be obstructed, which would be comparable to cannibalization. I feel deeply worried, so I have to reject and refute the ideas of Yang Zhu and Mo Tsu, so as to defend the morality of ancient saints. Duke Zhou would punish those people such as Yang Zhu and Mo Tsu, who does not respect their kings and parents. Therefore, I also need to clarify people's thoughts, eliminate heresy and rebuke ridiculous ideas. Am I really argumentative? No, I just have no other choice. Only I, the follower of saints, am qualified to oppose Yang Zhu and Mo Tsu with my arguments."

After hearing Mencius' words, we would develop much sympathy for him. After years of unsuccessful lobbying, Mencius felt hopeless but still refused to accept that, and therefore displayed strong passion to defend the Confucian ideas. What he worried most was the decaying of social morality and the spreading of heresy. Faced with the indulgence of dukes and the co-existence of various schools of thoughts, Mencius couldn't help defending the orthodox thoughts by claiming himself the disciple of saints to recall the achievements of ancient saints as well as criticize Yang Zhu and Mo Tsu. However, one of the highlights of the Warring States Period was its free and open atmosphere in thoughts and the co-existence of various schools of thoughts. Mencius regarded himself as the guardian of orthodox thoughts while regarding others as heresy, which was a bit over the top.

陈仲子的廉洁

　　陈仲子是齐国著名的"廉士"，一天，孟子的好朋友齐国将军匡章来到孟子住处拜访，两人聊起了陈仲子。
　　匡章说："陈仲子难道不是位廉洁之士吗？居住在於陵，三天不吃东西，耳朵听不见，眼睛看不见。井边有颗李子，被金龟吃去了大半，他才摸索着爬过去取来吃，吞咽了三口，耳朵才能听，眼睛才能看。"
　　孟子说："在齐国人中，我当然是把仲子看成是人品最突出的。然而，他怎么可能做得到廉洁呢？要完全符合他所要求的那种品行，恐怕只有蚯蚓才能做到。因为只有蚯蚓才吞食地面上的干土，喝地下的泉水。仲子居住的房屋，是伯夷所造的，还是盗跖（春秋时期有名的大盗）所造的呢？他吃的粟米，是伯夷所种的，还是盗跖所种的呢？谁知道呢？"孟子的意思是说，陈仲子总还是要吃要喝要住的，不可能做到他自己要求的那么苛刻的程度。

匡章说："这有什么关系呢？反正是他亲自编草鞋、妻子纺麻线所换来的。"孟子评论说，母亲给的食物不吃，妻子给的食物就吃吗？哥哥的房屋不住，於陵的房屋就可以住了吗？这能算得上真正做到了自己坚持的操守吗？所以，完全能做到的，只有地下的蚯蚓可以符合他要求的品了。

陈仲子厌恶权贵，甚至厌恶所有的物质生活，这种清心寡欲、淡泊执著的生活态度确有不少可敬之处，但若要推广，却是有问题的。即使是陈仲子本人，也未必能完全做到。凡事都有个度，过犹不及，陈仲子这样的行为，有点模仿不食周粟、而在首阳山被活活饿死的伯夷、叔齐，令人感到有些矫情。

CHEN ZHONGZI'S HONESTY AND INTEGRITY

Chen Zhongzi was famous for his honesty and integrity in the State of Qi. One day, Kuang Zhang, a general of Qi and good friend of Mencius, went to visit Mencius at his residence, and they talked about Chen Zhongzi.

Kuang Zhang said, "Isn't Chen Zhongzi a clean and honest scholar? He lives in Yuling; he didn't eat anything for three days and became blind and deaf. There was a plum beside the well, and had been mostly eaten by a turtle, and then Chen Zhongzi crawled to eat the rest of the plum before he regained his eyesight and hearing." Mencius said, "Of course, I deem Chen Zhongzi as outstanding in character among all Qi people, but how is it possible for him to be clean and honest? I am afraid only earthworms can meet his requirement for character, because only earthworms can eat the dirty soil and drink the spring water underground. Was the house of Zhongzi built by Boyi or Daozhi (an infamous thief in the Spring and Autumn Period)? Was the millet eaten by

Zhongzi planted by Boyi or Daozhi? Who knows?" What Mencius meant was that Chen Zhongzi, above all, needed to eat, drink and live, and he could not possibly be so critical of himself.

Kuang Zhang said, "Does that matter? He got the food by trading with the straw sandals made by himself and the linen cloth woven by his wife." Mencius commented, "Why did he refuse the food given by his mother but accept the food given by his wife? Why did he refuse to live in his brother's house but live in the house in Yuling? Has he really adhered to his principles all the time? Therefore, I think only earthworms can live up to his ethics."

Chen Zhongzi hated the rich and the powerful, and even hated all kinds of material well-being. His preference to a lifestyle without worldly desires was respectful in a certain aspect, but it would be difficult to make all the people accept this attitude. Even Chen Zhongzi himself couldn't fully carry out his own principles. We should always keep a sense of proportion and going beyond the limit is as bad as falling short. Chen Zhongzi's behavior reminds us of Boyi and Shuqi, who starved to death in Mount Shouyang because they refused to eat the food offered by the Zhou Dynasty. That was pretentious stubbornness indeed.

没有规矩，不能成方圆

齐宣王的政事总是不如意。究竟应该怎样治理国家？有一次他带着这个疑问来请教孟子，孟子趁机又发表了他的仁政主张。

孟子说，离娄有出众的视力，公输般有过人的技巧，但若没有圆规、矩尺是不能画成方圆的；师旷有敏锐的听力，但若不使用六律是不能校正五音的；尧舜虽然有大道，但若不实行仁政，也不能使天下得到安宁。现在有的国君虽然有仁爱的心、仁爱的美誉，然而民众却受不到他们的恩泽，不能被后世所效法。为什么呢？就在于他们不实行先王之道。所以说，仅有善心不足以治理国政，仅有法度不能使其自行实施。

遵循先王法度办事而犯错误，是从来就不曾有过的。圣人既然已竭尽了视力，再辅以圆规、矩尺、墨线，便可以随意地画出方圆平直；既然竭尽了听力，再辅以六律，便可以轻松地校正五音；既然竭尽了思虑，再加上怜惜民众的政治措施，那仁爱之政就可以使恩惠遍及天下了。所以说，筑高必须依傍山丘之势，掘深必须依傍河泽之利，处理政事不依靠先王之道能说是明智的吗？因此只有具备仁爱之心的人才适宜担任最高的职位，不仁的人在高位上就要把他的坏处传播给大家。在上的人如果没有行为准则作为衡量尺度，在下的人就不会遵循法度。朝廷不相信道德，百官不相信法度，君子触犯道义，小人触犯刑律，国家若是这样还能存在下去，那完全是侥幸。所以说，城郭不牢固，武器不充足，不是国家的灾难；土地没有得到开垦，财富没有积蓄，不是国家的祸害。要是在上的人不讲礼义，在下的人不受教育，作乱的小人就会兴起，国家的灭亡就不会有多远了，这才是真正的祸害。

工匠们纵使有过人的技巧，如果不凭借一定的工具，那也没法造出好的产品。一国之君即便有再强的能力，如果不能依照一定的法度做事，那肯定也是治理不好国家的，说不定还会招来杀身亡国之祸。规矩，是行事正确的条件；先圣制定的法度，是治理国家的准则。这个法度其实就是仁政。宣王一次次问政于孟子，却一直都没明白这个道理。

其实人类自古订立规矩，无非是为人们的社会活动定一个标准，规矩是成就自己人生乃至国家、社会的方圆的前提。但从历史上看，规矩一出，总是有人破坏。有能力破坏规矩的人首先是那些权贵们，无权无势的人破坏了规矩只能是死路一条，因此大都是守规矩的人。这就牵涉到规矩的普遍性问题，后来的法家韩非谈的治国之术，可以看成是孟子这一想法的延伸，尽管他们对规矩的看法是不同的。

NOTHING CAN BE ACCOMPLISHED WITHOUT NORMS

King Xuan of Qi was always unsatisfied with his own governance. Once on his visit to Mencius about how to run the state properly, Mencius promoted benevolent governance to him again.

Mencius said, "Li Lou had outstanding eyesight and Gongshu Ban had outstanding skills, but they couldn't draw circles and squares without rulers and compasses; Shi Kuang had acute hearing, but he couldn't correct his tones of music without referring to musical disciplines; Yao and Shun were virtuous kings, but they couldn't make the society peaceful and stable without benevolent governance. Now although many kings have hearts and reputation of benevolence, their subjects have not yet enjoyed the benefits of their benevolence, so they could not be emulated by later rulers. Their acts are not worthy of emulation by the later generations. Why is that? That is because they have not practiced the rule of former sage kings. Therefore, it is not enough to rule the country properly with a kind heart, nor is it enough to carry out benevolent governance with the system of laws.

"It is impossible to make mistakes if one follows the ways of former sage kings. That's because the saints have exhausted their eyesight, and utilized such important tools as compasses, rulers, and lines, so they can draw the geometrical symbols easily; they have exhausted their hearing while referring to the music rules, so they can easily correct the musical notes; they have exhausted their wisdom and adopted sympathetic political measures, so they can endow their subjects with felicity. Therefore, we must take advantage of the high hillside position to set up high buildings, and of the riverside position to dig deep holes. Can it be regarded as wise not to follow the ways of former sage kings? Therefore, only benevolent people are qualified to occupy the highest posts, and malevolent people would spread disasters if they were high-ranking officials. If the ruler doesn't refer to moral principles in their behaviors, their subordinates would not follow the laws; the court would not uphold morality; the officials would not believe in the laws; upright people would violate ethics; mean people would violate laws; it would be fluky if the country would continue to exist. Therefore, it would not lead to the real disaster of a state if the city wall is not firm enough, the weaponry is not abundant, the land is underdeveloped, or the wealth is not sufficiently accumulated. Actually it would be the source of catastrophe if the high-ranking officials didn't follow the etiquette, and the low-ranking ones didn't receive education. The unruly people would rise up and the state would meet its end shortly."

With excellent skills, though, the workers can't make good products without particular tools. Without certain laws capable kings can't rule his country well, and they may even cause tragic ends for themselves and their states. Rules are the prerequisite for one to behave properly and the rules set by the former saints are the principles for the governing of the states. This set of rules is the benevolent governance. King Xuan repeatedly asked Mencius for political advices, but failed to understand this.

Actually from time immemorial, humans set up the rules as the criteria for social activities. The rules are the preconditions for people to build up and manage families and even countries. In history there were always people who broke the rules. They were very often the rich and the powerful, because obscure people would be finished if they broke the rules, so they were always obedient. That's related with the viability of rules. Later, legalist Han Fei's ideas for governing countries actually carried the legacy of Mencius, although they defined rules in different ways.

反躬自问

　　一个人的修养如何,不单单是个人的事,而是关系到国家、天下和百姓的命运。修养有一条很重要,就是反躬自问。

　　假如有一个人,他爱别人,可是别人却不亲近他,那他就要反问自己,是否还不够仁爱呢?他想治理人民,而人民却不听从,那就要反问自己,是否自己的智慧和知识还不够呢?他有礼貌地对待他人却得不到回报,也要反问自己是否恭敬还不够呢?总之,凡是自己的所作所为得不到应有的效果,都要从自身来寻找原因,自身行为端正了,天下自然就归服了。

　　修养最高的标准是仁人君子。不仁的人见别人有了灾难,或者无动于衷,或者趁火打劫,或者投井下石,他们把荒淫暴虐当作乐事来追求,这样不仁的人能和他议论国事吗?有童谣唱道:"清澈的沧浪水啊,能够用来洗我的帽带;混浊的沧浪水啊,能用来洗我的双脚。"孔子听了这个歌谣后就对他的弟子们说:"水清洗帽子,水浊洗双脚,这都是水自身决定的。"人必定是有了自取侮辱的行为,然后别人才能侮辱你;家必是有了自己毁灭的原因,然后别人才能来毁坏你;国家必定是自己治理坏了,然后别人才能来攻伐你。

反躬自问,强调的是人的反省精神。孔子曾经说他一天要反省三次。我们不一定要完全照搬圣人的做法,但常常反省自己的行为,才能够意识到自己的缺点、错误和不足。常常反问自己到底想要什么,想过什么样的人生,才能使自己的自我修养达到完美的境界,做一个最好的自己。

EXAMINE ONESELF

According to Mencius, personal cultivation is not just related to the person himself, but also to the destiny of his country, the land under Heaven and all the people. It is very important to examine ourselves to achieve good personal cultivation.

If a person loves the people around him, but others still don't like him, then he needs to ask himself whether his kindness for people is sufficient or not. If a king wants to govern his subjects, but the subjects don't obey his orders, then the king needs to ask himself whether he has sufficient wisdom and knowledge. If he behaves politely to others, but his politeness is not returned, then he needs to ask himself whether his politeness is sufficient. In a word, a king needs to search for his own fault if his efforts don't pay off. Only when he has rectified himself, can he enjoy the obedience of his subjects.

The best-cultivated person boasts benevolence and integrity. Malevolent people, upon others' misfortunes, are indifferent, or fish in troubled waters or add fuel to flame; they seek fun from ridiculous and cruel acts. How can we discuss with malevolent people on how to run the state? A nursery rhyme has it, "clear water washes my hat belt and dirty water washes my feet." Confucius commented on this rhyme that it depended on the water itself as to whether it would be used for washing hat or feet. One would be insulted by others if his behavior has insulted himself. The home would be destroyed by others because the destructive seeds have been sowed within. The state would be invaded because it had been ruined by improper governance.

Examining ourselves stresses that we should have the soul-searching spirit. Confucius said he examined himself three times a day. We don't need to copy the way of the saint, but it is necessary to examine our own behaviors to realize our shortcomings, errors and weaknesses. Only by regularly asking ourselves what we want most and what kind of life we aspire for, can we achieve perfect personal cultivation and realize our full potential.

以道救天下

有一个善辩的纵横家淳于髡问孟子说:"男女授受不亲,这是礼。对吗?"孟子说:"是礼。"淳于髡接着又问:"那如果嫂嫂溺水了,应该伸手去援救吗?""嫂嫂溺水而不救,那是豺狼。男女授受不亲,是礼节;如果嫂嫂溺水而伸手救援,那是权宜之计。"

淳于髡趁势问道:"如今天下都溺水将亡了,夫子您为什么不伸手去救援呢?"

孟子的回答也很巧妙:"天下溺水将亡,应该用王道去援救,嫂嫂溺水了,那时才用手去援救——你难道想用手去救天下吗?"

孟子在这里其实是故意偷换了"伸手"的概念。淳于髡所说的"伸手"其实并不是真的把手伸出去的意思,而是出力帮助的意思。孟子故意地理解为把手伸出去,从而引出后面的意思,即个人的力量微不足道,必须用仁政的力量才能拯救天下。表面上看,这个故事反映了孟子的机智、善辩和幽默，但实际上也隐藏着很深的道理。孟子和当时一般的士人最大的不同就在于，他不是个只想着追求个人名誉、逞一时之快的英雄主义者。他关心的只有以仁义救世救民的大道理。

SAVE THE SOCIETY WITH MORALITY

Chunyu Kun, an eloquent strategist-turned-diplomat said to Mencius, "The body contact is not allowed between men and women according to the etiquette, right?" Mencius said, "Yes." Chunyu Kun asked again, "Suppose one's sister-in-law is drowning and should one reach for her with his hand?" Mencius answered, "If one doesn't reach for her with his hand to rescue her, one is barely human. Etiquette requires one not to have body contact with the opposite gender; but rescuing her by reaching one's hand is expediency."

Chunyu Kun pressed on, "Now the whole land under Heaven would be drowning, and why haven't you reached out with your hand to rescue it?"

Mencius answered skillfully, "We should rescue the land under Heaven with true royal ruling; a helping hand is only capable of rescuing the drowning sister-in-law. Do you plan to save the whole land under Heaven just with a hand?"

Mencius tactfully changed the definition of "reaching out with a hand". Actually what Chunyu Kun meant was offering assistance rather than reaching out with a hand. Mencius deliberately explained it in that way in order to bring out its implicit meaning, i.e., the capability of individuals was limited and the whole land under Heaven could only be saved by benevolent governance.

If looking superficially we can only see the wit, humor and eloquence of Mencius, but actually his words were pregnant with meaning. The biggest difference between Mencius and his peers was that he was not preoccupied with seeking for fame or flaunting his superiority. What he cared about was only the major principle: to save the country and people with benevolence and righteousness.

事亲如曾子

　　有一次孟子和学生又谈到孝道。孟子说，人侍奉谁最重要？当然侍奉父母最重要。守护什么最重要？当然是守护自己的品格最重要。侍奉的事都应该做，但是，侍奉父母是根本；守护的事都应该做，但是守护自己的品格最重要。他接着又讲了孔子的弟子曾子侍奉父亲的故事。

　　从前曾子侍奉他的父亲曾晳，每顿饭一定有酒有肉，撤除饭菜的时候，也一定要请示：剩下的给谁。曾晳如果问还有剩余吗？不管有没有剩余，曾子一定要回答说"有"。后来曾晳死了，儿子曾元供养曾子，每顿也必有酒有肉，但撤除的时候就不问剩下的给谁了。曾子若问还有剩余吗？曾元便说"没有了"，其实是留下一些预备以后用的。比较而言，曾子奉养父亲，才是真正的顺从父亲心意的奉养。侍奉父母要做到像曾子那样，才可以算作是真正的孝道。

可见，孟子对孝道的要求是很高的，不仅要侍奉父母的口、体之需，还要顺从父母的心意，才能称得上是真正的孝。当然，事亲如曾子这个事例还只是讲了孝道的一半，因为儒家的孝道除了奉养双亲，使他们身心愉快外，还有一个重要的内容是守护自身，不因自己牵累老人。

TREAT PARENTS AS ZENGZI DID

Once, Mencius talked about filial piety with his students. Mencius said, "Who are the most important people that we shall wait upon? Of course, parents. What are the most important things that we shall preserve? Of course, our own morals. We should wait upon other people, but parents are the most important ones for us to wait upon; we should preserve many things, but our own morals are the most important things for us to preserve. He then went on to mention the story of how Zengzi, a disciple of Confucius, had waited upon his father.

While serving his father Zeng Xi, Zengzi prepared meat and wine for each meal. While cleaning the table, he would also ask about how to deal with the remaining food. If Zeng Xi asked whether there was any food left, Zengzi would surely answer "yes". Later Zeng Xi passed away. Zengzi's son Zeng Yuan, while serving Zengzi, also prepared meat and wine for each meal, but he didn't ask Zengzi as how to deal with the remaining food. If Zengzi asked him whether there was any food left, he would say "no". Actually Zeng Yuan kept the remaining food and drink to prepare meals later. In comparison, only Zengzi served his father whole-heartedly. One could be regarded as filial only when he could serve his parents as Zengzi had done.

We can see that Mencius set up high criteria for filial piety. One should not only satisfy parents' appetite and physical comforts but also should act according to the parents' wishes. However, the story of Zengzi serving his father only revealed one dimension of real filial piety, because according to Confucianism, one not only need to serve his parents and make them healthy and happy, but also need to protect himself and don't implicate his parents into his own troubles.

乐正子见孟子

　　乐正子是孟子的学生,在鲁国为官。有一次,他跟随鲁国大臣於子敖到齐国办公事,就顺便去看看老师。他去见孟子的时候,孟子开口就说道:"你也来见我吗?"乐正子不解地问:"先生为什么这么说?"孟子问:"你来几天了?""昨天来的。""昨天?那我说这话难道不应该吗?"乐正子惶恐不安地回答:"我的住所没定。"孟子严厉地质问:"你听说过住所定了才去看望长者的吗?"乐正子终于认错道:"弟子有罪。"孟子意犹未尽,又继续批评乐正子:"你这次跟随於子敖来齐国,就是吃吃喝喝。没想到你学了那么多古时候的大道理,如今却用来吃吃喝喝!"

　　孟子严格遵守儒家学派对于君臣、父子(包括师生)、夫妻关系的规定,认为长幼、尊卑都有一定的次序。比如父亲呼叫儿子时,儿子应该不等答应就前去。乐正子是学生,到了齐国应该是第一时间就去看望自己的老师。可他却等到居所安顿好以后才去看老师，在孟子看来，这显然违背了礼制。

当然，孟子真正的不满还不只是乐正子没有马上去看他，他最不满的其实是乐正子跟於子敖在一起的所作所为没有尽到一个臣子应尽的责任。他本是带着公务来齐国的，但除了吃吃喝喝却没有干什么正经事，既然如此，却还不马上去见老师，这是让孟子最生气的，所以他批评弟子的语气也就比较严厉。

YUE ZHENGZI VISITING MENCIUS

Yue Zhengzi was Mencius' student and took public office in the State of Lu. Once he went to the State of Qi along with Yu Zi'ao, minister of Lu, and paid a call to his teacher. Mencius asked him immediately after seeing him, "You are here to see me?" Yue Zhengzi was puzzled and asked, "Master, why did you ask that?" Mencius asked, "How many days have you been here?" Yue Zhengzi said, "I arrived here yesterday." Mencius asked, "Yesterday? So why can't I blame you?" Yue Zhengzi was awed and replied, "Sorry, I didn't secure my accommodation here yesterday." Mencius said, "Have you heard of anybody who would only visit his teacher after he has secured the accommodation?" Yue Zhengzi finally admitted he was wrong. But Mencius continued to criticize him, "You came to Qi with Yu Zi'ao and indulged yourselves in extravagant drinking and dining. You have learnt so many major principles of the ancient times, but now you indulge yourself in extravagant dining and drinking."

Mencius rigorously obeyed Confucian principles regarding the relationship between the kings and the officials, the parents and the children (including masters and their disciples), the husbands and the wives. He believed in strict hierarchy between seniors and juniors, superiors and inferiors. For example, when one's father calls, he should be attending to him immediately. Yue Zhengzi was his student, so he should have visited Mencius once he arrived at Qi. His behavior of visiting Mencius until he had secured his accommodation was against the etiquette according to Mencius.

What annoyed Mencius most was not only that Yue Zhengzi didn't visit him in time, but that he indulged himself with Yu Zi'ao and failed to fulfill his duty as an official. He went to Qi on a business trip, but he didn't do anything except dining and drinking. That being said, he still did not visit Mencius in time. All these really annoyed Mencius. Therefore, Mencius criticized him harshly.

小惠不足以治国

子产做郑国宰相的时候,用他自己坐的车辇载行人过河。当时的人都称颂子产的仁德。但孟子却不以为然。他说:"子产对人的确算是有恩惠的,但他却不知道治理国家的要素。假如他十一月在河上架起木头造一个简易的桥,那样行人就可以过河了;再过一个月,扩大简易桥的规模,造出能供马车通行的桥梁,这样,老百姓哪里还会再苦于不得不趟水过河?身为君主的人,如果真的能把国家治理好,即使出行时让路人回避让道,也不算过分。如今子产给老百姓的只是小惠而已。用车帮人渡河,能把每个要过河的人都摆渡过去吗?这样看来,一个治理国家的人,如果要想让每个人都高兴,恐怕一辈子也做不到,更不用说将国家治理好了。"

这里孟子想说的是,小惠是不足以治国的。只有大惠才能解决根本问题。应该说历代的一些为官者并不明白这个道理,他们总是在做人上下工夫，善于施小惠于人，让人知恩图报，至于如何成就国家大事则常常是漫不经心的，结果，个人的名望提升了，大家的利益却丢失了许多。

SMALL FAVOR NOT ENOUGH TO GOVERN A STATE WELL

When Zichan was the prime minister of the State of Zheng, he carried people across the river with his own carriage. All the people then praised Zichan's benevolence, but Mencius didn't. He said, "Indeed, Zichan has offered favor to others, but he doesn't know the essences of how to govern a state. If he had built up a simple wooden bridge over the river in November, the passengers would have been able to cross the river; if a month later he had expanded the simple bridge and made it stronger, even the carriages would have been able to cross the river. Then how would it be possible for the people to be confronted with the difficulty of crossing the river? As a king who could rule his state properly, it would not be undue asking the passengers to make way for him. What Zichan has done is just doing a small favor to the people. Is it possible for him to carry everybody over the river with his carriage? Therefore, for one whose responsibility is to rule the state, he is doomed to fail if he wishes to make everyone happy, let alone run a state well."

What Mencius meant was that small favor was not enough to govern a state well, and only universal benefits can solve the fundamental problems. Many officials in ancient dynasties didn't fully understand this principle, and they paid great attention to the socializing, rendering small favors to others so as to make them grateful while ignoring the key issues concerning the governing of states. As a result, they enjoyed enhanced personal reputation and harmed the overall interests of the people.

君臣如何相待

　　齐伐燕的战争过去后,孟子对齐宣王的期望彻底破灭了。仁政的思想在他们那里不过是种高谈阔论罢了,根本不符合他们的利益。而齐宣王也由于孟子越来越尖锐的批评而心存不满。就这样,他们之间的关系渐渐冷淡了,孟子也于此时决意离去了。

　　既然决定离开,孟子的言论也就更加大胆而无所顾忌了。有一次在谈到君臣相处的原则时,孟子说:"如果君主把臣下看成自己的手足,那么臣下就会把君主当作自己的腹心。如果君主把臣下当狗和马一样的玩物看待时,那么臣下就会把君主当作路人看待。如果君主把臣下当作泥土草芥那么低贱,那么臣下就会把君主当作仇敌!"

　　这一段话即使在今天看来,我们仍然会佩服孟子的大胆。他直接地指出,君臣之间的关系并不是单纯的驾驭与效忠,而是要视对方的态度而定。君主固然可以高高在上、颐指气使,但臣下也有选择君主的权利。孟子的这番话其实是在向齐宣王传达一个信息，即君主如果不走仁政之道，总有一天会被他的臣下遗弃；面对不仁的君主，孟子随时可以选择离开。所以怪不得齐宣王听了这话很不高兴，就是几百年后，当明王朝的开国皇帝朱元璋读到《孟子》中的这段话时，据说也是"龙颜大怒，拍案而起"，操起毛笔就在书上胡乱涂抹，以宣泄自己的愤怒。看来孟子的话的确触到了统治者的要害。

HOW SHOULD THE KING AND HIS OFFICIALS TREAT EACH OTHER?

After Qi waged the war against Yan, Mencius became disillusioned with King Xuan of Qi. The king only enjoyed bragging about his preference for benevolent governance, which was actually against his interests. King Xuan also grew more and more unsatisfied with the sharp criticism from Mencius. Therefore, they were increasingly estranged and Mencius made his mind to leave Qi at that time.

Since he had made his mind to leave, Mencius' criticism became even bolder and without any restraint. Once when talking about the relationship between the king and his officials, Mencius said, "If the king sees his officials as his own siblings, the latter would regard the king as their own flesh and heart. If the king sees the officials as dogs and horses, the officials would see the king as a passer-by. If the king looks down upon the officials as earth and grass, the officials would treat the king as their enemy."

Even today, those courageous words of Mencius are still worth our admiration. He pointed out straightforwardly that the relationship between the king and his officials was not just governing and following; rather the relationship was interactive. If the king were superior and arrogant, his officials would be entitled to choose other kings to serve. He was delivering a message to King Xuan that if the king was not benevolent, he would be deserted by his officials sooner or later. For example, Mencius could choose to leave any time. No wonder King Xuan was very unhappy after hearing these words. Even hundreds of years later, Zhu Yuanzhang was said to have flew into a fury while reading this paragraph of *Mencius*, and scribbled angrily on the book to vent his anger. It seems that these words of Mencius have hit the weakness of kings.

公行子长子之吊

齐国大夫公行子的长子病故,百官纷纷前去吊丧。这些官员是公行子的同僚,他的儿子是晚辈,自然是用不着礼拜与祭祀,只要到府上表示慰问即可。齐国的权贵右师子敖也去公行子府中吊唁。进去之后,有的人走上前来跟右师说话,有的人来到他的座位旁与他搭讪。唯独孟子不跟右师套近乎。右师不高兴了,说:"大家都来和我打招呼,唯独这个孟子不来跟我说话,实在是太傲慢了。"后来孟子听说了这话,就回答说:"按照礼制,朝廷命官不能越过位次互相交谈,也不能隔着台阶相互作揖。我要按照礼制的规定来做,子敖却说我傲慢,这不是很奇怪吗?"

当今世上,趋炎附势、巴结权贵的人数不胜数,也十分寻常。反而是那些不事权贵、清高自重的人被视为异类,所以孟子不上前去跟右师搭讪,竟会被视为一件不正常的事情。孟子"舍生取义"、"穷则独善其身"的操守,使得他对这一套庸俗的风气早就具备了免疫力。你巴结你的，对我又有什么影响？当然孟子为自己找的借口也很难辩驳：我的所作所为都是依照礼制而来，你们又有什么话可说？这既表现出孟子的知识分子气概，也反映了他的机智与说话技巧。

THE CONDOLENCE FOR GONG XINGZI'S ELDEST SON

Gong Xingzi was the minister of the State of Qi and many officials went to the funeral of his eldest son who died of disease. Since those officials were his peers, they didn't need to observe bowing and to offer sacrifice to his son, instead, they just needed to pay condolence. Zi'ao, a powerful minister in Qi also went to the funeral. Many people went forward to talk with Zi'ao, and only Mencius didn't. Zi'ao was unhappy and criticized the arrogance of Mencius. After hearing his criticism, Mencius said, "According to the rules of the etiquette, officials should not talk with each other by overstepping their ranks or bow to each other standing on different stairs. I just want to obey the etiquette, but Zi'ao thought I was being arrogant. Isn't that strange?"

In our world, there are numerous people who flatter the rich and the powerful while most people have accepted that; instead, those who do not and hold respect for themselves are considered weird. Therefore, it was considered weird that Mencius had not gone forward to hold talks with Zi'ao. Mencius' upholding of high morals of "preserving righteousness even at the cost of death", and "trying to improve himself if not able to improve all the people" has presented him with immunity to the vulgar atmosphere then. He was not affected by those apple-polishers, and also he found himself a good excuse: he behaved according to the ancient etiquette, and none could challenge that. This story reflected his courage as an intellectual, and also his wisdom and eloquence.

匡章不孝

　　匡章是孟子在齐国交往最深的朋友。匡章出身将军世家，本人也是虎背熊腰的壮汉，然而却背上了一个不孝的罪名，不但亲朋远离，处处遭人白眼，而且得不到威王的信任和重用，无法建功立业。

　　一天，公都子问孟子："齐国的人都把匡章当不孝之子，您却与他交往密切、情同手足，不怕他坏了您的名誉吗？"孟子说："你知道为什么齐国人都说匡章不孝吗？"公都子回答说："因为他指出父亲的错误，父亲把他赶出家门，于是父子不再相见。"孟子说："那就是了。世间所说的不孝顺有五种：四体不勤，不养活父母；赌博嗜酒，不养活父母；贪婪财货，偏袒妻子儿女，不养活父母；纵情于声色，使父母蒙羞；好勇斗狠，使父母的安全处于危险之中。这五种不孝，匡章属于哪一种呢？"

　　原来，匡章的母亲得罪了丈夫，丈夫就把她杀了，然后埋在床底下。匡章知道了，就责备父亲不善，因此把关系搞僵了，父子从此不再相见。为了赎自己的"不孝"之罪，匡章甚至把自己的妻子儿女赶出了家门，以此来惩罚自己。

这样的人能说他不孝吗？孟子的学说在儒家属于思孟学派，最重视的是孝道。他为匡章辩护，正反映了他对孝道的正确理解，也为匡章重新赢得了信誉。后来匡章被威王委以重任，率兵抗秦，大获全胜，举国上下无不震动。

KUANG ZHANG WAS NOT FILIAL

Kuang Zhang was the closest friend of Mencius when he lived in Qi. Kuang Zhang came of a line of generals and grew up with a strong build. But he was infamous for not being a filial son and estranged by his relatives and friends. He was disdained by people everywhere, lost the trust and confidence of King Wei, and could not establish himself with great achievements.

One day, Gongduzi asked Mencius, "People in Qi regarded Kuang Zhang as not filial, but you keep a close relationship with him and treat him as your brother. Aren't you afraid that he would tarnish your reputation?" Mencius said, "Do you know why the people in Qi claim Kuang Zhang as not filial?" Gongduzi said, "Because he pointed out his father's error and was driven out of the family. From then on, the father and the son broke up." Mencius said, "Yes. There are five categories of being not filial: being too lazy to support and serve one's parents; getting indulgent in gambling and drinking and shying away from the responsibility of supporting one's parents; being greedy for wealth and partial for his wife and children, and unwilling to support and serve the parents; getting indulgent in women and music, as well as humiliating his parents;

being aggressive and endangering his parents. Which category do you think Kuang Zhang falls into?"

Actually Kuang Zhang's mother offended her husband and was killed and buried by him under the bed. Kuang Zhang blamed his father for this murder and their relationship was broken. Kuang Zhang drove out his wife and children to punish himself and to atone his guilt for not being filial.

Could other people blame him as not filial? Mencius' teachings, which belonged to the Simeng School of Confucianism, attached the greatest importance to filial piety. His defense for Kuang Zhang reflected his correct understanding of filial piety and also restored Kuang Zhang's reputation. Later, Kuang Zhang was entrusted with important missions by King Wei, and led the army to win over Qin's army. Their overwhelming victory in the fight made the whole state excited.

曾子与寇

　　孟子对弟子们说，先贤虽然行为不同，但他们遵循的原则是一致的。他举了两个例子来说明。

　　曾子居住在武城的时候，越国人来侵犯。有人说："敌寇来了，为何不离开这里呢？"曾子说："我只是不愿让那些人住在我的屋子里，毁坏我那些树木。"于是就离开了。等到敌寇退走，曾子就对弟子说，"我要整修我的院墙和屋子，这就回去了。"曾子的行为令弟子们不理解，他们说："武城的人对待先生那样忠诚、恭敬，可是敌寇来了，先生却为民众做了个带头离去的榜样，敌寇一退走，就又赶紧回去。这样做恐怕不合适吧？"其中一名弟子沈犹行说："这个你们就不知道了。从前先生住在我家的时候，有一次，一个叫负刍的家伙来我家捣乱，跟随先生的七十个人中，没有一个介入的呢。"

　　而子思居住在卫国的时候，也有齐国人来犯。有人也对子思说：

"敌寇来了，先生为何不离开呀？"子思回答说："连我都走了，国君和谁一起防守国家呢？"

孟子总结说，曾子和子思的行为是一个道理，只是他们的身份不同罢了。曾子在武城的地位是宾客，是老师，是武城人的父亲、兄长，所以遇到入侵时可以离去；而子思在卫国的身份是臣子，遇到入侵时自然必须留下尽责。曾子的离开和子思的留下，都是符合他们身份的行为。如果他们两人的位置换一下，他们同样也会这么做。所以，君子是不以利害关系来决定自己的行为的，他们的所作所为只和道理有关。正因为如此，换了位置身份，他们也同样会做符合自己身份的事情。这恐怕就是君子和普通人之间的差别吧。

ZENGZI AND THE INVADERS

Mencius said to his students that although the former saints had different sets of acts, they bore the same moral principles. He told two stories.

When Zengzi lived in Wucheng, the Yue people invaded into the city. Some people said, "The enemy came, why don't leave the place?" Zengzi said, "I just don't want those people to live in my house and destroy my trees." Then he left. After the enemy left, Zengzi said to his students, "I need to go back to renovate my house and wall." Zengzi's acts confused his students. They said, "The people in Wucheng were so loyal and respectful to you, but you set an example as an escapee when the enemy arrived. And you couldn't wait to go back when the enemy left. Is that proper?" Shen Youxing, one of the students replied, "You haven't understood our teacher. Our master used to live in my house; once a man called Fu Chu came to my house and caused disturbance. Not a single one of the seventy followers of our master got involved in the incident."

While Zisi lived in the State of Wei, the Qi people also invaded Wei. Some said to Zisi, "Why not leave?" Zisi answered, "If I leave, who would stay here with the king to defend for our state?"

Mencius concluded that "Zengzi and Zisi adhered to the same principle though in different capacities. Zengzi was a guest, an instructor, and an elder in Wucheng, and that's why he could leave when invaders came; but Zisi was an official in Wei, so he ought to stay to fulfill his duty. Their behaviors conformed to their respective capacity. They would do the same if they were in each other's shoes. Therefore, moral people don't determine their acts according to the benefits, rather according to the moral principles. That's why they would act according to their capacity. This is probably the difference between men with high morals and ordinary people.

终生之忧与一朝之患

孟子常常和学生们讨论君子的标准。有一次他说:"君子之所以不同于常人,就是因为他们的存心不同凡俗。"孟子认为君子的存心是仁和礼。怀有仁心的人爱护他人,有礼的人则尊敬他人。爱护他人的人,别人也反过来爱护他;尊敬他人的人,人们也总是尊敬他。如果有个人用蛮横无理的态度对待自己,君子必定会反躬自省:一定是我不够仁,不够有礼,否则怎么会遭遇这样的事呢?如果反躬自省的结果是自己的存心够仁,也够有礼,而那人蛮横的态度依然不改,那君子就会说:这不过是个狂人罢了。这样的人与禽兽有什么不同呢?对于禽兽又有什么必要去指责呢?因此,君子有终身的忧虑,而没有一时的担心。他忧虑的是:舜是人,我也是人,舜被天下的人所效仿,流芳百世,而我仍然是个乡里的普通人。这才是值得忧虑的事啊!至于一般人所担心的事,君子就没有了。凡是不合仁的事不干,不合礼的事不干,即使有一时的祸患,也用不着去担心了。这就叫"君子有终生之忧,无一朝之患"。

如何才是真君子?孟子提出了两个方面的内容:一是遇到问题首先应该检讨反省自己的错误或不足之处。二是只要自己行得正、站得直,问心无愧就够了,没有必要患得患失。君子唯一担忧的是,自己还没有达到圣贤的境界。至于突如其来的祸患,因为不是自己的过错,君子会坦然地面对,不会担忧什么。

遗憾的是,现代有些人的所作所为正好与古代君子相反。他们有无数并不值得的"一朝之患":患得患失,为得不到财富、地位而担心,为别人的评价、褒贬而担心,为眼前的利害、得失、安危而担心。而对于真正应该为之忧虑的事却又总是漫不经心,从来不为自己的行为、品德是否够得上正直、高尚而费一点心思。也许摆在现代人面前的一个问题就是:我们的物质财富在与日俱增,可是我们的精神财富呢?

LIFE-LONG CONCERN AND IMMEDIATE WORRIES

Mencius always discussed with his disciples about the moral standards of men with high morals. Once he said, "Men with high morals differentiate themselves with their outstanding characters." According to him, the outstanding character of men with high morals featured benevolence and ritual proprietary. People with benevolence care for other people, and people with ritual proprietary respect others. Those who care for and respect others would be reciprocated by other people. If someone behaves rudely to one with high morals, he would surely examine himself: It must be caused by my lack of benevolence and etiquette; otherwise why am I treated like this? If after examining himself, he is sure about his own benevolence and etiquette and that rude person doesn't change his attitude, the one with high morals would ignore him, because rude people are no different from beasts, and why should humans blame rude beasts? Therefore, a moral person bears life-long concerns, but he is free of immediate worries. He is concerned: Shun could be followed by all the people and his reputation passed down through generations, but why do I still remain an ordinary man? However, he is not burdened with the immediate worries as the other people. He would do none of the things which go against benevolence and etiquette; and he would not worry about immediate disasters. That's what we call "A man with high morals bears life-long concern, but he is free of immediate worries".

How can one become a real man with high morals? Mencius stressed two points: "Firstly, while facing any problem, we must examine ourselves and try to find our own faults. Secondly, we must behave morally and stand upright; if we are conscientious, we don't need to care too much about the gains and losses. The only concern for the moral people is that they haven't attained the morality of saints. And they will stand up to accidents and never get worried because those are not caused by their fault."

It is a shame that nowadays many people choose the opposite way from that of the men with high morals in ancient times. They have numberless superficial or immediate worries: they are preoccupied with wealth and status; they are bothered by other people's comments, criticism, immediate gains and losses as well as their personal safety. However, they ignore the important issues which are worthy of their attention — their own morals and integrity. We are faced with a question in our society now, that is, as our material wealth accumulates, how shall we accumulate our spiritual wealth?

大孝终生慕父母

　　孟子喜欢谈论孝道。有一次万章就问他:"听说舜曾经到田野之中向老天哭诉,他为什么要哭诉呢?" 孟子说:"因为怨恨和思慕。"万章又问:"曾子说:'父母喜爱,高兴而难以忘情;父母嫌恶,忧愁而不怨恨。'既然不应当怨恨,那舜为什么要怨恨呢?"

　　孟子解释说:孝子不得意于父母,自然会产生忧愁怨恨的心情,难道能满不在乎吗?我努力耕作,只需尽到做儿子的责任,父母不爱我,我又有什么错呢?尧帝派了他的九个儿子、两个女儿以及百官带着牛羊和粮食,到农田去侍奉舜,准备把整个天下都交付给他,但他并不以此为乐。为什么呢?因为得不到父母的爱,感到自己像穷困的人找不到归宿一样。被天下所喜爱,是众人所追求的,但这并不足以解除他的忧愁;美色是众人欲求的,他娶了尧帝的两个女儿也不足以解除他的忧愁;显贵,是众人所追求的,贵为天子也不足以解除他的忧愁。

大家都喜爱的美色富贵，都不能解除忧愁，只有得到父母的爱心才能解除忧愁。人们在年幼时是思慕父母的，到了懂得喜欢美色的时候就会思慕年轻美貌的女子，有了妻室就思慕妻子儿女，当了官就思慕君主，得不到君主的信任就会内心恐惧。而大孝的人一辈子都思慕父母，所以舜才会跑到田野里去哭诉自己得不到父母的爱。到五十岁仍在思慕父母的，我看只有舜做到了。

　　孟子的学说主张里，孝顺父母是其中很重要的一条，表现在言行上对父母双亲的顺从、侍奉，及双亲去世后举行符合身份的丧仪和遵照礼制的守丧。舜终生思慕父母，令孟子赞赏不已，认为这才是大孝。从另一个角度理解，孟子其实也告诉我们：对于根本原则的追求，要像古代圣贤那样不被任何外界事物所干扰诱惑，做到始终如一。

A FILIAL SON ADORES HIS PARENTS FOR HIS WHOLE LIFE

　　Mencius enjoyed discussing about filial piety. Once Wan Zhang asked him, "I heard Shun once went to the fields and cried and complained toward Heaven. Why did he do that?" Mencius replied, "Because of grievance and adoration." Wan Zhang asked again, "Zengzi said if being loved by our parents, we would be very happy; if being disliked by the parents, we would be sad but could not hold a grudge against them. Therefore, why did Shun act like that?"

　　Mencius explained, "It is natural that a filial son would feel sad if he is not adored by his parents. For example, if I have worked hard in farming and fulfilled my duty as a son but my parents just don't adore me, what's the fault of me? Yao sent his nine sons, two daughters, and hundreds of officials with the livestock and food to wait on Shun and intended to give the whole country to Shun, but

Shun was not excited. Why? Because he couldn't have his parents' love, just like some poverty-stricken people cannot have their home. He has won the love of the whole country which is everyone's dream, but even that could not relieve his sorrow; everyone seeks after beauty, but his marrying of the two daughters of Yao could not put an end to his sorrow; everyone seeks after fame and power, but even with the throne he was still bothered by sadness. Beauty and wealth which everyone adores could not relieve his sorrow, and only parents' love could free him from that. Many people adore their parents in childhood, adore young beauty in adulthood, adore wife and children after getting married, and adore the king after taking up official positions and would even feel scared without the king's confidence. The most filial sons adore their parents for their whole lives, and that explains why Shun went to the field to cry for not being able to enjoy the love of his parents. It seems that only Shun still adored his parents when he was already fifty years old."

In Mencius' philosophy, the filial piety to the parents is very important. It covered the obedience and attendance to one's parents when they are alive, and the appropriate funeral and mourning in line with the etiquette after their deaths. Shun adored his parents for his whole life, and that was highly acclaimed by Mencius as the utmost piety. From another perspective, Mencius also wanted to tell us that we must get rid of external disturbances and stick to the ultimate moral principles as those ancient sages have done.

舜以德报"象"怨

说到舜的孝顺，万章又想到一个问题："舜的弟弟象成天把杀害舜当成重要的事务来做，可是舜做了天子却没有杀他，只是把他放逐到远处去，为什么呢？"

舜是圣人贤君，是大孝子，然而在家的时候却不受父母喜爱。不仅如此，他的父亲、弟弟甚至还总想加害于他。父亲叫他去修谷仓，然后就抽去了梯子；派他去淘井，等其他人出来后，就把井口堵上；弟弟象则说：除掉了舜我就立功了。牛羊、粮仓都归父母，矛、盾、琴、弓都归我，两个嫂嫂也要让她们伺候我睡觉。

万章不明白，对于其他一些犯上作乱的人，如共工、三苗、鲧等，舜把他们流放的流放，诛杀的诛杀，天下人都没话说，因为是为民除害。可是对于象这样罪大恶极的弟弟，舜却不但不杀他，还给他在远方封地。这种行为是仁人该有的吗？别人有罪就惩罚，弟弟有罪就封地？

对于万章的这个问题，孟子这样解释：仁人对自己的弟弟，不存愤怒，不留怨恨，只有亲近、爱护。因为亲近、爱护弟弟，所以希望他显贵富有，于是给他封地。自己做了君王，弟弟还是一个平民，这怎么算得上是爱护自己的亲人呢？而象在他的封地也没有任何实权，舜派了官吏去治理他的封地，帮他缴纳贡税，所以这也跟放逐差不多，算是一点惩罚吧。

孟子的意思是，舜不因为象是自己的弟弟而放弃原则，也不因为要坚持原则而废弃了兄弟情义。在孟子眼里，圣人是没有过失的，不管怎么做，都能为他们找到合理的解释。只是，这样的解释是否能让自己的弟子信服呢？换个角度看，如果是在把天下当作自己私人财产的封建时代，天子想杀谁，想保谁，大概任何人都没有权力干涉。万章之所以质疑舜的行为，说明在他们的那个时代，君主的权力并不是至高无上的，百姓还是享有一定民主权益的。这一点比封建时代先进。

SHUN RETURNED XIANG'S MALICE WITH GRACE

The discussion about Shun's filial piety lead to Wan Zhang's another enquiry, "Shun's younger brother Xiang was determined on killing him. But Shun, who later ascended to the throne, didn't kill Xiang for revenge and just sent him into exile. Why?"

Shun was a sage king and a filial son, but was disliked by his parents. Furthermore, his father and younger brother always wanted to kill him. His father sent him to mend the barn, and stealthily put the ladder away; his father sent him to dig a well, and blocked the well after other people climbed out. His brother Xiang said, "It would be my feat if I killed Shun. The cattle and barn would go to my parents; the spear, shield, lyre and bow would be mine; two sisters-in-law would become my wives."

Wan Zhang didn't understand why for other rebels such as Gonggong, Sanmiao and Gun, Shun exiled or killed them, while for his own brother Xiang, instead of killing him, Shun granted him with fief in the remote area. The ordinary people supported Shun's punishment for the rebels since he had weeded out the evil for them, but was Shun's treatment of his own brother justified? Why did he punish the other criminals while grant his guilty brother with fief?

Mencius answered, "Moral people bear love and care for their brother instead of hatred and anger. Because Shun loved his brother, he hoped Xiang to become rich and powerful and thus granted him with the fief. How could Shun be regarded as being able to care for his own family while leaving his brother as an ordinary farmer after he ascended to the throne? Also, as a matter of fact, Xiang didn't have much say in his fief, because Shun sent for officials to manage the fief and collect the tax for him; therefore, it was not much different from exile and could be regarded as punishment."

What Mencius told us here was that Shun did not discard his own principles by being partial to his younger brother, nor did he discard fraternity for the adherence to his moral principles. In Mencius' eyes, those sacred people were error-free. No matter how they behaved, he could always justify their behaviors, but could he really convince his students with his justifications? From another point of view, in the feudalist era the king owned the whole country as his private property; others had no right to interfere with his decision of killing or favoring someone. Wan Zhang's challenge against Shun's behaviors showed that during that time the king's power was not supreme, and the general public still enjoyed some democratic rights, which was a bit more advanced than the feudalist dynasties.

民意为天

　　一般人的思想里都认为舜的天下是尧给的。万章曾就此事求教过孟子。孟子的回答是：天子不能把天下交给别人，只有上天才能把天下交给他人。上天虽然不说话，但却用行动和事实来示意。过去尧向上天推荐人，上天接受了，就把这个人推出来让百姓认识，百姓接受了，就是接受了上天的意思。

　　万章不明白这是什么意思。孟子又解释说：舜主持政务，治理国家，百姓都满意。这说明是百姓接受了他，他才能享有天子的地位。所以说，天子没有权力把天下交给别人，只有上天有这个权力。当年舜辅佐尧二十八年，尧去世后，舜服满三年的丧期，就跑到南河的南面来躲避尧的儿子。尽管这样，天下的诸侯前来朝见时，都去见舜，而不是尧的儿子；诉讼的人也都去找舜，而不去找尧的儿子；歌颂的人赞美的是舜，而不是尧的儿子。这样，舜才来到国都，登上了天子的座位。假如舜住在尧的宫室，逼迫尧的儿子让位，这就是篡夺，而不是民意，更不是天意了。所以，上天所见，依从民众所见；上天所听，依从民众所听。

万章又进一步问："人们都说到了禹的时候道德就败坏了，天下不传给贤人，而传给儿子了，是这样吗？"远古时代，尧传位给舜，舜传位给禹，而禹却把王位传给了自己的儿子启。因此万章认为这说明禹的时代社会风气已经开始转变了。

但孟子却摇摇头说，不是这样，上天的意思是把天下给贤人，如果儿子是贤人，那就把天下给儿子。如何判断是否贤人，只要看百姓的态度就知道了。尧是这样，舜是这样，禹也是这样。禹也向上天推荐了益，可是朝见、诉讼的人都只去见禹的儿子启，而不去见益；歌颂的人也只讴歌启，而不是益。尧舜的儿子品行都不好，禹的儿子启却很贤明，能够继承禹的德行。这一切百姓都能亲身体会到。所以没有人给他，他却得到了，这不是人力所能决定的，而是百姓的意愿所决定的，是天意。

儒家思想一向主张统治天下的资格取决于天意，而天意又是民意的体现。百姓拥护的人当了天子，这就是顺从天意。如果用不正当的手段篡夺了王位，必然会遭到百姓反对，王位自然也坐不稳，因为不合天意。孟子的这个说法虽然很唯心，但尊重民意，以民意为天意的思想却是进步的。

THE WILL OF THE PEOPLE IS THE WILL OF HEAVEN

Most people think Shun was bestowed with the land under Heaven by Yao. Wan Zhang also consulted this with Mencius. And Mencius answered, "The king can't confer his country to others, and only Heaven is entitled to grant it to others. Heaven does it not with words but with acts and facts. Heaven accepted the one recommended by Yao and made all the people get to know him. People's acceptance of Shun was actually the acceptance of the will of Heaven.

Wan Zhang still didn't understand, so Mencius continued to explain, "Shun presided over the running of the state and people were all very satisfied. That meant people accepted him, so that he could become the sovereign. Therefore, the son of Heaven could not give his country to others, and only Heaven could. Shun had assisted Yao for 28 years before Yao passed away. After observing three years' mourning for Yao, he went to the south of South River to evade the son of Yao. But even so, all the dukes went to pay respects to him instead of to Yao's son; the accusers all tried to seek help from Shun instead of Yao's son; the laudators all lauded Shun instead of Yao's son. In that case Shun went to the capital and ascended to the throne. Had Shun lived in Yao's palace and forced Yao's son to abdicate the throne, then it would be usurpation instead of following the will of people, even less following the will of Heaven. Therefore, Heaven sees and hears what the people see and hear."

Wan Zhang furthered his inquiry, "It is said that morality decayed during the reign of Yu, because the throne was not conferred to sages but to his son, is it true?" In ancient times, Yao passed down his throne to Shun, who then designated Yu as his successor, but Yu gave his throne to his own son Qi. Therefore, Wan Zhang thought the social morality had deteriorated in the era of Yu.

But Mencius shook his head and said, "Not really. Heaven wishes to put the country under the reign of the virtuous. And therefore there is nothing exceptionable to pass the throne to one's son, if his son is virtuous. You can look at the attitude of the public to see whether one is virtuous. Yao was, and so was Shun and Yu. Yu also recommended Yi to Heaven, but those inferior visitors and accusers all went to see Yu's son Qi instead of Yi, so did those laudators. Sons of Yao and Shun were not virtuous, but Yu's son Qi was. He could inherit the virtues of Yu and all the people experienced that. Therefore, nobody gave the throne to Qi, but he got it. It was not decided by the proposition of men, instead, it was decided by the will of Heaven and of all the people.

Confucianism holds the idea that the ruler is chosen by the will of Heaven, which is the reflection of the opinion of people. If the one supported by all the people took the throne, that would be in conformity with the will of Heaven. If anyone usurped the throne through improper means, they would surely be opposed by the people, and couldn't secure their throne, because they were against the will of Heaven. Despite the idealistic perspective of his words, Mencius' respect for people's opinion and reckoning that as the wish of Heaven was progressive.

致君为尧舜

万章对于先贤圣人的事迹总是会问个为什么。有一次在跟孟子谈到商汤的宰相伊尹时,万章问道:"人们都说伊尹是靠烹饪、切割之术来接近成汤的,是这样吗?"

孟子的立场向来都是维护古代圣贤的。他说,事情不是这样的,伊尹从前在莘国的郊野种田,以奉行尧舜之道为乐事,不合乎道义的事情,你就是拿整个天下作俸禄给他,他也不屑一顾。成汤派人用重金礼聘他,他满不在乎地说:"我要成汤的聘礼干什么?我栖身在这耕田之中,效仿尧舜之道,多快乐啊!"成汤一共派人去了三次,他才开始转变。他说:"与其栖身在这耕田之中,乐于尧舜之道,何不使这位君主成为尧舜那样的人呢?何不使这些百姓成为尧舜治下的人民呢?为何不在我的有生之年亲眼看到尧舜再现呢?上天哺育了这些百姓,有的人先明理,有的人后明理;有的人先觉悟,有的人后觉悟。我是先明理、先觉悟的人，我要用上天的大道来启发他们。除了我，还有谁能做这事呢？"伊尹就这样把天下的重任扛到了自己的肩上。孟子最后说，圣人的行为各不相同，有的疏远君主，有的接近君主，有的离去，有的留下，都有自己的准则。我只听说过伊尹用尧舜之道来接近成汤，没听说过什么切割、烹饪！

孟子维护圣人的立场一贯如一，他不能容忍别人诋毁圣人的所作所为。远古时代流传着很多圣人清高脱俗、避世逃世的美谈，似乎圣人贤者都应该厌弃功名，视金钱如粪土，即使入世从政，也该保有一份清高的姿态，否则就不够高尚有德行。后世"刘备三顾茅庐"，诸葛亮经三请四请才终于出山辅佐刘备，恐怕也有这层道理。

ASSISTING THE KING TO BECOME SAINTS LIKE YAO AND SHUN

Wan Zhang was always very curious about former sage kings' stories. Once talking about Yi Yin, the prime minister of King Tang of the Shang Dynasty, he asked Mencius, "People say Yi Yin got access to Cheng Tang relying on his cutting and cooking skills, is it true?"

Mencius always defended the ancient saints, so he said, "No. Yi Yin willingly followed the ways of such saints as Yao and Shun while planting crops in the fields of the suburbs of the State of Shen. He would never bend his moral principles even when he was offered with a salary worth the whole land under Heaven. When Cheng Tang (King Tang of the Shang Dynasty) wanted to recruit him with a high salary, he did not show any interest in it and said, 'Why do I need that? I am so happy living in the wild fields and following the ways of Yao and Shun.' King Tang sent messengers to invite him for three times before he finally changed his mind. He said, 'If I just live here in the fields, I can only carry out moral principles myself, but if I assist the king, I can try to make the king emulate ancient saints such as Yao and Shun. Why not let people enjoy the benefits of living under the benevolent governance as in the era of Yao and Shun? Why not enable myself to witness the prosperity of Yao and Shun's era in my lifetime? Heaven breeds all the people and some of them have been enlightened earlier than others. I myself belong to the former category and so I need to enlighten others with the major principles of Heaven. Who can achieve that besides me?' Yi Yin, therefore, shouldered that grand responsibility on himself." At last Mencius also said, "Saints might act differently. Some were estranged from the kings while some chose to be closer; some left while some stayed. They all had their principles. I only heard that Yi Yin had access to King Tang with the principles of Yao and Shun, but I never heard about such things as his cutting or cooking skills."

Mencius was consistent in his position to defend the saints, and he couldn't stand other people to speak ill of them. There were many much-lauded stories about the saints being lofty-minded and choosing reclusive lifestyles; it seemed that all the saints and the virtuous should disdain fame and wealth and even if they had taken up official positions, they would have to hold themselves aloof, otherwise they could not be reckoned as men with high morals. The story had it that during the Three Kingdoms Period, Liu Bei, the king of Shu Kingdom, visited and invited Zhuge Liang for three times before the latter finally agreed to assist him in ruling his kingdom, which might have also mirrored this mentality.

好事者为之

　　痈疽是卫国国君的亲信,瘠环是齐国的宠臣宦官,在士人中的名声都不好。可是有人说,孔子在卫国和齐国时分别是受这两人的接待。孟子自然要为自己最崇拜敬重的圣人辩护了。他说根本不是这么回事,这是好事之徒胡编乱造的。

　　孔子当年在卫国是受颜雠由接待的,颜雠由是卫国的贤大夫。当时有个叫弥子的卫君宠臣,其妻和孔子的学生子路之妻是姐妹。这个弥子就对子路说:"你的老师要是由我来接待的话,我肯定能让他当上卫国的国卿。"子路就把这话告诉了他的老师孔子,孔子听了说:"我当不当国卿取决于命运。"孔子行事处处依据礼义,对于官位从不强求,认为一切取决于天命,所以对弥子的话并不以为然,更不会因此去接近讨好弥子。

　　孔子在鲁国、卫国都不顺心,在宋国又遇上一个叫司马桓魋的人要拦截杀害他，只好改变装束离开宋国，处境困难的时候，受到贤臣司城贞子的接待，于是当了陈国的臣子。

因此，观察在朝的臣子，要看他都接待什么样的宾客，观察外来的士人，要看他受什么样的人接待。如果孔子受宠臣痈疽和宦官瘠环的接待，那还能称得上是孔子吗？所以圣人的行为总是依据礼义的原则，无论处境多么困难，也不会放弃原则去讨好迁就那些权贵。好事者所编造的那些流言，在孟子看来，简直就是对孔子人格的侮辱。

由此可知，古人对于人的交往对象这一点看得很重。所谓物以类聚、人以群分，一个人所结交的人群属于哪一类，往往代表着他自己的内心喜好。我们根据这一点，常常可以判断出谁是君子，谁是小人。

TROUBLEMAKERS STARTED THE RUMOR

Yong Ju was a minion of the State of Wei, while Ji Huan was a eunuch favored by the Duke of Qi. Both had bad reputations, but some people said Confucius had been received by them while he was in Wei and Qi. So it was natural for Mencius to defend the saint who he most respected and adored. He said that was all groundless rumor made up deliberately by the busybodies.

He said, "While Confucius was in Wei, he was received by Yan Chouyou, a virtuous official there. The wife of Mizi, a minion of the Duke of Wei, was the sister of the wife of Zilu, Confucius' student. Mizi said to Zilu, 'If I received your teacher, I would make him become the prime minister of Wei.' Zilu told this to his teacher and Confucius said, 'Whether I could become the prime minister or not depends on my fate.' Confucius always followed moral principles in his acts, and never deliberately sought for official positions, because he thought everything was disposed by Heaven. Therefore, he was not interested in Mizi's words, let alone flattering him.

After the unpleasant stay in the States of Lu and Wei, Confucius had to put on a disguise and left the State of Song also, because a man named Sima Huantui there stalked and planned to kill him. During this difficult time, he was received by Sicheng Zhenzi, a virtuous minister in the State of Chen, and he took public office there.

Therefore, while accessing the officials in the court, we should see what kind of guests he receives; while accessing scholars coming from other states, we should see they are received by what kind of people. If Confucius had really been received by such minions as Yong Ju and Ji Huan, he would have been unworthy of his reputation. Therefore, saints would never discard their moral principles to flatter the rich and the powerful even when they were in difficulty." The rumor fabricated by the troublemakers was regarded by Mencius as an insult to Confucius.

Hereby, we can see that the ancients attached great importance to their contacts. Birds of a feather flock together and like attracts like. One's friends could be a mirror of oneself. By that we can tell the moral from the immoral.

集大成者

　　有一天,孟子与公孙丑讨论什么是圣人的问题,他就几位先贤谈了自己的看法:

　　伯夷眼不看不好的颜色,耳不听不善的声音。非自己的君主不侍奉,非自己的朋友不交往,非自己的百姓不使唤。天下太平就出来做官,天下混乱就归隐山林。暴政所在,暴民所处的地方,坚决不停留。不站在恶人的朝廷里,不与恶人说话。如果让他站在恶人的朝廷里,与恶人说话,那简直就是让他穿着整齐的衣冠,坐在黑污的地上一样。他这种讨厌恶人的心理扩大开来,就到了这样的地步:跟同乡人站在一起,见别人衣冠不整,就隔着老远说话,好像人家会把他弄脏似的。诸侯中有善于辞令者来拜访他,他也不接待。不接待的原因其实是不屑,是看不起。

　　关于伊尹,伊尹的看法是:"侍奉谁不是侍奉君主?使唤谁不是使唤臣民？"因此，世道好时他出来做官，乱世时也出来做官。还说，"上天之所以生养这么多人，正是让先知先觉的人来启发他们。我就是天生的先知先觉之人，我要用我的大道来使世人觉悟。"他看到天底下有一个人没有享受到尧舜美德的教化，就好像是自己把他们推到沟壑中一样。他就是如此地以天下为己任。

而柳下惠不以侍奉恶君为羞，不以官职小而自卑。出仕不隐藏自己的贤能，被免职也不埋怨，处境穷困也从不自怜。与普通人交谈，和悦亲切，好像不愿离开一样。他说，"你是你，我是我，就算你袒胸露体地在我身旁，又怎么能够污染我？"于是依然心情很好地与别人在一起，保持着自己的操守。人家留他，他就留下。留他而不走，其实也是不屑于离开啊。因此，凡听到柳下惠的风范的，鄙陋的人变得更加宽容，刻薄的人也变得更为敦厚。

这三个人都是古代圣贤者的榜样。比较起来，孟子认为伯夷太狭隘，柳下惠太玩世不恭，而伊尹又不懂得自如地进退。狭隘与玩世不恭，都不是君子该有的行为。真正的君子，那标准是很严格的，就算是伯夷、伊尹、柳下惠这样品德高尚的人，也还是有缺陷的。

孟子最后评论说，只有孔子是圣人中的典范。离开齐国时，不等米淘好下锅就匆匆上路。离开鲁国时，却慢慢地走，因为那是父母之邦。可以快就快，可以慢就慢，可以继续就继续；云游诸侯时可以独处就独处，可以出仕就出仕。所以他是圣人中的识时务者，是集圣人之大成的人。如果用射箭来打比方的话，伯夷、伊尹、柳下惠都只是在力量与技艺上各有所长罢了，只有孔子既具备力量，又拥有技艺，所作所为从容自如，而且都符合圣贤的标准。

"集圣人之大成"是孟子对孔子的评价。古时敲钟击磬，敲钟为起音，击磬为收尾，前者为智，后者为圣。孟子的意思是，孔子是集智圣之大成。他对孔子的崇拜恐怕无人能及。现在我们说的"集大成"，意思是集中了某类事物的各个方面，达到相当完备的程度。

EPITOME OF WISDOM AND SANCTITY

One day Mencius discussed with Gongsun Chou about the qualities of saints and he commented on some ancient saints.

Mencius said, "Boyi didn't look at bad colors, nor did he listen to bad voices. He only served his own king, communicated with his own friends, and ordered his own subjects. He took up official positions in peaceful times and secluded himself in deep forests during political turmoil. He didn't stay with tyrants or mobsters. He didn't participate in the court with evil officials, nor did he even talk with those people; otherwise he would feel like standing well-groomed on the dirty ground. He expanded his hatred for evil people to such extent that while talking with his town folks who were not well-groomed, he would keep a long distance between, as if he would be dirtied by them. He refused to receive those visiting dukes with silver tongues, because he despised them."

"Yi Yin thought no matter who he served and to whom he gave order, it was all the same. Therefore, he took public office whether there was good or bad governance. He also said, 'Heaven feeds so many people because he intends to let those enlightened to inspire the rest. I am enlightened and I must inspire the rest with my moral philosophy.' When seeing those who had not been edified by the moral principles of Yao and Shun, he felt like he had pushed them into deep ravines. He shouldered the responsibility of inspiring all people with the major moral principles."

"However, Liu Xiahui was not ashamed of serving bad kings or taking up minor official positions. He didn't conceal his own wisdom or talent while in office nor did he complain if being dismissed or living in poverty. He talked with the ordinary people in an easygoing and pleasant manner as if he were reluctant to finish their conversation. He said, 'We are different individuals. Even if you were naked by my side, I would not be tainted by you.' Therefore, he was in a happy mood staying with others, while adhering to his own principles. He followed others' invitation to stay longer because he didn't want to leave anybody. After hearing his principles, mean people became more tolerant and caustic people became more sincere."

All the three people were exemplars among ancient saints. Comparatively speaking, Mencius thought of Boyi as narrow-minded, Liu Xiahui too sly, while Yi Yin inflexible. Narrow-mindedness and slyness should not be found in men with high morals. The standards for real men with high morals were extremely strict and even people with high morals such as Boyi, Yi Yin, and Liu Xiahui were yet to improve themselves.

In the end Mencius commented, "Only Confucius was the exemplar among saints. While leaving Qi, he couldn't wait until the meal was cooked. While leaving Lu, he walked slowly, because that was his homeland. While he should leave quickly, he did it quickly; while slowly, slowly; while he should continue, he continued. In his wandering lobbying experience, he chose reclusive life and public life according to the circumstances. He discerned the social trends, and therefore, he was profound in lofty principles. Taking archery for instance, Boyi, Yi Yin and Liu Xiahui all had their own advantages either in strength or in skills, but only Confucius was equipped with both, so he could act calmly and live up to saints' principles all the time.

Mencius regarded Confucius as the epitome of the qualities of saints. Now when we say something has epitomized certain qualities, we mean it has integrated the essences of various aspects and become perfect. In ancient times while playing music, people started knocking at the bell and ended with hitting the percussion instrument; the former could be taken as wisdom, and the latter could be taken as sanctity. Mencius, by claiming that Confucius has epitomized wisdom and sanctity, displayed his unparalleled admiration for Confucius.

却之不恭

　　万章问孟子："请问对人之间的交际来往应该怀有怎样的心理？"孟子说："恭敬。""那为什么推辞不接受别人送来的礼物就是不恭敬呢？"万章又问。"假如尊长送给你礼物，你推辞不肯受，会让人觉得你怀疑这礼物得来是否正当，这样就显得轻慢而不恭敬了，所以不要推却才好。"孟子回答。"那我心里这样想，并不明白说出来，只用别的借口来拒绝，这难道也不可以吗？""只要人家是以礼相待、以道交往，即使是孔子也会接受的。"孟子答道。万章想了想，又问道："如今有一个人在国都的郊野拦路抢劫，可是他在你这里却以道交往，以礼馈赠，这种情形也该接受吗？"孟子说："不可以。杀人越货，强横不怕死，人民没有不痛恨的。这种人的礼物怎么可以接受呢？""那么今天这些诸侯，四处搜刮百姓钱财，也和拦路抢劫差不多。假如他也很重视礼节，而君子就接受了他的馈赠，那又是什么道理呢？"原来万章问了老半天，兜了一个大圈子，这才是他真正想问的话。

孟子回答这个问题也颇费心思。他说，不是自己所有而拿别人的，叫做盗。说诸侯是盗，其实是把这个意思延伸到了最大边缘，不能说是真盗。真要这么说的话，孔子以前在鲁国做官时也随同大家一起出去打猎，较量各自所获猎物的多少。这种不合理的"猎较"风俗，孔子也跟从了，何况接受诸侯所赐的礼物呢？君子做官，先得试行一下。如果他的主张可以行得通，而君主却不肯实行，那就离开，所以孔子不曾在一个国家呆满三年的。孔子做官，有的是因为看到可以实行道义，有的是因为国君接待有礼，有的是因为国君诚意养贤。

万章听到这里终于明白孟子曾说过的"中道而行"的意思。真正的君子，虽然可以因环境的改变而改变，但是最根本的原则是不能放弃的。拒绝一件礼物不一定就代表正直公正，当大道不能行于天下时，毅然离去，不与当局者苟且，不贪图已经在手的官位俸禄，这才是真正的正人君子所为。孟子虽然是夸赞孔子，其实也是在表明自己的处世态度。

NOT RESPECTFUL TO REFUSE GIFTS

Wan Zhang asked Mencius, "With what mentality shall we communicate with others?" Mencius said, "With respect." Wan asked, "Why refusing others' gift was disrespectful?" Mencius answered, "If your seniors and superiors send you gifts and you refuse to accept them, they may think that you are suspecting those gifts were obtained through improper means. Therefore, it seems to them you are not respectful to them, so you'd better accept the gifts." Wan continued to question, "If I really have this concern, I could cover it and refuse the gifts under some other excuses. Wasn't that viable?" Mencius replied,

"Even Confucius would accept the gifts sent in polite and moral manners." Wan thought for a moment and said, "If one robbed in the suburbs of the capital, and he socialized with you here with gifts, would you still accept them?" Mencius said, "No. Everybody hates murderers, robbers and mobsters. How could we accept gifts from them?" After beating around the bush, Wan Zhang finally revealed his real question, "Nowadays the dukes exploited people ruthlessly and their behaviors were no different from the robbers. If the dukes followed the etiquette, and men with high morals would accept their gifts, how could you explain that?"

Mencius thought carefully before answering this question. He said, "Those who take things not possessed by them are robbers. Regarding the dukes as robbers is actually too extreme, because they are not real robbers. While Confucius was taking office in the State of Lu, he always followed others in hunting and they competed with each other about the prey. Confucius accepted this irrational custom of "competing about prey", let alone accepting the gifts from the lords. A man with high morals would have a try before officially taking the public office. If his ideas are feasible but the kings refuse to implement, then he would leave. Therefore, Confucius has never stayed in any single state for over three years. Confucius took up official positions sometimes because of the prospects of implementing his benevolent governance, sometimes because of the politeness of the king in receiving him and sometimes because of the king's sincerity in supporting the virtuous."

Wan Zhang finally understood "following the middle course" put forward by Mencius before. A real moral person would never discard the fundamental principles although he could adapt himself to the changing environment. Refusing to accept a gift doesn't necessarily mean being upright. A real man with high morals should quit the public office determinedly despite the decent salary offered by the rulers if the moral principles could not prevail. Mencius was illustrating his own attitudes while praising Confucius.

君子的人格

谈到君子的人格问题时,孟子曾经说,君子担任官职不是因为贫困,但有时是因为贫困;娶妻不是为了奉养父母,但有时是为了奉养父母。如果是因为贫困而担任官职,那就要推辞高位而担任低职,推辞高薪而接受薄禄。孔子就曾当过管仓库的小吏,做一些核算之类的事;曾子当过管畜牧的小吏,只是统计一下牛羊的数目。在其位、谋其政。职位低而过问高位的事,是不合礼义的;处于高位而不能使大道得到施行,同样也是耻辱的。

为了生计而出任官职,那么职务高低应与维持生活相当,这时候当然也谈不上施行大道。如果国君敬重君子,方式也要适当。像子思,当年没有在鲁缪公的朝廷任职,但鲁缪公却很仰慕他,总是派人送这送那的,搞得子思很不高兴,最后一次,竟把来人赶出大门,不肯接受鲁缪公的馈赠了。子思认为,如果鲁缪公喜好贤能之人,那就应该任用他们。既然不能任用，却又不断地馈赠礼物，让贤者不在官位而得到俸禄，对于大道的施行却什么也做不了，这跟畜养狗马没有什么两样，是对贤者的侮辱啊！所以，尊敬贤者，最关键的是要施行他们的主张。否则，待遇再优厚，也跟畜养牲畜一样，君子是以此为耻的。

孔子有一个贡献，那就是区分君子与小人，从而使君子具有道德的意义，但君子的标准还不是很确定的，而孟子则明确地把行大道、施仁义作为贤人君子的标准。在其位，就一定要谋其政，大道不行，就视为自己的耻辱。后人说的"当官不为民做主，不如回家卖红薯，"也是这一标准的通俗表述。

CHARACTER OF A MAN WITH HIGH MORALS

While talking about the character of men with high morals, Mencius said, "Moral people take up official positions not necessarily to relieve their poverty, just like some people marry wives not necessarily to serve their parents. If they really need to go to officialdom to relieve the poverty, they must refuse high-ranking positions with high salaries and only take the lower positions with low salaries. Confucius worked as a minor official responsible for keeping accounts of a barn; Zengzi worked as a minor official taking care of the livestock and calculating the number of cows and sheep. Everybody must fulfill his duty on his own position. It would be against etiquette if the low-ranking officials interfere into responsibilities of their superiors; it would be humiliating if the high-ranking officials can't implement the major principles.

If taking up official positions just for supporting one's living, then his ranking should be in line with the level of his basic livelihood, and of course the implementation of major principles is beyond him. If a king respects moral people, he should do so through proper manners. Zisi did not hold any public office in the court of Duke Miao of Lu. Nevertheless, the Duke admired Zisi very much and always sent gifts to him which annoyed him. In the end, he even drove the messenger away and rejected all the gifts. Zisi thought if Duke Miao really admired the virtuous, then he should recruit them. Not recruiting them while keeping sending gifts and giving them salaries without accompanying positions, and denying them of opportunities to implement the major principles was as if they were feeding the livestock, which is an insult to the virtuous. Therefore, the ultimate respect for the virtuous is to implement their political ideas. Otherwise, it is like they are feeding the livestock, which is a shame for the moral people."

Confucius contributed to the discrimination between the moral and the vile and the moral aspect was imbedded into the definition of men with high morals. However, he didn't define them with the explicit criteria, while Mencius defined men with high morals as those who could implement major principles and practice benevolence. One must be earnest in fulfilling his duties while he occupies a position, and he should regard his failure of promoting the major moral principles as his shame. Nowadays, there is a common expression for Mencius' idea, i.e., if one takes public office without defending the interests of people, he'd better quit his post and become a peddler instead.

人性与善

　　孟子认为人人都具有天生的善性，向善之心是人类原有的良知良能。然而在动荡不安的战国时期，一切传统的信仰、理想、价值观都在发生动摇，人们对人性的善恶也有不同的认识。告子是和孟子同时代的一位思想家，他就认为人性无善也无不善。

　　有一次，告子对孟子说：人性就好比急流水，哪儿有缺口就往哪儿流。东西南北，只要有缺口，无不流去。所以人性是没有善与不善可言的，就像这流水不分东西南北一样。孟子接住告子的话题说：你这水就算是不分东西南北，难道也不分上下么？人性的善，就像这水流向下一样。水没有不向下流的，所以人性没有不向善的。当然，如果拍击水使它跳起来，它也可以高过额角。筑一道堤把水拦住，也可以使它逆流而上。但这难道是水的本性吗？不过是外力使它改变了本性而已。同样的道理，环境可以使一个人干坏事，这就是改变了人的本性。如果人们能够顺着自己的本性好好培养自己的向善之心，不被环境左右，那么人人都可以成为尧舜那样的人。

　　孟子的用心是良苦的，也是很简单的：那就是要拯救那个日益败坏的世道人心，要拯救那个充满"恶"的社会。而这一切必须依靠"善"人。要"创造"这样的"善"人，就必须唤起人们对"善"的良知，意识到自身善的存在。如果人人都有善的本性，那么人人都可以成为君子，成为圣人，要想实施孔子的仁爱也就不难了。

HUMAN NATURE AND BENEVOLENCE

　　Mencius believed that everyone had inborn goodness of human nature, which was the original conscience of men. But in the turbulent Warring States Period, all the traditional faiths, ideals and world values were challenged and people's views were divided on the human nature. Gaozi was a contemporary of Mencius and he believed that there was neither goodness nor evilness of human nature.

　　Once Gaozi said to Mencius, "Human nature can be compared to rushing water which flows into any cracks regardless of the directions. Accordingly, there is neither malevolence nor benevolence for human nature, just like there is no set direction for the rushing water." Mencius followed Gaozi's words, "Water can flow towards the south, the north, the west or the east, but doesn't it distinguish the upward and downward direction? The benevolence of human nature is like rushing water's tendency of flowing downwards. Water always flows downwards, just like human nature, which is always oriented toward benevolence. Of course if the water is stirred, it could splash even higher than our forehead; if we build up a dyke to block the water, we can also make a U-turn of the water's flow. But is it the nature of water itself? No, it is only changed by the external force. Likewise, external environment might induce people into making mistakes, and change the original goodness of human nature. If people can foster their benevolence following their own original goodness of human nature, and resist the external temptations, then they all can become sages like Yao and Shun.

Mencius has given much thought on this issue and his idea was simple: We should rescue the decaying social morality and save this society full of evils. All that needs to be done by people with good nature. In order to "create" such "people", we have to arouse the conscience of people and make them realize their own goodness of human nature. If everybody is gifted with the good human nature, then all could become men with high morals or even saints, and the implementation of Confucius' benevolent theory would be ensured in theory.

君子与小人

　　面对人们日益追求物质利益,忽略道德培养的时弊,孟子曾经痛心地感叹:人总是懂得爱惜自己,但问题是爱惜自己的什么呢?是名利?是生理感官的享受?还是有更值得爱惜的东西呢?一个人的无名指不能弯曲了,即使不影响他的工作生活,他也会不管路途遥远而去求医;可是道德心性丢失了,却不晓得去找回来,真是不知道轻重啊!

　　针对这个现象,公都子问:"同样是人,为什么有些人成了君子,有些人却成了小人呢?"孟子说:"能注意满足自己的心志需要的就是君子;而只注意满足自己的生理需要的就是小人。""那同样是人,为什么有的人注意满足自己的心志需要,有的人却只知道满足自己的生理需要呢?"公都子又问道。孟子说,耳朵、眼睛这类器官是不会思考的,因此容易被外界事物蒙蔽,也容易被引向歧途。而心这个器官是用来思考的,思考就会得到善性,不思考就得不到。这个器官是天赋予我们人类的，是人重要的器官，应当好好培养。如果心志足够强大的话，那么耳朵、眼睛这样的器官就不会把人的心志和善性夺走了。这样就能成为君子了。

现代社会的人类从大体上区分的话，也有这么两类。一类注重精神生活，另一类则只追求物质享受。所谓"声色犬马"，也就是物质享受，最容易引发人的感官追求，让人沉醉其中而迷失方向。精神境界高尚的人有能力驾驭自己的生理欲望，培养出高于普通人的心志和品德。俗人则蝇营狗苟，一心追求物质欲望的满足，却丧失了做人应有的善良本性和朴素的本质。如果整个社会都由这样一群人组成或者驾驭，那这个社会的崩溃就为期不远了。

THE MORAL AND THE VILE

Witnessing people's greater focus on material wealth and negligence of the fostering of morality, Mencius sighed deeply in grief, "People all cherish themselves, but what shall they cherish? Is it fame, fortune, physiological satisfaction, or something more precious? If one's ring finger was incapable of bending, he would go all the way to consult a doctor even though his life or work wouldn't be affected; but if one lost his morals, he would not care to retrieve it. He who did so was really incapable of distinguishing the important from the trivial."

Gongduzi inquired about that, "Why do some people become moral ones while others become the vile?" Mencius said, "Those who have tried to satisfy the needs of their hearts are people with high morals, while those who only have tried to satisfy their physiological needs become the vile." "Why can some attend to the needs of their hearts, while others could only satisfy the physiological needs?" asked Gongduzi. Mencius said, "Our sensory organs such as eyes and ears cannot think and are prone to be misguided and go astray. But our heart is the organ supposed to carry out the thinking and through thinking we can retain the goodness of human nature, otherwise we would not retain it. Heart, as an important human organ, is endowed by Heaven, which deserves our earnest attention. If the will of our heart is strong enough, we wouldn't be deprived of our benevolence and conscience by the misleading eyes and ears. And in this way we can become moral people."

Generally speaking, in our modern society, people can be divided into two categories. One category focuses on spiritual life and the other seeks material comfort.

The phenomenon of the so-called "Music, beauty, keeping dogs and riding horses (*sheng se quan ma*)" refers to the material comforts, which are the most appealing sensual pleasures easily reducing people to self-indulgence and making them get lost. People with high morals can control their physiological lust and cultivate high morality and virtues, distinguishing themselves from immoral ones. The immoral are preoccupied with seeking the material comforts, but have lost the due qualities of benevolence and frugality. If the whole society were to be composed of or controlled by these people, it would meet its ultimate collapse very shortly.

礼义与食色

　　孔子曾经说过:"食色,性也"。食、色固然是人的本性,那么如果跟礼义相比,哪一个重要呢?有一个任国人便拿这个问题去为难孟子的弟子屋庐子。屋庐子一直遵从孟子的教诲,当然回答说是礼义重要。任国人有备而来,接着又问:"如果遵从礼义的原则就得饿死,不遵从礼义的原则就能得到食物,那也一定要遵从礼义吗?依照礼仪迎亲却娶不到老婆,不依照礼仪迎亲就能娶到老婆,那也一定要依照礼仪迎亲吗?"

　　屋庐子回答不了这个问题,连忙跑去见老师。孟子说,这个问题有什么难回答的?打个比方说,一寸厚的木块可以高过尖顶高楼,是因为没有度量它们的根基啊。说金子比羽毛重,难道是一丁点金子相对于一车羽毛而言吗?这个任国人拿饮食、色欲的重要因素跟礼义的轻微成分相比,自然是饮食、色欲重要了。你去答复他的时候这么问他:"扭断兄长的胳膊去抢夺他的东西就能得到食物,不这么做就得不到食物,他会做吗?翻越邻居家的墙头去搂抱邻家女子就能满足色欲,不那么做就满足不了,你问他去不去做?"

饮食、性欲代表的是人最基本的需求,礼义代表的是道德品质,前者说的是物质,后者是人的精神需求。孟子想说的是,当人们最基本的生存需求得到满足时,人的精神应该怎样支配自己的欲望?人是否是自己欲望的奴隶?人之所以为人的本质是什么?孟子在反驳任国人的命题时,强调事物比较的条件,强调事物的可比性,是颇有价值的。

ETIQUETTE AND RIGHTEOUSNESS VS. FOOD AND BEAUTY

Confucius said, "It is human nature to seek food and beauty." However, compared with etiquette and righteousness, which is more important? Once, a man from the State of Ren challenged Wulu Zi, a student of Mencius, with this question. Wulu Zi always followed Mencius' teaching, so naturally he replied that etiquette and morality was more important. That man was fully prepared to challenge him, so he pressed on, "I would starve to death if I observed the principles of etiquette and morality, and I could gain food if disobeying them, so shall I still observe them? If I observed the etiquette of wedding, I would not be able to marry a woman but I could get one if disobeying it, so shall I still observe it?"

Wulu Zi could not answer this question and immediately turned to his teacher for help. Mencius said, "Was it that difficult? Take an instance; a wood chip can stand higher than the tip of a high building, because we don't take into consideration the bases where they are placed. We say gold is heavier than feather, but is a little bit of gold still heavier than a carriage of feathers? The man from Ren compared the important elements of food and the lust for beauty with the insignificant elements of morality and etiquette, and of course in this sense food and the lust for beauty was more important. You can answer him by asking him that, 'If you broke your brother's arms, then you could get food and if you climbed over the wall to the neighboring girl's house and hugged her, then your sexual needs could be satisfied, would you act in that way or not?'"

Food and the lust for beauty represent the most fundamental needs of men, while righteousness and etiquette reflect the moral aspect. The former refers to material comforts while the latter refers to the spiritual needs. What Mencius wanted to say was that once the fundamental needs for survival were satisfied, how should people control their lusts? Are humans the slaves of our own lusts? What are the most essential characteristics for humans? While refuting the man from Ren, Mencius stressed the preconditions for the comparison as well as the comparability of different issues, which was of significance.

人人都可成尧舜

曹交是古代曹国贵族的后裔。有一天他去见孟子,请教怎样才能有尧舜那样的成就。孟子告诉他,这一点都不难办。比如,如果有人认为自己连提起一只小鸡的力气都没有的话,那他就是没有力气的人;如果他认为自己可以举起三千斤的重量,那他就是个力气很大的人;如果他认为自己可以举起像大力士乌获能举起的重量,那他就是和乌获一样的大力士。就看他自己愿不愿意做了。尧舜之道,无非是孝悌。孝敬父母、尊敬长者,这个做不到吗?很多人只是不去做罢了。比如有个老人走在你前面,你跟在后面走,这就是悌。抢到老人前面走,就是不悌。你想做到悌,那就跟在老人后面慢慢走好了,不是很容易做到的事吗?可是很多人就是不愿意做啊。你穿尧舜一样的衣服,说尧舜那样的话,做尧舜那样的事,你就可以成为尧舜那样的人了。相反,你穿桀那样的衣服,说桀一样的话,做桀一样的事,那就会成为桀一样的人，很简单的道理。

听孟子这么一说，曹交突然明白了好多，于是赶紧说要去拜见邹国国君，请他给自己一个住所，好留在孟子身边，聆听他的教诲。孟子马上说，这种道理其实很简单，只是你没有想清楚，不去身体力行罢了。你回去做做就会发现这不难做到。要找老师，那天下可多得很呢，未必一定要找我啊。

人人都可以当尧舜？这话听起来让人有点疑惑。曹交总觉得这里应该有很深的学问，所以要拜孟子为师。但孟子却认为这只是个能否身体力行的简单问题。既然你想做，那你就去做，然后就能实现你所希望的。只想不做，那就是空想。

EVERYBODY COULD BECOME SAGES AS YAO AND SHUN

Cao Jiao was the descendent of the noble family of the State of Cao. One day he went to visit Mencius and consulted him about how to score the achievements as great as those of Yao and Shun. Mencius answered, "It is not difficult at all. If one thinks he can't even lift a chick, then he will never make it; but if he thinks he can lift things weighing 1,500 kilos, then he will become a man of great strength; if he thinks he could become as powerful as Wu Huo who was with unusual strength, then he will really have that great strength. Therefore, all is up to him. The focus of the principles of Yao and Shun is filial piety. Can't people respect their parents and elders? Most people just don't bother to do so. For example, suppose an old person walks ahead of you and you follow behind him, then you could be regarded as having followed the filial piety; if you surpass him then you couldn't. Therefore, it would be easy to follow filial piety by just following behind the old man but many people just don't want to do that. If you wear clothes, speak and behave following the examples of Yao and Shun, you will become as virtuous as them, but if you follow the example of Jie, the tyrant, then you will become as tyrannical as Jie. That is as simple as that."

After hearing Mencius' words, Cao Jiao suddenly became enlightened and immediately said that he was going to seek an audience of the king of the State of Zou to request to be accommodated so as to follow Mencius and hear his teachings. Mencius said to him, "The idea is very simple. You just have not considered it seriously and have failed to implement it. If you go back and implement the idea by yourself, you would find it not that difficult. There are so many people who can teach you, and you don't necessarily need to follow me."

Can everybody become sages as Yao and Shun? This might sound a bit confusing. Cao Jiao thought that idea should be profound, so he wanted to study under Mencius. But Mencius thought it was only a simple matter of whether one would translate the principles into acts. If you want to realize your hope, then you need to make actual efforts to make them come true. If you only hope without making any endeavors, then you'll only be daydreaming.

石丘遇宋牼

　　孟子率领众弟子走在去宋国的路上,一边议论着秦国和楚国之间即将发生的一场大规模的战事。当时,齐国和秦国是分别位于东、西方的两个强国,南方的楚国也是个强国,所以它的一举一动就显得举足轻重。当时楚国的朝廷分为亲齐派和亲秦派,最初是亲齐派占上风。后来秦惠王为了破坏齐楚之间的关系,就派人对楚怀王说,如果楚国跟齐国断交的话,秦国就送给楚国六百里的土地。楚怀王看见这么好的条件,就答应跟齐国断交了。可是这时候秦国又反悔了,只同意给楚国六里地。楚怀王知道自己上当受骗了,十分生气,就调动军队,准备进攻秦国。眼看一场战争就要爆发了,形势十分紧张。

　　孟子和他的弟子们一路议论着,不知不觉来到了一个叫石丘的地方,凑巧的是他们在这里遇见了宋牼。宋牼是一位融合了法家和道家思想的著名学者，同时也是一名和平主义者。他正准备去楚国，碰巧也在石丘休息。于是孟子就和他谈论起来。

孟子问宋牼准备去哪里？宋牼回答说："我听说秦楚之间要开战，我打算拜见楚王，劝他罢兵。如果楚王不听，我就去拜见秦王，劝他罢兵。两国君王中，总会有一个听我的。"孟子问宋牼打算怎样进言？宋牼回答："我打算说，两国交战是不利的。"

孟子说："您的愿望的确很伟大，可是您的说法却不行。您以利害关系为目的向秦楚两位国君进言，如果两位国君认为有利可图才罢兵休战，那么下面的官兵也都会认为罢兵是因为有利可图。照这样的想法，那做臣子的也会抱着有利可图的目的来侍奉君主，做儿子的也抱着有利可图的想法来侍奉父母，做弟弟的也抱着有利可图的观念来侍奉兄长，这样下去，君臣之间、父子之间、兄弟之间就不存在仁义，只剩下利益关系了，国家总有一天也会灭亡的。相反，如果您一开始就以仁义的观念来说服两位君主，那么两国上下都会知道是因仁义而罢兵休战，从而明白仁义的好处。这样君臣之间、父子之间、兄弟之间就都会抱着仁义的观念来互相对待，国家也就能以德政统治天下了。您何必一开口就跟他们谈利呢？"

就像战国时代各国诸侯开口就谈利一样，孟子也是一开口就说仁义。在多年的游说生涯中，孟子一直高举着仁义的大旗，屡战屡败、屡败屡战，尽管不断遭受挫折，但却始终幻想着有一位贤德的君主能接受他的仁政思想。只要这位君主愿意实行仁政方针，那就是战无不胜的法宝，统一天下也毫无问题。可是孟子没有想过，对于可以为了六百里土地而与盟国断交，也可以为了六里地而互相开战的秦楚两国国君来说，让他们为仁义而罢兵休战，有可能吗？孟子的仁政思想跟现实一碰撞，就显得十分的天真了。

ENCOUNTERING SONG KENG AT SHIQIU

Mencius was leading his students on the way to the State of Song, while discussing the looming war between the States of Qin and Chu. At that time Qi and Qin were two strong states in the east and the west respectively. Chu, lying in the south, was also a strong one, so it could tip the balance for the situation. The court of Chu was divided into two groups, one favoring Qi while another favoring Qin. At first the group biased towards Qi gained the upper hand. Later King Hui of Qin, with the intention of ruining the relations between Qi and Chu, cheated King Huai of Chu that Qin would give a land extending six hundred *li* to Chu if he broke the relations with Qi. King Huai agreed to his offer and broke the ties with Qi. But then, the king of Qin went back on his words and only agreed to give Chu a land extending only six *li*. King Huai, after realizing this trap, was so annoyed that he deployed armies to prepare for a war against Qin. The war was looming and the situation was very tense.

Mencius was discussing all the way with his students and reached a place called Shiqiu where they encountered Song Keng, a pacifist and famous scholar who integrated the ideas of Legalism and Taoism. He was heading for Chu and happened to take a rest in Shiqiu then, so Mencius began to discuss with him.

Mencius asked where Song Keng was heading for. He answered, "I heard a war would break out between Qin and Chu, so I decided to visit the king of Chu and suggest him not to wage the war. If he doesn't follow my advice, I will go to visit the king of Qin and suggest him not to have the war. I am sure at least one of them will follow my advice." Mencius asked how he would suggest the kings. Song Keng said he would tell them the war would be unfavorable for both states.

Mencius said, "Your hopes are lofty, but your ways of persuasion are not feasible. You said you would suggest the two kings not to wage the war on the account of benefits. If the two kings stop the war only for benefits, then so would their officials and troops. Had this mentality prevail, then all the officials would serve their king for benefits, and sons and younger brothers would serve their fathers and elder brothers respectively based on those. In this way, the whole country would be deprived of benevolence among the king and his ministers, fathers and sons, elder and younger brothers and only left with interests. Then the country will meet its end before long. On the contrary, if you start by persuading the two kings to stop the war for benevolence and righteousness, all the people would know that it is benevolence and righteousness that bring about peace, thus they will understand the benefits of benevolence and righteousness. Then benevolence and righteousness would prevail in the relationship between the king and his ministers, fathers and sons, elder and younger brothers, and then the whole country would be governed with the moral rule. So why mention profits and benefits at first?"

Mencius always centered his talks on benevolence and righteousness, just like the dukes during the Warring States Period who centered their talks on profits and benefits. During the long period as a wandering lobbyist, Mencius kept upholding the principles of benevolence and righteousness and kept his hope of the acceptance of his ideas of benevolent governance by a virtuous king. He thought that benevolent governance would enable a state to become inconvincible and even unify the whole land under Heaven. However, Mencius had neglected one fact, i.e., it would never be possible for the kings, such as those of Qin and Chu, who could cut relations with their allies just for a land extending six hundred *li* and wage a war against each other for a land extending only six *li*, to stop the war just for benevolence and righteousness. Mencius' idea of benevolent governance seemed too naive while facing the reality.

什么是良臣

　　战国时代的风气是诸侯之间相互争城掠地，杀人建功。所以侍奉君主的文武大臣也总是对诸侯说"我能为国君开辟土地，充实国库"之类的话，以此来得到国君的宠幸和重用。孟子批评这种所谓"良臣"，其实是古代所说的民贼。当他听说鲁国打算任用刚刚率兵打了胜仗的慎子做将军，就当面直言批评道："不教导民众而任意使唤他们，在古代这叫殃民，是尧舜时代所不容的。就算是一仗战胜了齐国，据有了南阳，也一样不被尧舜所容。"慎子听了这话自然很不高兴，说："这话我就不明白了。"

　　孟子说："那我就明白地告诉你。天子的土地应该是方圆千里，没有千里就不足以接待诸侯；诸侯的土地方圆百里，没有达到就不足以奉守宗庙的典册文书。当年周公分封给鲁国是方圆百里的土地，分封给齐国也是方圆百里的土地。可如今，鲁国的土地已经是五倍于百里，现在若有称王天下的明君出现，你觉得他是会削减鲁国的土地，还是会增加鲁国的土地？白白获取别处的土地给自己，仁者尚且不干，何况是通过杀人来取得土地呢？君子侍奉君主，就是要致力于引导自己的君主走仁义的路啊！你不去做这样的事，却帮助国君邀结盟国争地以战，谋取利益，你这样简直是辅佐夏桀啊。不改变这样的风气，你就是把整个天下都交给他，恐怕连一天都不能安生吧。"

慎子自以为能争城夺地，就是有功于国家，因此得到重用也是理所应当的。不料孟子给他浇了一盆冷水，告诫他侍奉君主最重要的是引导君主施行仁义，而不是穷兵黩武。可叹孟子，一生为仁义奔走呼唤，却始终得不到重用。而能够得到重用的人凭借的优势却总是孟子所反对的。孟子只能一遍一遍地把自己的主张传达给这些人。

WHAT CONSTITUTES A GOOD OFFICIAL?

Invasion for plundering others' land and killing for gaining individual laurels were prevalent in the Warring States Period. Therefore, most officials bragged in front of their kings that they could expand territory and enrich the treasury to win the king's favor and confidence. Mencius criticized that such so-called good officials were actually branded as traitors to the people in ancient times. He criticized Shenzi straightforwardly to his face, who was promoted to be the general by the State of Lu after his recent victory in a war, "You didn't instruct the people, instead willfully ordered them about. This in the past was regarded as ruining the people, which was not accepted in the era of Yao and Shun. Even if you were to defeat Qi in a war and to gain the city of Nanyang, you would never be tolerated by sage kings such as Yao and Shun." Shenzi was surely very unhappy at these words and said, "I couldn't understand your word."

Mencius said, "Let me tell you clearly. The land of the son of Heaven should occupy a land over a radius of a thousand *li*, otherwise, it would not be enough to receive the dukes; the land of a duke should occupy a land over a radius of a hundred *li*, otherwise, it would not be enough to keep the books and scripts of the ancestral halls. Lu was granted by Duke Zhou with a land covering a radius of a hundred *li*, so was Qi. But now Lu has expanded its land by five folds, so if a wise sovereign were to emerge now and to rule the whole country, would he cut Lu's land or enlarge it? Benevolent people would never agree to gain land without proper reasons, let alone getting that by killing. The responsibility of people with high morals in serving their king is to guide him onto the road of benevolence and righteousness. Instead of doing that, you assisted your king to unite with other states in waging wars to plunder others' land and seek after profits, which is no different from assisting the tyrannical King Jie of the Xia Dynasty. Without the shift of such tendency, even if you could provide him with the whole land under Heaven, you could not leave the country in peace for even a single day."

Shenzi thought he had made great contributions to the state by plundering other states' cities and land. Therefore, he deserved the king's trust and confidence. However, Mencius' word poured cold water on his ideas. Also Mencius exhorted him that the top priority of serving the king was to inspire him to implement benevolence and righteousness rather than resort to military power and wars. What a shame that despite his lifelong endeavors for promoting benevolence and righteousness, Mencius had never been entrusted with substantial responsibilities! And "those strengths" with which the officials won trust from their kings were always the very aspects Mencius despised. Therefore, in order to persuade the kings to implement his ideas, Mencius had to pass on his ideas through those officials time and time again.

孟子批评白圭

　　白圭是魏惠王的大臣,善于修筑堤防,主张减轻田税。他以为自己的主张必定能得到孟子的支持,就对孟子说:"我想把田税减为二十分之一,您觉得怎么样?"不料孟子回答:"你的办法是貉国的办法。我问你,假如一个有万户居民的国家,只有一个人制作陶器行吗?"白圭回答说不行。孟子趁势说:"貉国是异族,他们国家不产庄稼,只产黍子,没有城邑、房屋、宗庙和祭祀的礼仪,没有官吏衙门,也没有诸侯间来往的礼物和宴请,所以税收取二十分之一就够了。像我们中原这样的国家,摈弃人伦,不要君主,可能吗?陶器不够尚且会有大问题,何况没有君子呢?税率比尧舜还低,那是大貉小貉;比尧舜高,那是大桀小桀。"这番话说得白圭半天张不了口。

　　过了一会儿白圭又说:"我治水胜过了大禹。"战国时代各国治水的方法就是在河流上建筑堤坝,以防洪水,利于自国,却以邻为壑。所以孟子回答道:"你又错了。大禹治水,是让水归于正道,是疏导,所以他把四海当作沟壑。可如今你却把邻国当作沟壑,让水逆流,变成洪水,损害别国谋取自利。这可是仁人君子所憎恨的,所以你错了。"

　　白圭以贤臣自居,却在孟子那里碰了一鼻子灰,很是狼狈。对白圭减税的批评,反映的是孟子所主张的什一税,即收取十分之一的税。他认为税过高过低都不恰当,过高会损害百姓利益,过低国家就无法运转,无法具备应有的国力和礼仪。对白圭治水的批评,反对的是只图自己一方的利益,把困难或祸害转嫁给别人的做法,成语"以邻为壑"就是由此而来的。

MENCIUS CRITICIZED BAI GUI

　　Bai Gui, an official under King Hui of Wei, was good at building dams and advocated reducing the land tax. He took it for granted that his ideas would be supported by Mencius, so he said to Mencius, "I want to reduce the land tax to one twentieth of its current rate. What do you think about it?" Mencius answered, "Your method is applicable to the State of He. Suppose only one person makes pottery for a state with ten thousand households, would that be practical?" Bai Gui said no. Mencius illustrated further, "The State of He is made up of an ethnic minority. They don't plant crops, and only have wild rice; they don't have cities, houses, ancestral halls, sacrificial ceremonies, government offices; there are no socializing activities such as exchanging gifts and hosting dinners which are common to our dukes. Therefore, one twentieth land tax would suffice for that state. However, in the states located in central China like ours, we can't possibly be isolated from all the socializing or leave our kings alone. The lack of pottery would bring about big problems, let alone the lack of people with high morals. Lower taxation than that in the era of Yao and Shun would only be practical in the states of ethnic minorities such as the State of He, and higher taxation than that in the era of Yao and Shun would make the king become as tyrannical as King Jie in Xia Dynasty." Mencius' words made Bai Gui lost for words for a while.

Later Bai Gui said, "I was better than the ancient sage King Yu in controlling flood." In the Warring States Period, most states built dams over rivers to prevent themselves from the floods, but the waters would pour into the neighboring states. Mencius replied, "You are wrong again. King Yu channeled water through its appropriate watercourses into the four seas; you, on the contrary, reverse the flow of water and make them flood other states, benefiting your own state at the cost of others. These acts are hated by all moral people, and that's why you are wrong."

Bai Gui always considered himself as a virtuous official, and he was extremely embarrassed by Mencius' words. Mencius criticized Bai Gui's proposal on taxation because Mencius himself advocated the one tenth land tax rate. He thought neither the too high nor the too low land tax was proper. Excessively high tax rate would harm the interests of the ordinary people, while extremely low tax rate would affect the functioning of a state, depriving it of its due strength or etiquette. Mencius criticized Bai Gui for his improper water control measures, because he only considered the interests of his own state and shifted the problems and disasters to others. That's where the idiom "confining benefits within one's own borders (*yi lin wei he*)" originated from.

乐正子执政

　　鲁国准备让孟子的学生乐正子执政,孟子听了高兴得不得了,连觉都睡不着。公孙丑问道:"乐正子能力很强吗?"孟子回答说"不是。"公孙丑又问:"那他能够深谋远虑吗?"孟子仍回答说"不是。"公孙丑紧接着问:"那么乐正子知识渊博吗?"孟子还是回答说"不是。"公孙丑奇怪了:"那您为什么那么高兴啊?"孟子回答道:"他是个好善的人。""好善就够了吗?"公孙丑毫不放松地问道。于是孟子就解释了他的看法。

　　好善的人能给天下带来好处,何况是小小的鲁国呢?如果执政者好善,那么四海之内的人们就会不远千里赶来报告他的善行。如果执政者不好善,那么人们也会说,我已经知道了,这个人傲慢无礼,不懂装懂。傲慢无礼、自以为是的表现往往是拒人于千里之外,有识之士也会止步于千里之外,而阿谀奉承、排斥异己的小人就来了。跟阿谀奉承的小人在一起，想把国家治理好，可能吗？

孟子无时无刻不相信人性本善，也无时无刻不期待君主臣子为善天下。如今他的学生乐正子就要为鲁国执政了，而乐正子的好善，正符合孟子的心意。他期待自己的弟子能够在鲁国实行他一直主张的仁政。孟子等了几十年没有等到的机会，如今在自己的学生那里看到了，他怎么能不激动得睡不着觉呢？看来以善治国还真不容易推广。

YUE ZHENGZI TO GOVERN THE STATE

The State of Lu decided to appoint Yue Zhengzi, a disciple of Mencius, to govern its politics. After hearing that, Mencius became too excited to fall asleep. Gongsun Chou asked, "Is Yue Zhengzi of great capability?" Mencius answered, "Not really." Gongsun Chou then asked, "Does he have great vision and insight?" Mencius still said, "No." Gongsun Chou asked, "Is he erudite?" Mencius again said, "No." Then Gongsun Chou was puzzled and asked, "Then why are you so excited?" Mencius said, "Because he is benevolent." Gongsun Chou pressed on, "Is being benevolent enough?"

Then Mencius illustrated his idea, "Benevolent people can bring benefits to the whole land under Heaven, let alone the small state Lu. If the ruler is benevolent, then all the people in the country would come all the way to report his benevolent practices; if the ruler is not benevolent, his subjects would say they have already known he was arrogant and pretentious. Their arrogant air and pretentious manners often keep themselves a good distance from others, so the people with high morals would not demean themselves to approach, while the vile with flattering lips and those with exclusive mentality would come and fill the court. Is it really possible to rule the state properly with the company of the vile with flattering lips?"

Mencius believed in the goodness of human nature, and aspired to see the benevolent governance of the kings and officials all the time. At that time, his student Yue Zhengzi was to come into power in Lu soon, whose benevolence was just what Mencius advocated. So Mencius was looking forward to the implementation of his ideas of benevolent governance in Lu by his disciple. The opportunities Mencius had waited for over decades of years finally presented themselves before his own disciple at that time. How could he help getting excited! We could also see from this story how difficult it was to implement the benevolent governance.

生于忧患,死于安乐

　　孟子虽然肯定人人都有成为尧舜的可能,但要真正成为尧舜那样的贤士,是需要经历各种艰难困苦的考验的,这就是孟子所强调的忧患意识。许多先贤圣人其实都经历了从艰难困苦中成长起来的过程。比如:舜是从田间农夫的生活中成长起来的;傅说原本是从一名筑墙工匠的位置中提拔起来的;胶鬲是从鱼盐商贩的地位上提拔而成名的;管夷吾是由监狱的囚犯中选拔出来的;孙叔敖是隐居在海边被发现的;百里奚是从市场上被赎出来的。因此,上天若要降大任于某一个人,一定先磨砺他的心志,劳累他的筋骨,使他的身体忍受饥饿,使他穷困贫乏,处处不顺,然后用这些来触动他的灵魂,增强他的心性,使他宽容大量,让他具有原来没有的能力。

　　"生于忧患,死于安乐"是说,忧愁困苦可以使人奋起,让人生活得更好;安逸快乐只会消磨人的意志,使人趋于灭亡。这有点类似于我们现在说的挫折教育，逆境容易成材，一帆风顺常常半途而废。因为这样，孟子认为人不怕犯过错，只要随后改正就好。心境困窘，思虑不顺，才会奋发有所作为。"自古英雄出寒门"说的就是这个道理。

TO THRIVE IN CALAMITY AND PERISH IN A SOFT LIFE

Though Mencius believed everyone had the potential to become as virtuous as Yao and Shun, one had to weather the tests of various ordeals and frustrations before reaching sagehood. That was why Mencius called for the awareness of facing adversity. Many ancient saints had grown by overcoming all the ordeals and difficulties. For example, Shun grew up from a farmer; Fu Yue was promoted from a bricklayer; Jiao Ge rose to fame from a fish merchant; Guan Yiwu was selected out of prisoners; Sun Shu'ao was spotted from a recluse by the sea; Baili Xi was redeemed from market peddlers. Therefore, if someone were to be chosen by Heaven to be entrusted with great missions, he would surely have his mind being exercised, his sinews and bones being exhausted, his body being exposed to hunger, and also he would be subjected to poverty and all frustrations in order to inspire his mind, strengthen his fortitude, enhance his tolerance and expand his competency.

The saying of "To thrive in calamity and perish in a soft life" means that sufferings and difficulties could stimulate one's potentials and make people live better while comforts and leisure would sap one's will and lead people to devastation. That has something in common with the "adversity education" we advocate today, which claims that adversity provides a better environment for the fostering of talents while favorable circumstances often make people give up halfway. Therefore, Mencius believed people should not be afraid of making mistakes, only if they could rectify themselves afterwards. As the saying goes, "Ever since the ancient times, heroes have come from humble background". This tells us that only with the suffering of the body and spirit as well as the obstacles in one's thoughts could one exert himself to score great achievements.

独善其身

　　孟子很厌恶纵横家的游说活动,认为他们都是为了自己的私利而四处奔窜,搬弄是非,使得诸侯间战乱不断,百姓不得安宁,但是对宋勾践却十分热心。一方面这个宋勾践不是坏人,另一方面也可以借助他的口去宣传仁政思想,扩大仁政的影响。所以,他就对宋勾践说:"你喜欢游说是吗?那我就来和你说说游说的事。别人理解我,我也悠然自得、清心寡欲;别人不理解我,我也悠然自得、清心寡欲。"

　　宋勾践说:"那怎么才能做到悠然自得、清心寡欲呢?"

　　孟子回答:"崇尚德,喜爱义,就可以做到了。士人在穷困的时候不丧失义,富贵显达的时候不背离道。穷困时不丧失义,就能自得其乐,不失去自己的节操;显贵时不背离道,就不会让百姓失望。古时的君子,得意的时候,把恩惠广施于百姓;不得意时,就修养个人的品德。所以,穷困时使自己做到善,显达时就使天下人都做到善。"

这就是孟子的"穷则独善其身，达则兼善天下"的著名思想。这句话在过去的两千年里影响了中国从古至今无数的读书人。真正的君子，无论自己的处境如何，都不能放弃君子所应该追求的道义。这样，即使身处困境，也不会动摇自己的个人追求，富贵显赫的时候也不会违背自己的主张，而让天下百姓都得到恩惠。应该说，兼善天下是不容易做到的，并不是每个人都有那么多的机会去帮助民众。但独善其身则不难，管好自己，修养自己的品德，应该是每个有精神追求的人都应该努力去做到的。

CULTIVATE ONE'S OWN CHARACTER

Mencius detested the lobbying activities of the strategists-turned-diplomats because he thought they wandered among the states with the preoccupation with their own profit seeking by sowing discord among dukes which led to incessant wars disturbing people's lives. However, he kept close contacts with Song Goujian, because on the one hand this man was not evil, and on the other hand the idea of benevolent governance could reach to more people through him. Therefore, he said to Song Goujian, "You like lobbying, don't you? Then let's discuss about it. If people understand me, I would be carefree and content with a pure mind and few desires; and if they do not, I would still be so."

Song Goujian asked, "How could you attain that mentality?"

Mencius replied, "You can attain that by valuing virtues and adoring righteousness. People with high morals would neither discard righteousness in poverty nor deviate from moral norms in richness and eminence. They can enjoy themselves and maintain their integrity if they adhere to righteousness in poverty; they won't disappoint people if they don't deviate from morality in eminence. In ancient times, the moral people when in favorable circumstances would spread their benefits to all the people, and would cultivate their own morality while in poverty. Therefore, when in poverty, one should practice benevolence by himself; while in eminence, make all the people practice benevolence. "

This is Mencius' famous idea of "cultivating one's own character in poverty and spreading benevolence to all in eminence". This idea has influenced numberless Chinese intellectuals in the past two thousand years. Real moral people will never discard the morals they seek after regardless of their circumstances. Thus, even when in adversity, they will never waver their pursuits and when in eminence, never betray their own beliefs so as to spread the benefits to all the people. It is fair to say the ambition of spreading benevolence to the whole country is not easy to realize since not all the people have such opportunities, but it is not so hard to cultivate one's own character. Therefore, each person with spiritual pursuits should behave oneself and nurture his own virtues.

君子有三乐

在十多年的奔走游历之后,孟子产生了一种疲倦的感觉,他发现政治原来是那么虚幻,唯有教育才能使人心灵净化,才能使人看到希望。所以他对学生说:君子有三乐,父母健在、兄弟平安,这是一乐;仰头无愧于天,低头无愧于地,这是二乐;能够教育天下优秀人才,这是三乐。而王天下之乐并不在其中。

对于受教育的对象,孟子是有所选择的。有一次,滕文公的弟弟滕更向孟子求教,就遭到孟子的回绝。公都子不理解:"滕更到您的门下来求教,您似乎应该礼待他,可您却不回答他的问题,为什么呢?"孟子回答说:"凡是自恃尊贵来问的,自恃贤能来问的,自恃年长来问的,自恃老交情来问的,我都不回答。这几条里,滕更已经占了两条。再说,我不屑去教育他,这本身也是一种教育方法,这叫不教之教。""不教之教"其实是在用无声的方式提醒学习者应当怀有虚心求教、尊重知识的心态和诚意。

此外，孟子还谈到一个有趣的教育现象，他说，古时候的人，常常彼此交换儿子来进行教育，为什么呢？原来亲生父母教育孩子有一个弊端，即在讲解道理的时候如果没有效果，往往会发怒责备，而孩子就会说，您拿大道理来教训我，自己却做不到。这样一来，就有可能导致父子之间相互伤害感情。交换孩子来教育，就可以避免伤害亲情。因为教育而伤害父子感情是不值得的，所以古时候的君子都不亲自教育自己的孩子。

学习者不虚心，就不能接纳新的东西；基于亲情之上的教育，常常会省略必要的认识程序，犯简单化的毛病。"易子而教"可以有效地控制教育者的情绪，形成的是一种既让孩子懂得道理，又不伤害彼此感情的教育方式。孟子关于教育的这些看法，在我们今天看来，仍然很有价值。

THREE DELIGHTS OF PEOPLE WITH HIGH MORALS

After his wandering experience of over a dozen years, Mencius felt tired and realized that politics was too hollow and only education could purify people's hearts and present hopes to people.

Therefore, he told his students, "People with high morals have three delights: one is to have their parents alive and healthy, their brothers safe and sound; second is to have oneself free from guilt while facing Heaven and Land; third is to be able to educate the excellent talents. But the delight of ruling the whole country was excluded by Mencius here.

Mencius was selective about choosing who he wanted to teach. Once Teng

Geng, the younger brother of Duke Wen of Teng, wanted to consult Mencius but was refused. Gongdu Zi didn't understand why and asked Mencius, "Teng Geng called on you for counsel. It seemed that you should have respected him, but you even refused to answer his questions. Why?" Mencius answered, "I don't answer questions from those who capitalize on their status, capability, seniority or old friendship. Teng Geng capitalized on two of them. Furthermore, my refusal to teach him is also another form of education, which is called 'education without teaching'. It actually reminds students to bear the mentality of modesty in seeking advice and learning as well as sincerity in respecting knowledge."

Mencius also mentioned an interesting phenomenon of education. He said, "In ancient times, people often exchanged their sons with others in instruction. Why? Because there is a shortcoming in educating one's own children: if the instruction could not be well received by their own children, the parents might get angry and blame the children while their children would retort them by saying, 'you can't live up to those principles yourself, so why blame me for my failure?' Thus the bond between father and son would probably be hurt and by exchanging their own children with others' in education, they could avoid that from happening. It was not worth harming the relationships of father and son on the account of education, therefore people with high morals in the past did not teach their own children."

Without modesty, students could not accommodate new things; and teaching delivered by one's own family tends to ignore necessary processes of learning, thus simplifying the instruction. Therefore, the swapping of children in education is an effective method to keep the sentiments of teachers under control. Through this method, students could learn properly without hurting the relations between parents and children. These views of Mencius on education are still of great value in our time.

乡愿之人

孟子、万章师徒有一天谈论孔子时,万章想到一个问题:"孔子在陈国遭遇困境时曾经感叹:我的家乡还有一群志气高而缺乏阅历的青年,我为何不回去呢!我不明白,孔子在陈国为什么会想念这些狂放的人?"

孟子说:"孔子也想找到中规中矩的人来传授知识,可是得不到,便想找到这些次一等的人来传授。毕竟狂者有进取心,狷者有所不为。狂放的人志高言大,动不动就是'古人啊,古人啊'什么的。而狷介的人就又次一等,他们的好处是不屑于干坏事。孔子最厌恶的恐怕就是乡愿之人了,认为他们是破坏道德的人。"

万章就问:"怎样才算是乡愿之人呢?"

孟子说:"乡愿之人批评狂者说'为什么这样志气高远呢?言语不顾及行为,行为不顾及言语。'又批评狷者说:'处事为什么落落寡合呢？生在这个世道，就迎合这个世道，过得去就行了。'这种八面玲珑、四处献媚讨好世人的人，就是乡愿之人。"

万章又问："整个乡里都称赞的人，无论到哪里都得到称赞的人，孔子却认为是德行的破坏者，为什么呢？"

孟子说："这种人，要指责他，却举不出缺点，责骂他，却找不到理由。看起来为人似乎忠诚守信，处事似乎端正洁净，大家也都喜欢他，他自己也认为自己很正确，但实际上却与尧舜之道完全背离，所以说是德行的败坏者。孔子说他憎恶似是而非的东西：憎恶莠草，是怕它混淆禾苗；憎恶自作聪明，是怕它混淆正义；憎恶强辩，是怕它混淆忠信；憎恶郑国的乐曲，是怕它混淆了雅乐；憎恶紫色，是怕它混淆了朱红色；憎恶乡愿之人，是怕它混淆了德行。君子只是让一切都回归到正道罢了。正道可以使民众奋发向上，这样就没有邪恶的藏身之地了。"

"乡愿"这个词语我们比较陌生，它的构成来源于"乡里的人都称赞他符合大家的愿望"这个含义。孔子所谓的"乡愿"大概是指伪君子，指那些貌似忠厚，其实没有一点道德原则，只知道媚俗趋势的人。孟子所指的意思则是当面一套、背后一套，四处讨好、八面玲珑的人。生活中有些人表面上善良、忠诚、不偏不倚，但实际上却是随波逐流、趋炎附势的虚伪之徒。这不是善，而是伪善，是最大的恶。俗话说的"伪君子比真小人更可怕"，表明了人们对乡愿的普遍厌恶。

PEOPLE WHO TRY TO PLEASE EVERY TOWN FOLK

Once talking about Confucius, Wan Zhang asked his teacher Mencius, "When Confucius was frustrated in the State of Chen, he sighed, 'There are many ambitious but inexperienced youngsters in my hometown, so why don't I go back?' I just cannot understand why he was still missing those arrogant scholars during his stay in Chen?"

Mencius said, "Confucius also wanted to find those who could pursue the true medium to instruct, but he couldn't make it. Thus he had to find those who were a little inferior to them to educate. After all, those arrogant people were ambitious and those overcautious people considered some behaviors were beneath them. The arrogant held great ambitions, enjoyed bragging, and they frequently commented on the ancients. While the overcautious were even inferior to the arrogant, but their merit was that they would not do anything beneath them. The ones Confucius detested most were those who want to flatter all their town folks, blaming them for undermining morality."

Wan Zhang asked, "What kind of people do you refer to?"

Mencius said, "Those people criticized the arrogant, 'Why should they hold such great ambitions? Their words could not respect their acts and their acts could not honor their words.' They also criticized the overcautious, 'Why being so particular over dealing with people? Born in this society, you have to be adapted to it and don't be so particular.' Therefore, I refer to those who were slick and tried everything they could to flatter others."

Wan Zhang asked, "Those people were praised by all their town folks and by the people anywhere they went, but Confucius deemed them as the wreakers of morality, why?"

Mencius said, "If you blamed them, you could not find their shortcomings; if you criticized them, you could not find any reasons. They are seemingly honest and credible, and their behaviors are also seemingly proper and pure. People adore them and they also think themselves highly. However, they actually completely deviate from the principles of Yao and Shun, so they are the wreckers of virtues. Confucius said he hated ambiguity by claiming, 'I hate the darnel, lest it be confounded with the corn; I hate pretentiousness, lest it be confounded with justice; I hate sophistry, lest it be confounded with sincerity; I hate the songs from the State of Zheng, lest they be confounded with the refined music; I hate purple, lest it be confounded with vermilion; I hate those who want to flatter all their town folks, lest they be confounded with the virtuous.' What men with high morals do is just to bring everything back to the proper path. This rightful path could inspire people to improve themselves, thus there would be no hiding places for the wickedness."

The term of "trying to please every town folk" sounds unfamiliar to us, which originated from the phrase "All one's town folks acclaim one as being able to satisfy the people's wishes". Confucius referred to those people as hypocrites, who seemed to be honest and sincere but actually were just weathercocks without any respect to moral principles. Mencius referred to those as the two-faced and slick apple-polishers. There are some who look kind, loyal and unbiased, but are actually hypocrites who curry favor with the powerful. They are not kind, but just pretend to be so, therefore they are the evilest. The common saying that "A hypocrite is even more dreadful than an obvious vile man" is a manifestation of people's widespread detestation of such people.

五十步笑百步

　　孟子刚到魏国的时候,梁惠王的态度有一点轻慢。经过几次交谈,梁惠王对孟子的态度已经有了一些改变。有一次,他很有点卖弄地对孟子说:"我对于国家,算是很尽心了吧?河内发生饥荒,我就把那里的百姓迁移到没有饥荒的河东去,并把河东的粮食运到河内去,如果河东发生饥荒时也是这样办。我研究过邻国的政治,没有像我这样为老百姓尽心尽力的。可是邻国的百姓并不见减少,我的百姓也没有增多,这是什么原因呢?"

　　孟子答道:"大王喜好打仗,我就用打仗来做比喻吧。战鼓咚咚擂响,双方交战开始了,战败的士兵丢盔弃甲拖着武器逃跑,有的跑了一百步才停下,有的跑了五十步就停下了。那个跑了五十步的士兵却讥笑跑了一百步的士兵,这事您怎么看呢?"惠王说:"这不行,他只不过没有跑到一百步而已,但同样是逃跑啊。"孟子说:"大王如果知道这个道理，就不要指望您的百姓比邻国多了。"

战国时代的国君致力于征战，农民既是耕田的劳动力，又是战争的兵力。所以增加人口一直是各国统治者十分关心的事。孟子对于这一点看得很清楚，但他并没有直接说出来，而是用了一个"五十步笑百步"的故事来打比方，机智地给梁惠王设了一个圈套。梁惠王自满于自己的一点点功德，却不知道自己的根本问题是什么。孟子要让梁惠王充分地认识到，移民、输粮固然是好事，但也只是头痛医头，脚痛医脚的办法，比邻国好不了多少。只有解决老百姓的生老病死，让他们真正过上安定富庶的生活，才能成就国家千秋万代的功业。

THOSE WHO HAD RETREATED FIFTY PACES LAUGHED AT THOSE WHO HAD RETREATED A HUNDRED

When Mencius just arrived at Wei, King Hui snubbed him slightly. After several conversations, King Hui's attitude towards him improved. Once he boasted in front of Mencius, "I have tried my best in running the state, haven't I? When the inner reaches of the river suffered famine, I moved the people there to the east side of the river, which was free from the famine and I also sent food to that famine-stricken area from the east. If the east side was also to suffer famine, I would do the same. I have closely observed the governance of the neighboring states, and I could not find any king who tried so hard for the well-being of their subjects as I do. However, I didn't see the number of people in neighboring states decrease, nor have I found the number of people in my state increase. Why is that?"

Mencius answered, "King, you are fond of wars, so I can explain that by drawing an analogy related to wars. With the beating of war drums, the fighting began. Then the soldiers of the defeated side fled pellmell. Some of them stopped after having retreated a hundred paces, some after fifty paces. And one who retreated fifty paces laughed at another who had retreated a hundred, how would you comment on this?" King Hui said, "He could not laugh at others just for the longer distance; after all, he also fled." Mencius said, "King, since you have realized this, you should not count on the increase of your population through the immigration of subjects from other states."

The kings in the Warring States Period focused on waging wars. The farmers were both the laborers for farming and soldiers on battlefields. Therefore, all the rulers were all highly concerned about the increase of population. Mencius was fully aware of that, but he did not point that out explicitly. Instead, he drew an analogy through the story of "those who had retreated fifty paces laughed at those who had retreated a hundred" to force the king to admit the truth.

King Hui was contented with his small contribution, but failed to understand the key of his problem. Mencius wanted the king to fully understand that though his practices of moving people to better places and sending food to the stricken area were laudable, they were only expedients. His governance was not so much better than that of others. Only by solving the problems closely related to people's well-beings and providing them with stability and prosperity, can the rulers score great achievements with the influence lasting thousands of years.

缘木求鱼

  孟子有一次问齐宣王最大的愿望是什么。齐宣王笑而不答。孟子继续追问："是为了肥美的食物不够吃？轻暖的衣服不够穿？还是美丽的色彩不够看？美妙的音乐不够听？手下的侍从不够使唤？这些大王的臣子都充分地供应了，大王难道会是为了这些吗？"齐宣王摇头说："不，我不是为了这些。"

  孟子说："那么大王的愿望我已经知道了。是想开辟疆土，威慑秦楚，君临天下，安抚四方夷狄吧。可是，以大王的所作所为而想达到这样的愿望，那就好比是爬到树上去抓鱼一样不可能啊。"

  齐宣王吃惊了："有那么严重吗？"孟子回答说："恐怕还更严重呢！爬到树上去抓鱼，虽然抓不到鱼，但不会有灾祸。可是凭陛下的所作所为，想实现愿望，就算尽心尽力，也必然招来灾祸呢！"

  齐宣王大惊失色，说："我心思很混乱，希望您帮助我，教导我。

我虽然不贤,但愿意照您所说的去尝试。"

孟子见齐宣王挺诚恳的,心中十分高兴,便趁机对齐宣王论述"仁政"强国的必要性。他认为,没有固定产业的人能坚持道德原则的只有读书明理的人才能做到。一般老百姓如果没有固定的产业收入,生活没有保障,就不可能保持向善的心态,甚至可能违法干坏事。等到他们犯了罪,再去惩罚他们,这不等于是故意陷害他们吗?所以贤明的君主一定要让老百姓有固定的收入,使他们上足以赡养父母,下足以养活妻子儿女。年成好的时候,可以丰衣足食;年成不好的时候,也不会饿死。生活有了保障,再教育他们向善,那就很容易了。孟子接着就为齐宣王提出了一系列的施行仁政的方针。但齐宣王会不会实行,就不是那么容易的事了。

"缘木求鱼"这个成语我们至今仍在使用。那些想要达到目的的人,却使用了错误的方法,结果就是离目标越来越远,就像爬到树上去抓鱼一样,肯定是徒劳无益的。孟子的这个比喻难道不是很恰当吗?

CLIMBING THE TREES TO CATCH FISH

Mencius once asked King Xuan of Qi what was his biggest wish. King Xuan smiled without answering him. Mencius continued to ask, "Do you want to take more delicious food, wear warmer and lighter clothes, see more beautiful colors, enjoy more wonderful music or order more attendants and servants? Your officials have already ensured those supplies. Is the acquisition of those comforts your biggest wish?" King Xuan shook his head and said no.

Mencius said, "Now, I know what your biggest wish is. You want to expand Qi's territory to overawe Qin and Chu, to rule over the whole country and to conquer ethnic minorities, such as Yi and Di. However, your current approach to realize such wish is like to climb trees to catch fish, which is impossible."

King Xuan was astonished and asked whether the mistake of his approach was really so serious. Mencius answered, "Even more serious than that. You won't be caught in disaster if you can't catch fish on the trees. However, even with your utmost efforts, your approach would surely invite disasters."

King Xuan was astounded and said, "I am totally at a loss now. I hope you can assist and instruct me. Though I am not virtuous, I would make attempts by following your advices."

Mencius was pleased for the sincerity of King Xuan and therefore he took the opportunity to illustrate the necessity of benevolent governance. He said, "Without any fixed assets, only those well-educated and judicious could adhere to moral principles. The ordinary people, with neither stable income from assets nor any guarantee for livelihood, could not possibly maintain their inclination towards benevolence, and they might even commit crimes. If you were to punish them after they committed crimes, isn't it like you are deliberately persecuting them? Therefore, a virtuous king should ensure that people have fixed income to support their parents, wives and children. So in bumper harvest years, people could have ample food and clothing while in bad years, they would at least be saved from starvation to death. Once their basic living is ensured, it would be much easier for us to educate them and guide them toward benevolence." Mencius immediately put forward a series of policies on benevolent governance, but it would not be so easy for King Xuan to implement them.

Even now, we still often refer to the idiom "catching fish on the trees (*yuan mu qiu yu*)". Those who use wrong approaches to meet their goals would deviate from their targets even further just like catching fish by climbing the trees, which is doomed to be futile. Isn't this an appropriate analogy?

王顾左右而言他

　　孟子对齐宣王屡次正面宣讲王道都不起作用后,就改变了策略。有一天他对齐宣王说:"假如大王有一个臣下要去楚国,将他的妻子儿女托付给他的一个朋友照料。等他回来时,却发现自己的妻子儿女在挨饿受冻,他应当怎样对待这个朋友呢?"齐宣王回答说:"跟这个朋友断交。"孟子接着说:"长官管理不好属下,怎么办?"齐宣王说:"罢免他。"孟子说:"那么一个君王没有治理好政事,又该怎么办呢?"齐宣王不敢正对孟子,只好扭头去看左右侍从,岔开话题说起别的事来了。

　　这就是我们现在常说的"王顾左右而言他"这个成语的由来。一句"王顾左右而言他",把齐宣王尴尬心虚的难堪神态刻画得惟妙惟肖。一个人如果在内心深处知道自己的行为有过失,但又没有勇气坦白承认自己的错误时,往往会选择逃避性的肢体语言。齐宣王不敢正视孟子,眼睛往别处看,把话题扯开,正好暴露了他内心的不安和不自信。

从这个小故事里也可以看出，战国时期君臣之间还是存在着相对平等的关系，并不像后世的独裁者那么专制暴戾、一意孤行。

KING LOOKING ASIDE AND TALKING ABOUT OTHER THINGS

Mencius repeatedly failed to persuade King Xuan to adopt benevolent governance through the straightforward manner, so he changed his strategy.

One day he said to King Xuan, "If one of your ministers had asked his friend to take care of his wife and children during his trip to the State of Chu, and when he came back, he found that his wife and children had been suffering from hunger and cold. Then how should he treat this friend?" King Xuan answered, "To break up with him." Mencius continued, "What if an official could not manage his subordinates?" King Xuan said, "Dismiss him." Mencius then said, "What if a king could not rule his state well?" King Xuan was unable to look Mencius in the eyes and had to turn to his subordinates and to turn aside from that topic.

The popular idiom of "king looking aside and shifting to other topics" originated from this story.

This expression vividly reflected the king's embarrassment, guilty conscience and awkwardness. Usually one tends to use evasive body language when he has a guilty conscience while lacking the courage to admit his mistakes. King Xuan was unable to look Mencius in the eyes and deviated from the topic, and this revealed his lack of confidence and uneasiness.

We can see from this story that during the Warring States Period, kings kept an equal relationship with their officials, unlike those arbitrary and tyrannical dictators in the following dynasties.

拔苗助长

公孙丑问孟子最擅长于什么？孟子说，"我善养我浩然之气。"那什么是浩然之气呢？孟子解释说，浩然之气很难用语言表达清楚。它刚直、宏大，如果用正确的方法培养它，不伤害它，它就会充塞于天地之间。这种气要和正义感融合在一起，才会有气势。

公孙丑问孟子如何才能培养浩然之气。孟子没有直接回答他，而是给他讲了一个故事：从前有个宋国人，担心禾苗不长而去拔高它，然后把自己累得惨兮兮地回到家里，对家人说："今天累坏了，我帮助禾苗生长了。"他的儿子连忙跑到田里一看，结果禾苗都枯萎了。

"浩然之气"是我们至今常用的概念，"养气"的说法则比较接近我们说的意志培养的问题，同时也包含养生、气功等中国传统理论。一身正气的人往往具有这种不同于"勇气"的浩然之气，它是在道德良知的基础上养成的。"拔苗助长"固然反映了拔苗者强烈的主观能动性，但它脱离了现实，最后的结局往往与愿望相背。

PULL SEEDLINGS TO HELP THEM GROW UP

Gongsun Chou asked Mencius what he was best at. Mencius said he was good at nurturing the natural greatness of a soul which he said was hard to describe with words. It was upright, magnanimous, and if you foster it through the proper means without undermining it, it would fill the whole space between Heaven and Earth. It would only gain its momentum when it has been integrated with the sense of justice.

Gongsun Chou asked Mencius how to cultivate it. Instead of answering him directly, Mencius told him a story, "A man in the State of Song was worried that the crop seedlings would not grow, so he pulled them out from the earth a bit to make them look higher. Then he went back home exhausted and told his family, 'I am so tired because I helped the seedlings to grow.' After hearing that his son went to the field immediately and found all the crops had withered already."

We still often mention the concept of "the natural greatness of a soul" nowadays. The idea of "cultivating the natural greatness of a soul" is quite similar to the issue of cultivating our will. Also it is related to the traditional Chinese theories of preserving one's health and traditional Chinese breathing exercise.

People with dignity and honor often have this "natural greatness of a soul" which is different from "courage" and is fostered on the basis of morality and conscience. "Pulling the seedlings to help them grow (*ba miao zhu zhang*)", though reflecting people's strongly proactive attitude, is unrealistic; therefore the result would turn out to be the opposite.

天时地利不如人和

　　有一次,在和弟子论说民心问题时,孟子举了一个军事方面的例子。他说,比如有一座城池,内城城墙方圆三里,外城城墙方圆七里,把它团团围住却攻打不下来。既然能够团团包围着攻打,必然是得到了天时的有利条件;如果得到了天时仍没有攻打下来,证明这一方的天时不如另一方的地利重要。再比如有一座城池,城墙不是不高,护城河不是不深,武器不是不锋利,盔甲不是不坚固,粮食也不是不充足,可是敌人一进攻,士兵就放弃城池逃走了,这证明地利之便,又不如人和重要啊。

　　所以说,想让民众安居乐业,不在于划定边界,限制他们来往;要使国家稳固,不能光靠山川河流的险要;要威震天下不能光靠武器设备的先进。拥有道义的人自然会得到众人的帮助,失去道义的人帮助他的人自然就少。失道到了极点的时候,就连亲人也会背叛他。得道到了极点的时候，天下的人也都会归顺他。用整个天下都来归顺的力量去攻打那些众叛亲离者，那仁德的君王不用战争手段也就罢了，一旦用了，那就一定会获胜的。这就叫"天时不如地利重要，地利不如人和重要"。

"天时地利人和"、"得道者多助，失道者寡助"这两句名言，就出自孟子的这一段话。他强调了战争胜败的关键在于人心的向背。能把人民团结在自己的周围，就具备了人和的优越性。当然，这两句话其实并不局限于军事斗争，也适用于现代社会中各行各业的发展。一个国家的进步，是否符合正义，能否取得民心，至关重要。

PEOPLE'S SUPPORT IS MORE IMPORTANT THAN OPPORTUNITIES GRANTED BY HEAVEN AND FAVORABLE GEOGRAPHICAL POSITIONS

Once talking about the support of people, Mencius cited an example about military affairs. He said, "A city has an inner city wall extending for three *li*, and an outer city wall extending for seven *li*. It is surrounded but can't be conquered. Since the invaders have surrounded that city, they must have good opportunities granted by Heaven. However, despite that, they have failed to conquer it, which indicates that the geographical positions are more important than Heavenly opportunities. Suppose there is another city with high city walls, a deep moat, sharp weapons, strong helmets, and sufficient stock of food, but it would still be conquered if its people immediately flee from the city once being attacked. This proves that people's support is more important than favorable geographical positions."

Therefore, to let people live and work in peace and happiness, a king cannot depend on setting strict boundaries and limiting the communication between people of different states; to defend one's state, a king cannot only rely on the natural barriers of deep rivers and high mountains; to deter the land under Heaven, a king cannot only count on the sophistication of the weaponry. Those who are with high morals will surely win the help of others, and those who have lost morality will have little support. For one who has completely deviated from the moral principles, even his family will betray him; for one who has exactly followed the moral principles, all people on the land under Heaven would follow him.

When a moral king wages a war against the one who has been deserted by all he will surely secure the victory by relying on the support of all the people. This is why we say, 'Opportunities granted by Heaven are less important than favorable geographical positions, and which in turn are less important than people's support.'"

The two famous sayings of "favorable climatic, geographical and human conditions" and "He who follows moral principles enjoys abundant support while he who deviates from moral principles finds little support" both originated from these words of Mencius. He stressed that the result of a war depended on the support of the people. He who could unite people around him could enjoy the favorable human condition. Of course, the two sayings are not only applicable to military aspects, but also to the development of all trades and professions in the modern society. The development of a state relies on whether its cause is of moral justice and has enjoyed the people's support.

一傅众咻

　　戴不胜与薛居州都是宋国的大臣。当时的宋国，正处于周围大国的包围之中，宋国君臣都想振兴国运，却又找不到好办法。于是戴不胜便去向孟子请教。

　　孟子对戴不胜说："你想让你的君王向善靠拢吗？我问你：有个楚国大夫想让他儿子学会说齐国话，是让齐国人教他呢？还是让楚国人教他呢？""让齐国人教。""一个齐国人教他说齐国话，十个楚国人在旁边跟他说楚国语，即使天天鞭打他，让他学说齐国话，也是不可能做到的。你要是把他放到齐国的闹市里，几年后，想让他再说楚国话，即使天天鞭打他，也是改不过来的。你说薛居州是个品德善良的人，那就让他住在王宫里。在王宫里，如果不论年龄大小、地位高低，都是像薛居州那样善良的人，那君王便不可能与别人做不好的事。相反，在王宫，如果不论年龄大小、地位高低，都不像薛居州那样，那君王又能与谁一起去做好事呢？一个薛居州又能改变宋王多少呢？"

孟子用了一个楚人学说齐语的故事，最直接的意义是说语言学习与语言环境的关系，深层次的意义说的就是环境对人的巨大影响力。从政治上说，只有多吸纳像薛居州那样的贤士，创造好的环境，才能让君王多做好事。通常人们所说的"近墨者黑，近朱者赤"说的也是这个道理。

ONE TEACHING AND MANY DISTURBING

Dai Busheng and Xue Juzhou were both officials of the State of Song, which was surrounded by its strong neighboring states. The king and the officials in Song all wanted to strengthen their state, but couldn't find any effective measures. Therefore, Dai Busheng went to consult Mencius for advice.

Mencius said, "Do you want your king to be closer to benevolence? Let me ask you a question: if an official in the State of Chu wants his son to speak the dialect of the State of Qi, should the father invite a teacher from Chu or from Qi?" Dai said a teacher from Qi would be suitable. Mencius replied, "If there is only one man from Qi to teach him the Qi dialect and a dozen of Chu people talk with him in the local dialect, he wouldn't possibly acquire Qi dialect even under the threat of whipping. If you let him stay in the bustling marketplace of Qi, then after a few years, he would not be able to speak his mother tongue, the Chu dialect, even at the cost of being whipped by you every day. You said Xue Juzhou was a benevolent person, so please let him live in the king's palace. If the palace can be filled with people, young or old, superior or inferior, of the same level of benevolence as him, then it would be impossible for the king to involve in wrongdoings. On the contrary, if the palace be filled with people, young or old, superior or inferior, different from Xue, then with whom could the king do good deeds? Xue himself as one single person could not really exert much influence on the king."

The explicit meaning of Mencius' example of "learning Qi dialect by a native Chu" is about the relationship between language learning and the language environment. Its implicit meaning refers to the great influence of environment on people. In terms of politics, only by creating a better environment through attracting more virtuous talents like Xue Juzhou can the kings pursue more benign causes. What people often say by "He who handles vermilion will be reddened and he who touches ink will be blackened" is also based on the same argument.

为何等到明年

宋国大夫戴盈之对孟子说:"田租只收十分之一,取消关市的征税,现在还做不到;我先减轻税收的比例,等到明年再彻底实行,怎么样?"

孟子回答说:"如今有一个人每天偷他家邻居的鸡,有人忠告他说:'这可不是君子之道。'他回答说:'请允许我先少偷一点,每月偷一只鸡吧,等到明年我就一只也不偷了。'你觉得怎么样?既然知道自己的所作所为不合道义,那就快点改正,为何要等到明年!"

知道错误而及时改正,才是真诚的认错。"月攘一鸡"的故事是对那些知过而不改的人的辛辣讽刺。

WHY WAIT UNTIL NEXT YEAR

Dai Yingzhi, an official of the State of Song said to Mencius, "It is impossible now to levy only one tenth of the due land rent and to abolish the taxes on the markets and at the passes. May I just reduce the tax rate for now and then to rescind it next year?"

Mencius replied, "Suppose there was a man who stole one chick from his neighbor each day and people admonished him for violating the moral principles. He replied to them, 'Please tolerate my wrongdoings this year and I will steal only one chick each month and I will never steal anything next year.' What do you think of that? Since you have already realized your behaviors are against morality and righteousness, why wait until next year to correct them instead of now?"

Only by rectifying the mistakes immediately after one saw them, can one be regarded as having sincerely admitted his mistakes. The story of "stealing one chick one month" is a caustic satire to those people who don't want to rectify themselves after being aware of their fault.

三年之艾

　　有一次,孟子跟齐王谈起了为君之道,他从桀纣的失天下说起。桀纣之所以失天下,是因为失去了百姓的支持。之所以失去百姓的支持,是因为失去了民心。获得天下其实并不难,只要获得百姓的支持就够了。得到老百姓的支持也不难,得到他们的心就够了。得到民心是难事吗?老百姓想要的,你给他们;老百姓讨厌的,你不要施加在他们头上,就这么简单啊。百姓归附仁政,就像水往下流,野兽在旷野奔跑一样自然。

　　所以,把鱼赶进深水里的是水獭;把鸟雀赶进树林的是鹰鹯;使老百姓归顺汤武的是桀纣啊。如今天下的君主如果有爱好仁义的,那么其他诸侯统治下的老百姓都会归顺过来,即使他不想称王天下都难。可是你看看现在那些想称王天下的人,一个个就像患了七年的病,却用三年的艾草来医治,你说能有用吗?平时不积累,一辈子都不可能办到。同样的道理，假如不行仁政，一定会终身受辱，甚至会像桀纣一样招来杀身之祸呢。

不行仁政就会导致自己的灭亡。孟子在这里并不是危言耸听，夏桀商纣国破身亡的例子就是很好的证明。可惜不爱护百姓的统治者向来不相信他们的下场会如此不幸。他们就好比病入膏肓的人，什么药都治不了了。"七年之病求三年之艾"，孟子用了一个很好的比喻，说明统治者不行仁政的行为，是没有任何办法可以改变他最终的悲惨结局的。

THREE-YEAR-OLD WORMWOOD

Once Mencius discussed with the king of Qi the ways of being a king and he started with the loss of sovereign power by King Jie of the Xia Dynasty and King Zhou of the Shang Dynasty. Mencius said, "They lost their countries because they had lost the support of their people. It is not difficult to win the whole country as long as the king could win the support of its people. It is also not difficult to win people's support. You just need to satisfy their wishes, and don't impose upon them anything that they detest. It is as simple as that. The people are willing to obey benevolent rulers, just as water naturally flows downward, and the wild animals run in the wildness.

Therefore, otters drive fish into the depth of water; hawks drive birds into the forest; King Jie and King Zhou drove their people to follow King Tang and King Wu. If a king were to practice benevolent governance, people from other states would come to follow him and the whole country would submit itself to the rule of him even he himself did not intend to. But now all those who want to rule the whole country are acting like people who have been ill for seven years, yet taking the three-year-old wormwood as their cure. Do you think that would be possible? Without regular treatment, it would be impossible to cure their disease. Likewise, if one doesn't implement benevolent governance, he is bound to be humiliated all his life and might even invite a fatal disaster as King Jie and King Zhou had."

  Failure to practice benevolent governance will lead to one's own destruction. Mencius was not exaggerating the potential danger. The doom of the two kings and their countries were telling evidence. It is a pity that those rulers who didn't care for their subjects would never be able to envisage their tragic ends, just as those who with fatal disease were beyond cure. Through the appropriate analogy of "trying to treat one's seven-year-old disease with three-year-old wormwood", Mencius illustrated that those rulers who refused to practice benevolent governance were doomed to meet their tragic ends.

逢蒙学射

　　远古时代，有个叫逢蒙的人跟着后羿学习射箭，最终掌握了后羿全部的技巧。这时逢蒙想到天底下只有后羿比自己的射箭技术高明，就突然生出了歹念，把后羿谋害了。逢蒙忘恩负义，恩将仇报，自然遭到世人唾骂。而后羿历来都是公认的完美英雄。但有一次，孟子和学生们谈起这件事，孟子却评论说："这个结果之所以会发生，后羿自己也有责任啊。"孟子的学生公明仪不同意老师的看法，说道："后羿不应该有什么过错吧？"孟子说："只不过错小点而已，怎能说没有错呢？"接下来孟子就讲了一个故事。
　　从前，郑国派子濯孺子侵犯卫国，卫国派庾公之斯追击他。子濯孺子说："坏了，今天我的旧病发作了，胳膊抬不起来，弓拉不开。我就要死在敌人的手里了。"于是问他的侍从："追我的人是谁？"侍从说："庾公之斯。"不料子濯孺子听了竟说："这下我能活命了。""庾公之斯是卫国有名的射手。您却说您能活命了，这是什么意思？"侍从不解地问。子濯孺子回答："庾公之斯的老师是尹公之他，尹公之他又是我的徒弟。我知道尹公之他是个正派的人，他收的徒弟肯定也是正派的人。"

说话间，庾公之斯追上来了，见到子濯孺子却并没有动手射箭，而是问他："先生为什么不张弓射箭？"子濯孺子说："今天我旧病复发了，拉不开弓，射不了箭。""我的老师是尹公之他，尹公之他是您的徒弟。我不忍心用您的射术来伤害您。话虽这么说，但我今日执行的是国事，我不敢不做一下表示。"庾公之斯一边说着，一边拔出四枝箭，除去箭头，向子濯孺子的战车射了四下，便转身走了。

孟子用这个故事告诉我们，交友、择徒都要慎重。只有真正信得过的有德行的正派人，才能引为知己、朋友和亲近的人。如果是因为自己选错了人，那么出了问题的话，自己也要负一定的责任。这个道理放在今天来说也是很有意义的。

FENG MENG LEARNT ARCHERY

In ancient times, a man named Feng Meng learned archery under Hou Yi and finally acquired all the skills of his teacher. When Feng Meng thought only Hou Yi surpassed him in archery on the whole land under Heaven, an evil idea came across his mind and he murdered his teacher. Of course, Feng Meng's ungratefulness and returning kindness with hatred have been reviled by all the people, while Hou Yi was always widely accepted as a perfect hero. However, when Mencius discussed this with his disciples, he said Hou Yi himself should be partially responsible for his own tragedy. Gongming Yi, one of his disciples disagreed and said it was not the fault of Hou Yi. Mencius said, "Hou Yi also made a mistake. We could not deny that even though it was a small one." Then Mencius told a revealing story.

"The State of Zheng sent Zizhuo Ruzi to attack the State of Wei, which sent Yugong Zhisi to fight back. Zizhuo Ruzi said, 'My old disease recurred and I wouldn't be able to lift my arm to stretch the bow, so I was going to be killed by the enemy.' He asked his subordinates, 'who are pursuing and attacking us?' They told him, 'Yugong Zhisi.' After hearing that, he said, 'Now, I am safe.' 'Yugong Zhisi is a famous archer of the State of Wei, but you said you would be safe, why?' asked the puzzled subordinates. Zizhuo Ruzi answered, 'His teacher is Yingong Zhita, who is my disciple. I know Yingong Zhita is a decent man, therefore his disciple should be a decent man as well.'"

At that very moment, Yugong Zhisi caught up with them. Instead of stretching the bow to attack Zizhuo Ruzi, he asked, "Sir, why not stretch your bow?" The reply was, "My old disease came back, so I could not stretch my bow to shoot." "My master is Yingong Zhita, who is your student. How can I possibly harm you with your shooting skills? However, what I am executing now is state affairs, so I have to do something to strike my attitude." Then he fetched out four arrows, removed their points, and then shot towards Zizhuo Ruzi's carriage before leaving.

Through this story, Mencius told us that we must be careful in making friends and recruiting students. Only those decent people with credibility and high morals are eligible to become our confidants, friends and members of our intimate circle. If we trusted a wrong person who then made mistakes, then we ourselves should also be responsible for that. These words of Mencius are still highly meaningful in today's world.

齐人骄妻

有一天，孟子给弟子们讲了一个很有名的寓言故事。

从前有个齐国人，家里有一妻一妾。这个人每天出门，都要酒足饭饱后才醉醺醺地回来。他妻子问与他一起吃饭的人是谁，他说都是富贵之人。他的妻子有点怀疑，到了晚上，就偷偷对妾说："咱们的夫君每天出去，都是酒足饭饱才回。问他和什么人一块吃饭，他说都是富贵子弟。但我们可从来没有看见有地位的人拜访过咱家。因此我要跟踪调查夫君的行踪，看看他究竟在干什么。"

第二天早上起来，齐人之妻待其夫君出去后，便远远跟在后面，结果发现整个城中竟没有一个愿意与她丈夫说话的人。到了中午，跟到城东郊外的墓地中，她才看到她丈夫走到祭坟的人那里乞讨剩余的酒肉。不够吃，又东张西望跑到别的地方乞讨。原来这就是他酒足饭饱的方法。

齐人的妻子回到家中,如实地把看到的情况告诉了他的妾,并说道:"夫君是咱们一生的依靠,现在他却这样!"两个人骂了好一会儿,相对哭泣了起来。可是,这个齐人还不知道他的家人了解了内幕,仍旧洋洋自得地回来,又在他的妻妾面前摆威风。

孟子讲的这个故事在一定程度上反映了当时的社会状况。在孟子生活的年代,那些追求富贵显达的人,其在外的丑行能够不使家人感到羞愧哭泣的,恐怕太少了。孟子便借此抨击那些表面上衣冠楚楚、洋洋自得,背地里却为求富贵而行为卑鄙、无所不为的人。人们千万不要被他们所炫耀的那些表面现象蒙住了眼。

A MAN OF QI BOASTED IN FRONT OF HIS WIFE

One day, Mencius told a famous fable to his disciples.

A man of Qi had a wife and a concubine. The man went out every day, and he would always get himself dined to satiety and tipsy before he came back. On his wife's asking him with whom he had dined, he would always tell her that they were all people of wealth and rank. His wife became a bit suspicious and said to the concubine secretly at night, "When our husband goes out every day, he is sure to come back having partaken plentifully of wine and food. I asked with whom he dined, and they are all, according to him, people of wealth and rank. And yet we have never seen people of distinction ever visit us. So, I will tail after him to find out what he is doing."

The next day, she got up early in the morning, and stalked him from a distance after her husband went out. Then she found out, throughout the whole city, there was no single person who was willing to talk to her husband. At noon, after following him to a graveyard located at the suburban area in the east end of the city, she finally saw him come to those who were sacrificing to the deceased, and beg for the sacrificial food and wine they had left over. Not enough, he went to other places to beg. It turned out that was his way of getting himself dined and wined to satiety.

His wife returned, and informed the concubine truthfully of what she had seen, "Our husband is supposed to be the one for us to count on for the whole life, but he turns out to be a man like this!" The two of them reviled their husband for quite a while before weeping together. The man, knowing nothing of all this, still came home with a jaunty air, carrying himself proudly to his wife and concubine.

Mencius' story to a certain extent mirrored the reality of society during that time. During the period when Mencius lived, few of those who sought after wealth and rank conducted outside home in a way that could save their family from feeling ashamed of and weeping. Through this story, Mencius assailed the ones who were smartly dressed and contented with themselves while secretly employing contemptible means and committing all manners of crimes as a way to seek wealth and rank. We should never be blinded by their ostentations.

得其所哉

　　万章有一回问孟子:"舜被父母和弟弟陷害,大难不死回到家后,弟弟象却还在他面前装出一副乖巧的样子,说自己非常想念舜。这时候,舜到底知道不知道象要谋杀他呢?"孟子于是给万章讲了一个故事:

　　从前有人送给郑国的子产一条活鱼,子产让管理池塘的小吏把鱼养在池塘里,那小吏却把鱼煮着吃了。然后报告子产说:"那鱼刚放到池塘里的时候还半死不活的,过了一会儿就摇摇尾巴活动起来,很快游走不见了。"子产听了高兴地说:"那它是去到了它该去的地方啊。"小吏出去后就对别人说:"谁说子产聪明啊?我把鱼煮了吃了,他还说'到了好地方啊,到了好地方啊。'"

　　孟子讲完这个故事就总结说,真正的君子行的都是正道,不会懂得小人的阴谋诡计。内心光明的人,看待别人的行为也以为同样是光明的，不会产生怀疑。象看见舜的时候装出一副敬爱和想念舜的样子，内心光明磊落的舜自然不会怀疑自己的弟弟，所以马上就相信了象。舜因此而常常遭受欺骗、甚至陷害而浑然不觉。这就是人们常说的"明枪易躲，暗箭难防"，君子也难防暗中使坏的小人。

HAVE GOT TO THE RIGHT PLACE

Wan Zhang once asked Mencius, "Shun had been framed by his parents and younger brother. When he came back home after surviving all the dangers, his younger brother Xiang even put up an appearance of happiness in front of him and said he had missed Shun so much. I am wondering that at that time whether Shun was indeed ignorant of Xiang's plot of killing him or not." Mencius replied by telling a story.

"Formerly, someone sent a gift of a live fish to Zichan of the State of Zheng. Zichan ordered his pond-keeper to keep it in the pond, but the pond-keeper cooked and ate it. Then he reported to Zichan , 'When I first put it to the pond, the fish was barely alive, but after a while it revived and began to swing its tail before it finally swam away.' Zichan was pleased after hearing that and said, 'It went to the place where it should belong!' The pond-keeper then went out and told others, 'Who calls Zichan a wise man? After I had cooked and eaten the fish, he said, 'It went to a good place. It went to a good place.'"

Mencius concluded after he told the story, "Men with high morals only follow the right track, and they have no idea about the tricks and plots of the vile. He who is honest regards others' behaviors as the same without suspicion. Thus in front of his younger brother's seeming respect and longing for him, Shun, who was honest, believed Xiang immediately without the slightest suspicion for him. For this reason, Shun was often subject to deceits and frame-ups without any knowledge of them." This is what we often say, "A visible spear is easily withstood, but an unseen arrow is hard to dodge against." Therefore, it is hard for men with high morals to guard against the dirty tricks played by the vile in secrecy.

牛山之木

　　孟子一直强调人人都有善性,那么为什么世间还会有那么多的恶行呢?有一次,孟子的弟子公都子就问道:"告子说:'本性没有善,没有不善。'有人说:'本性可以成为善,可以成为不善。所以,文王武王在位,民众就崇尚善;幽王厉王在位,民众就崇尚暴。'还有人说:'有的人本性善,有的人本性不善。所以,尧这样贤明的君主却有象这样的坏儿子,瞽瞍这样的恶父亲却有舜这样的好儿子,纣这样的暴君却有微子启、王子比干这样的贤兄。'如今老师认为性善,那他们都错了吗?"

　　面对这样的质疑,孟子回答:"按人们的实际情况确实是能够向善的,这就是我们所说的人人性善。至于有的人变成不善,并不是资质的问题。同情之心人人都有,羞耻之心人人都有,恭敬之心人人都有,是非之心人人都有。同情之心属仁,羞耻之心属义,恭敬之心属礼,是非之心属智。仁、义、礼、智不是从外部注入的，是人本来就有的，只是有的人不曾去领悟罢了。所以说，追求就能得到，放弃就会失去，人与人之间的能力或德行相差一倍、五倍甚至无数倍的原因，就在于有的人没有充分发挥他们天生的善性。孟子接着又举了一个例子来说明：

齐国国都临淄的南方有一座牛山，曾经林木茂盛，郁郁苍苍。然而因为靠近都城的缘故，常常遭到人们的砍伐，所以如今几乎是光秃秃的了。当然，那里的树木仍然在继续生长，加上雨露的滋润，并不是没有长出新枝嫩芽。可是那些放牛牧羊的人又去糟蹋了一番，于是就变成寸草不生的模样了。大家看见牛山的这副模样就认为它不曾长过树木，就认为寸草不生就是这山的本性，这难道对吗？

人其实也一样。人的善良之心就像牛山上的树木一样，天天用斧子去砍伐，当然就会越来越少。日夜砍伐，而不去培养，这样，他的善性就会日益淡薄，以至于完全丧失，行为跟禽兽没有什么两样了。但如果你看见他现在的行为跟禽兽一样，就认为他从来不曾有过善良的本性，这难道是对的吗？所以，如果能得到应有的培养，没有什么东西不能生长；要是失去了应有的培养，那就什么东西都会消失。

孟子的这段话说明，人的善良本性就像牛山的树木一样，得到保护培养和雨露滋润，就能够根深叶茂。相反，一味地任自己的恶性发展，不去培养自己的善性，那它们终有一天会消失干净，原来善良的人就会变成恶人，跟禽兽没有两样了。

THE TREES ON MOUNT NIU

Mencius always stressed that the nature of everyone was good, but why were there still so many acts of malice in the world? Once Mencius' disciple Gongduzi asked him, "Gaozi said, 'There is neither good human nature nor evil one.' Some said, 'Human nature can become either good or evil. Therefore, during the reign of King Wen and King Wu, the people advocated goodness, while during that of King You and King Li, the people worshipped cruelty.' Others said, 'Some have good human nature while others have evil one. For this reason, the sage king Yao had an evil son like Xiang, while the immoral man like Gu Sou had a virtuous son like Shun, and tyrant Zhou had virtuous brothers as Viscount Wei and prince Bi Gan.' Now, master, you hold that human nature is good, so do you think they are all wrong?"

Mencius answered, "According to the real conditions, men could indeed be goodness-oriented; that is why we claim that the human nature for each person is good. Natural endowments could not be held accountable for one's failure to remain good. Everyone has the heart of sympathy, of shame, of deference and of judgment. The heart of sympathy belongs to benevolence; the heart of shame belongs to righteousness; the heart of deference belongs to propriety; the heart of judgment belongs to wisdom. Benevolence, shame, righteousness and propriety, instead of being acquired externally, are inborn qualities of all the people; only some have not tried to comprehend them. Therefore, you can get them if you aspire after them, but lose them if you give up. The reason why there is a gap of one or five or even numerous folds in terms of the capability or virtues among people is that some have not fully lived up to their inborn goodness of human nature."

Mencius continued by giving another example: "Located at the south of Linzi, capital of the State of Qi, Mount Niu was once covered with a wild profusion of trees. But being situated near the capital, it nearly becomes bare for its trees have been felled by people all the time. Of course the trees there are still growing and with the nourishment of rain and dew, they are not without buds and sprouts springing forth. Unfortunately, it is then ruined by those who graze sheep and cattle there and finally not even a blade of grass grows there. Now when people see it, they think it has never been finely wooded and the nature of this mount is barren, so is this observation justified?"

"The same logic applies to us human beings. The way through which a man loses his proper goodness of nature is the same as the way through which the trees on Mount Niu were felled by axes every day. Being hewn down day after day instead of being nurtured, surely the trees would become less and less in number; without being nurtured, the goodness of human nature decays day and night. When he has totally lost his goodness, he would become no different from the beasts. But do you think it's justified for you to think he has never had the good nature just because now you see him act like the beasts? Therefore, with proper nurturing, there is nothing which will not grow; while being deprived of it, there is nothing which will not decay away."

What Mencius told us was that the goodness of human nature, blessed with protection and nurturing, like the trees of Mount Niu blessed with the nurturing of rain and dew, could flourish and witness vigorous development. On the contrary, if people let their evil aspects expand excessively, without nurturing their natural goodness, in the end they would become evil men with none of the good nature left, making themselves no different from the beasts.

一暴十寒

　　齐宣王总是不能实行仁政,孟子对此评论说:不能怪大王不明智。即使有天下最容易生长的植物,你拿去暴晒一天,再冻它十天,也不可能活下来。我见大王的次数本来就很少,我刚退下,那些泼冷水的人就又来了,齐王即使产生了一点行仁政的念头,我又能怎么样呢?这好比下围棋,围棋作为技艺,是一种很小的技艺,但如果不专心致志去学就学不好。弈秋,是全国最好的棋手。如果让弈秋教两个人下棋,其中一个人专心致志,听从弈秋的教诲。另一个人虽然也在听,但心里却在想着如果天鹅飞来了,就要拿弓箭去射它。虽然他也与别人一起在学习,但成绩却赶不上别人的好,这是因为他的智力赶不上别人吗?并非如此啊。

　　孟子所说的"一日暴之,十日寒之"由后人精简成成语"一暴十寒",用来比喻修学、做事没有恒心,作辍无常。生活经验告诉我们,努力的人不一定会成功，但成功的人一定经过了超人的努力。世上没有不劳而获的事，只有经过了汗水的辛勤浇灌，才有可能让自己的希望之园结出果实。一暴十寒，三心二意，三天打鱼两天晒网，缺乏持久的努力，最终的结果只能是白费力气，徒劳无功。

ONE SCORCH AND TEN COLDS

Mencius commented on King Xuan of Qi's failure to practice benevolent governance, "Don't blame the king and this is not because the king lacks intelligence! Suppose we get the easiest plant to grow; if you leave it under the blazing sun for one day, and then expose it to freezing weather for ten days, it won't survive. It is but seldom that I have an audience of the king, and after I retire, there come all those who pour cold water on my ideas. Though the ideas of benevolent governance flashed into the king's mind, of what avail is it? It is also like playing chess. Chess-playing is only a simple art, but you could not master it without your full attention. Yi Qiu is the best chess player in the whole state. Suppose that he is teaching two men to play it. One gives his whole attention and follows the instructions of Yi Qiu, while the other man, although he seems to be listening, is daydreaming that if a swan comes he would shoot it with his arrow and bow. Although he is learning along with the other, he could not come up to the other in achievement. Is it because his intelligence is not equal? Not so."

Mencius' saying that "leave it under the blazing sun for one day, and then expose it to the freezing weather for ten days" has been condensed into the idiom "one scorch and ten colds (*yi pu shi han*)" which is used metaphorically to describe those people who lack perseverance, working and studying by fits and starts. Our experience tells us that those who work hard might not necessarily succeed, but those who are successful must have made extraordinary efforts. There is no such thing as gains without pains in the world. Only through the irrigation with one's perspiration, can our garden of hope bear fruits. Working by fits and starts and changing one's mind constantly with no persistent efforts is doomed to come to naught and prove futile.

鱼与熊掌

　　孟子认为，人的本性虽然善，但有时候也会迫于形势与私欲，而做出不善的事情来，这样就失去了应有的本心。所以君子时刻都要反省自己的所作所为。孟子举了一个例子来说明这个观点。
　　孟子说，鱼是我所喜爱的，熊掌也是我所喜爱的。二者不能同时得到，便舍弃鱼而取熊掌。生命是我所追求的，正义也是我所追求的。二者不能同时得到，便舍弃生命而奉行正道。生命虽是我所追求的，但有比生命更为令人向往的，因此决不苟且偷生。死亡虽是我所厌恶的，但有比死亡更令人厌恶的，因此，面临祸患时决不苟且逃避。如果人所追求的没有比生命更为重要的，那凡可以获生的手段无不可用。如果人所厌恶的没有超过死亡的，那凡可以避患的手段无不可用。由此来看，虽有时可以获得生命，但人们宁死不生；虽有时可以避患获生，但人们宁死不逃。因此，有比生命更为令人向往的，也有比死亡更为令人厌恶的。其实并不仅仅是贤人君子有这种人生态度,人皆有之,只不过贤人君子能保持这种心境而不丧失罢了。

一筐食物或一罐羹汤,得到了便能活命,得不到就要饿死。呼喝着给予路边行人,路人不会接受;扔到地上,踩上一脚,送给乞丐,乞丐也不会接受。由此看来,一万石粮食如果不考虑一下合不合乎礼义便接受了,又意味着什么呢?一万石粮食又能给我带来什么呢?难道为了让宫室房屋更美,妻妾生活得更好吗?还是施舍给穷人,让他们感激我呢?这种不合礼义的东西,小到一筐食,一罐汤,也宁可饿死而不接受;变成一万石粮食时,便因为房屋、妻妾或穷人的感激而接受下来,这到底是一种什么心态呢?难道不应该想想可不可以这样做吗?这样做的人真是失去了他的本心啊。

鱼与熊掌不可得兼,我们在做出选择的时候往往需要取舍。在鱼与熊掌之间做出取舍也许不太难,而面对生存与正义,人们该怎样取舍呢?在孟子看来,知识分子固然要有崇高的理想,但更应该具备在逆境中坚持的勇气,所以他的答案是:放弃生命,追求正义。现实生活中人们并非一定会面临这样的选择,但利益与理想的冲突不可避免,那时你该怎么做呢?

FISH OR BEARS' PAWS

Mencius believed that despite the goodness of human nature, sometimes driven by the situation and selfish desire, people would do some malicious deeds at the cost of losing their original human nature. Therefore, people with high morals should reflect on themselves all the time. Mencius explained this through a revealing example.

Mencius said, "I like fish, and I also like bears' paws. If I cannot have the two together, I will choose the bears' paws and give up fish. The same is for life and righteousness. If I cannot keep the two together, I will give up life, and choose righteousness. I like life indeed, but there is that which I like more than life, and therefore, I will not seek to possess it by any improper ways. I dislike death indeed, but there is that which I dislike more than death, and therefore in case of disaster or danger, I would not seek any improper means to sue for life. If among the things which man likes there is nothing more valuable than life, why should he not use every means to preserve it? If among the things which man dislikes there is nothing more undesired than death, why should he not do everything to avoid it? However, there are cases when men by a certain course might preserve life, but they just do not employ it and when by certain means they might avoid death, but they will not do that. Therefore, men have something they like more than life, and something they dislike more than death. Not only the sages and people with high morals have this attitude towards life, actually everyone has it. But only the sages and people with high morals could preserve it and prevent it from being lost."

"Suppose that there is a small basket of food or a jar of soup, and getting them would mean the survival of life. But if you offer them by bawling to the passers-by, they will not accept them, or if you toss them aside on the road and tread upon them, then give them to the beggars, they will not take them either. Therefore, what is the implication of my accepting ten thousand dan of grain without any consideration of propriety or righteousness? What benefits can the ten thousand dan of grain bring to me? Is it that I may make the rooms more magnificent and improve the lives of my wife and concubines? Or earn gratitude from the poor and needy by being charitable towards them? Those bounties which are not consistent with propriety or righteousness, even as small as a basket of food or a jar of soup, could not be accepted though it could save dying lives from hunger. If there is a bounty of ten thousand dan of grain, one accepts it on the account of having more magnificent rooms, improving the lives of his wife and concubines, and getting gratitude from the needy. Then what kind of man is he? Shouldn't he think about whether he should do this or not? He who has acted this way did lose the proper nature of his mind."

One cannot have fish and bears' paws together, so we often have to make a choice from some alternatives. It might not be so difficult to make a choice between fish and bears' paws, but how should people make a choice between survival and justice? According to Mencius, no doubt scholars should have lofty ideals, but more importantly they should have the courage to persevere in adversity. Therefore, his choice was giving up life for the pursuit of justice. In our real life, people might not face such life-or-death choices, but the conflicts between interests and ideals are unavoidable. How should you act on such occasions?

茅草塞心

有个叫高子的读书人,听说孟子很有学问,就去拜他为师。孟子将他收为弟子,对他讲授儒家的学问知识。可是过了一段时间,这个高子就开始走神了,对其他的事物发生了兴趣,而且在孟子讲课的时候三心二意,很不用功。

孟子发现这个情况,就对高子说了一个比喻:布满茅草的山间小路虽然很狭窄,但走路的人多了,小路就渐渐被踏宽了,变成了一条大路。但是如果没人再去走它,过不了多久,茅草又会长满这条山路,最终将它堵塞,以前所做的一切努力就都白费了。高子听了孟子的这番话,有点似懂非懂。看他那个样子,孟子接着又说:"也许现在茅草已经把你的心给堵塞了吧!"高子听到这里才明白了孟子的意思,感到很不好意思,于是下决心努力学习。

孟子用山间小道之所以成为大路来作比喻,勉励高子对于大道要持续不断地追求，不能有任何松懈、疏忽和间断，否则的话，就会如同被茅草塞住一样，永远也走不到通向大道的路。

这个故事如今已经被引申出了两个语义。一是"茅塞顿开"这个成语，即经过孟子的一番教导，高子一下就明白了其中的道理，好像堵塞山路的茅草一下子被扫除了一样，道路变得通畅开阔，高子的内心也豁然开朗了。还有一个就是鲁迅先生说的名言：世上本无路，走的人多了，也就成了路。这告诫我们不要因循守旧，要勇于开拓、创造，走出新的人生道路。

THE HEART FILLED UP WITH WEEDS

There was a scholar called Gao Zi. He paid respects to Mencius and requested him to become his master when learning about his immense erudition. Mencius agreed to his request and instructed him on Confucian doctrines. But after a while, Gao Zi was distracted and began to be interested in other things. He even got absent-minded when attending Mencius' lectures.

Mencius noticed that and drew an analogy, "There are footpaths along the hills; if more and more people walk on them, they will be broadened and become roads; and if no one walks on them, they will be filled up and blocked up by the wild weeds after a short while, thus wasting all the previous efforts ." Hearing that, Gao Zi looked to be quite hazy. Therefore, Mencius went on, "Now perhaps your heart has already been filled up by the wild weeds!" Then Mencius' intention finally dawned on him and he was embarrassed and made up his mind to study harder.

Mencius, through the analogy of making a narrow footpath into a wide road, encouraged Gao Zi to persevere in his pursuit without any slack, negligence or interruption. Otherwise, he would be like a footpath being blocked up by wild weeds, never leading towards the wide road.

This story has been extended to two different meanings. One refers to the idiom of "become enlightened at once (*mao se dun kai*)", i.e., with Mencius' guidance, Gao Zi realized its meaning and his mind was suddenly enlightened just like a footpath that became broadened and unobstructed after the wild weeds on it were cleared. Another meaning refers to the famous remark of Lu Xun: There used to be no road on earth but a road forms when a lot of people had walked on it. It tells us not to follow the beaten track, instead, we should have the daring to blaze new trails and innovate and create a new path for our life.

再作冯妇

　　齐国闹饥荒。陈臻对孟子说:"国内百姓都以为夫子您会再次劝说齐王打开粮仓拯救灾民,我想您恐怕不会那么做了吧?"

　　孟子回答说:"再那么做我就成了冯妇一样的人了。"

　　冯妇是晋国人,很善于打虎。后来他宣布再也不打虎了,从此专心读书。一天他与朋友去郊外玩,看见一只老虎靠着山角。很多人围着它,却没有人敢上前捉它。人们远远看见冯妇来了,就快步上前去迎接他。冯妇就挽起衣袖,露出胳膊下了车,杀死了老虎。人们都很高兴他这样做,可是士人却讥笑他又重操旧业。

　　孟子讲这个故事的用意是什么呢?其实很简单。假如反复提出自己的主张而不被采纳接受,遭到冷遇,却还要不顾一切地去继续劝谏,那就会跟冯妇一样遭世人讥笑了。即使是像孟子这样的圣人,也有普通人的一面:我干么要去做那种吃力而不讨好的事呢?

DO IT AGAIN WOULD BE ACTING LIKE FENG FU

When Qi was suffering from a famine, Chen Zhen said to Mencius, "The people are all thinking that you, Master, would once again try to persuade the King of Qi to open the granary to provide relief to the affected people. But I don't think you will do that again."

Mencius replied, "To do it again would be acting like Feng Fu."

Feng Fu was a native of the State of Jin, famous for his skills in subduing tigers. Later he announced that he would never again fight a tiger. Instead, he would devote himself wholeheartedly to reading books. One day, when he was out with a friend in the suburbs, he saw a tiger taking refuge in the corner of a hill. The tiger was surrounded by a lot of people, but no one dared to attack it. When the people saw Feng Fu, they walked quickly towards him to greet him. Feng Fu immediately bared his arms, descended from his carriage, and killed the tiger. People were so pleased with him for doing that, while the scholars laughed at him for taking up his old trade again.

Why did Mencius mention this story? The reason was quite simple. If one continues to make remonstration despite the fact that his suggestions have been ignored repeatedly, he will be mocked at by others as Feng Fu once was. Even sages like Mencius would share similar sentiments with the ordinary people by thinking, "Why should I do those hard and thankless jobs?"